Exploring the Media

Text, Industry, Audience

Second Edition

Exploring the Media

Text, Industry, Audience

Second Edition

Edited by Barbara Connell

auteur

EXPLORING THE MEDIA

This edition first published in 2010 by Auteur, The Old Surgery, 9 Pulford Road, Leighton Buzzard LU7 1AB
www.auteur.co.uk
Copyright © Auteur 2010

First edition published in 2008, reprinted in 2009 and 2010

Design: Nikki Hamlett
Stills research and production assistance: Tom Cabot (www.ketchup-productions.co.uk)
Set by AMP Ltd, Dunstable, Bedfordshire
Printed and bound by Scotprint, Haddington, Scotland

British Library Cataloguing-in-Publication Data
A catalogue record for this book is available from the British Library

ISBN 978-1-906733-47-6 (paperback)

Contents

List of Contributors

BARBARA CONNELL is Subject Leader for Media Studies, Coleg Glan Hafren, Cardiff and Chief Examiner, A Level Media Studies, WJEC.

CHRISTINE BELL is Head of Media Studies, Heaton Manor School, Newcastle-upon-Tyne and is Principal Examiner, A Level Media Studies, WJEC.

COLIN DEAR is Head of Media Studies, Royal Russell School, Croydon, and is a Team Leader, A Level Media Studies, WJEC.

WENDY HELSBY taught Media and Film at Queen Mary's College, Basingstoke and is also a tutor for the Open University.

NAOMI HODKINSON is Lecturer in Media Studies, Coleg Glan Hafren, Cardiff, and is an Examiner, A Level Media Studies, WJEC.

DEBORAH JONES is Head of Media Studies at Cardiff High School and an Examiner for A Level Media Studies, WJEC.

SAMANTHA WILLIAMS teaches at Cardiff High School and is an Examiner for A Level Media Studies, WJEC.

Editor's Introduction

This second edition of *Exploring the Media* has been written by a group of practising teachers of Media Studies and reflects some of the changes that have occurred in the AS and A Levels and in Media teaching in Britain over the past few years. Producing a second edition has given us the opportunity to develop our ideas, add new sections and chapters and to pass on what we have learnt from our experiences of teaching the new A Level Specification.

The book is based on what the writers see as the central concepts informing the study of the media: 'texts' (a general term to describe all products of the media), their audiences and the industries which produce them. We believe that these concepts are fundamental to a study of the media and are at the heart of what you need to learn and understand. We also think it is important not only to study products of the media – broadly by asking questions about their genre, narrative and the representation issues they raise – but also to ask questions about how those media products are shaped by the audiences they're produced for and the industries which produce them. It's only through considering all of those elements that we can begin to understand the role that the media may play in shaping the way we think and feel.

You will realise early on in your Media Studies course that the media do not just provide a 'window on reality', they provide us with representations of the world we live in – versions of that 'reality'. When you explore those representations you will begin to see that representations are, at their simplest, images of 'reality' coupled with points of view about them. They are what the writers of this book refer to as 'ideological representations' – representations which incorporate attitudes, values and beliefs. All representations are influenced by the audiences they appeal to and the organisations which produced them. So, a television drama like *The Wire*, for example, will give you a very different representation of crime, the police and criminals from an episode of the popular crime series *Midsomer Murders*. That is partly to do with the fact that *Midsomer Murders* is produced by ITV1 for mainstream television viewing whereas *The Wire* was originally produced by HBO (Home Box Office, part of the massive Time Warner empire), who have a tradition of creating challenging dramas for an American pay-TV audience who like riskier television.

Expanding the concepts

So, thinking about media 'texts' in relation to their audiences and producers is important. But the concepts underlying the study of the media themselves change as the media changes and becomes ever more convergent. Consequently, the way we relate to the media is also changing. We are all beginning to combine being audiences in the traditional sense – like watching television or going to a film – with being interactive users, and often at the same time! For example, you may watch a television programme on your computer and simultaneously open up various interactive windows at the same time as emailing a friend. Our media usage is more exciting and dynamic than it's ever been – new technologies are expanding our choices and our methods of consumption.

Convergence within the media and the ways in which audiences are using it have several implications for the way we study 'texts'. We might, for example, think about the way we explore media texts by considering their genre – what kind of text they are, why genres have developed and how audiences and industries 'use' them. You could describe a television programme like *skins* as a 'teen drama', with more than a touch of soap; but you could also talk about it as a 'multiplatform' drama with viewers watching online or attending some of the parties the show sponsored. Or you might be one of the many who produced their own scenes from it or picked up 'mobisodes' or deleted scenes on mobile phones or the web. The 'kind' of programme you're studying has changed from being a simple television programme creating particular expectations in audiences and following particular 'rules' to a multiplatform experience.

Equally, you might think of how computer games are immersing us all in different kinds of narrative. At their simplest, game narratives are less about beginnings, middles and ends and more about following up different possibilities. The 'linear' narrative is often replaced by parallel and multi-layered narratives.

The book's structure: text, industry and audiences/users

The first section of the book introduces the concepts of genre, narrative and representation as the main ways of exploring the media and analysing texts. This section emphasises representation issues and starts to ask questions about how audiences and users respond to – and are potentially influenced by – those representations. You will find references to Stuart Hall who has formalised the way audiences respond to the media in terms of positioning: the representations underlying media texts encourage audiences and users to take up particular points of view, particular 'positions'. Not all audiences, of course, adopt those points of view and some only partly agree with them (what Hall called preferred, oppositional and negotiated 'readings' of media texts). What Hall (amongst others) importantly introduced was the way the media can be interpreted by different audiences in different ways – ways which reflect their social and cultural backgrounds. This seems to us a very important idea – that not everybody interprets the media in the same way and there is therefore not one single meaning to any media text but rather a number of different ways a text can be interpreted or used by audiences.

Having concentrated on media texts and the way audiences and users interpret them, the second section of the book considers the industry context. You will therefore progress from the focus on texts and their audiences and users to considering the role of industries in affecting the nature of those texts. Writers have concentrated on eight industries: television, computer games, film, music, radio, magazines, newspapers and advertising. Each writer has started by looking at a contrasting range of media texts and has then raised questions about what those texts suggest about the industries which produce and distribute them as well as about their audiences. Obviously in a book designed primarily for A Level students, it is impossible to cover everything so the writers have tried to provide you with a good starting point from which you will be able to develop your own ideas through further research. Consequently, the writers have indicated important books, websites, magazines and relevant DVD sources to help you.

The relationship between studying and creating media is an important one. Your study will clearly be reinforced by creating a product and creating is informed by study and research. Creative work is such an important part of all approaches to the media that the third part of this book focuses entirely on researching, creating and evaluating. Here we have tried to give practical advice on some of aspects of planning for and creating media products as well as reinforcing, in a similarly practical way, some of the research methods you might use to produce a more informed approach to your work.

You might like to approach any creative work in two stages: the first stage is where you aim to become technically proficient in the medium you have chosen to work in and where you need to do some research into the kinds of products you are aiming to produce. The second stage, leading to a more informed approach to media production, involves investigating aspects of the media (text, industry and audiences) which you will aim to reflect in your media production.

Concepts, ideas, theories and the theoretical

This book is clearly informed by a conceptual approach to studying the media and much of the book's emphasis is on exploring the texts of the media. All writers refer to some common theoretical issues and theories underlying Media Studies but most writers suggest that an understanding of the issues underlying theoretical perspectives is more important than a simple reproduction of 'theories'. Certainly, we would like to encourage a critical approach to theoretical perspectives – asking how valid they are, what thinking underlies them and how they can be seen in the context of studying the contemporary media – but we equally seek to avoid the mindless recitation of theory for its own sake. Hopefully this book will encourage you to become critical, independent audiences, users and producers.

Acknowledgements

It goes without saying that I thank all those who have contributed to this book and also Mandy Esseen, Pip Jones and Vivienne Clark who contributed to our first edition (Vivienne's case study on *This is England* has been retained in the otherwise wholly new 'Film' sub-section in this edition). They have all been very generous with their time and approached all aspects of the work with humour and good grace.

I would also like the thank Jeremy Points for his support and advice and John Atkinson at Auteur for never doubting we could manage it!

It has been a pleasure working with everyone.

Barbara Connell

July 2010

APPROACHING THE MEDIA

Genre

Christine Bell

In this Section

- What do we mean by genre?

- Using generic conventions to analyse texts.

- Understanding sub-genres and hybrids.

KEY TERMS TOOLKIT

Genre – the word genre derives from French and means 'type' or 'kind'. In a study of media texts it is used to divide texts into easily identifiable categories. It is a way of classifying media products according to the elements that they share.

Genre Conventions – these are the repertoire of elements that texts belonging to the same genre have in common. They are the aspects that an audience expect to see in a specific media text. They help audiences to recognise the genre and have been built up over a period of time so that they are easily recognisable. For example, the use of hand-held cameras is a convention of some documentaries used to suggest realism.

Hybrid / sub-genre – a text that combines or subverts the conventions of an existing genre to create a new one. For example, the reality television genre combines, in some cases, aspects of the documentary and game show genres.

Introduction

Genre analysis is often centred on the formats of media and television, but all media texts can be categorised according to their key features including magazines, computer games and radio programmes. Genre, however, is not purely a term created to help media studies students to analyse texts; establishing the genre of a text is also essential to the media industry and to the *producers* of media texts. Genre is inextricably linked also to industry and audience, key concepts related to a study of the media in all its forms. Clearly establishing the genre of a media text allows producers to attract audiences to products. Audiences recognise the features of a genre and are attracted through recognition, repetition of conventions and therefore expectation of what is to come. Audiences feel comfortable when they know what to expect and return often for 'more of the same'. A good example is the film industry where films tend to establish the genre clearly to attract audiences through familiarity and recognition. The genre of the film is made clear in marketing material including posters and trailers. It is also the case that actors become associated with certain genres, for example, Matt Damon with action / thriller films or Jennifer Aniston with romantic comedies. The mere inclusion of the actor's name in the publicity material will signify to an audience what to expect from the film. The audience's pleasures and enjoyment of a text are further enhanced by recognising key conventions of a particular genre, allowing them to predict narrative outcomes and to anticipate how characters will react and behave in certain situations. Audiences will accept that a character suddenly bursts into song as they understand this is a convention of the musical. This also explains the reliance of the television and film industries on sequels and spin-offs – these often have guaranteed success because the producers replicate pre-existing successful formulas already endorsed by audiences:

> 'Genres are good for media industries because their potential audience, and consequently their potential profit, can easily be assessed.' (Bell et al., 2005: 223)

However, it must also be understood that genres are fluid and changing, and adapt to the changes in society and audiences. Producers are also always looking for new formulas and adapting existing ones in order to continue to attract audiences and to re-invent themselves for new generations of viewers, readers and users. Hence, the advent in recent years of hybrid genres like the docu-soap and reality television formats and the establishment of the conventions of new genres including computer games and web pages.

Learning Point: In film and television clearly establishing the genre of the text is important in attracting an appropriate audience.

Zoning – the placing together of programmes of the same genre to encourage audiences to stay watching that channel, e.g. Channel 4 comedy programmes on a Friday evening and Channel 5 crime dramas *NCIS*, *Law and Order: Special Victims Unit*, *Law and Order: Criminal Intent*.

Stripping – placing programmes at the same time every evening so that audiences get used to watching them as part of their evening's viewing, e.g. *Coronation Street* 7.30pm and *EastEnders* at 8.00pm.

TASK

Look at the film listings in a magazine where the films are described to the audience. Can you establish the genre of the film from the description and / or the stars? How does the description of the film establish the genre for the audience? Find specific examples.

Now look at the scheduling guide for a day's viewing:

- What can you discover about the scheduling time of particular genres? For example, which genres tend to appear on day time television?

- Which genres have regular 'slots'?

- Can you come to any conclusions about the popularity of certain genres for particular channels or for specific days?

- Can you find any evidence of zoning or stripping?

- Are there channels that devote air time to specific genres?

Genre Conventions

We have already established that conventions are the common features of media texts that situate them in a particular genre. Although we have focused upon texts related to television and film, all media texts are constructed using recognisable conventions.

TASK

Look at two CD covers.

List the common features on the front and back covers – such as a central image.

- Are these conventions common to all the CD covers?

- What are the similarities and differences between them?

- Can you think of any CD covers which do not use these conventions? Why?

Genre conventions can be grouped under the following headings:

- Characters.

- Narrative events.

- Iconography.

- Setting.

- Technical and audio codes.

Characters

Certain characters become associated, through repetition, with a specific genre. Their appearance advances the narrative because the audience recognise them and as a result have expectations about their behaviour and the narratives in which they may be involved. Some of these characters may be types or 'stereotypes'. Stereotypes are established through repetition and are linked to the ways in which specific audiences respond to them.

However, it is also true that certain genres rely on using stereotypes as a quick way of communicating information. This is particularly true of advertisements where there is a limited amount of time to convey messages and to attract the audience. Character 'types' are used to save time as they are easily recognised and interpreted by audiences; this is often due to their intertextuality.

Characters in specific genres also have a function or a purpose and how the audience respond to them is very important for the success of the text.

skins

Spooks

What expectations would an audience have of these characters?

TASK

Complete the table below suggesting the expectations you have of a particular genre.
Consider how audiences may respond to these conventions:

GENRE	CHARACTERS	NARRATIVE PLOT SITUATIONS	ICONOGRAPHY	AUDIENCE / APPEAL RESPONSE
TV news	Anchor		Suits	Expert
Reality TV	Presenter			Interaction
Action film		Car chase		
Crime drama	Pathologist		Police cars	
Gossip Magazines		'Uncovered'		Celebrity interest

What conclusions can you draw from the table?

- Do certain genres use character types more regularly?

- Are the genre conventions the same across a range of examples from the same genre?

- How do the genre conventions elicit different responses from audiences?

TASK

Create a new character for one of the following television genres that either challenges or conforms to the stereotypical representation of that character type in that genre:

- A soap opera.
- A police series.
- A hospital drama.

Consider:

- Appearance.
- Relationships with other characters.
- Role and function within the text.
- Audience response to the character.

Learning Point: Specific characters are typical of particular genres, and their role and function are recognised and understood by audiences.

Narrative events

These are the plot situations that an audience will expect to see in a particular genre. Again, the audience will be familiar with the structure of the plot and will anticipate events and situations that will occur within the overall narrative. Each of these then becomes a convention associated with the genre. Narrative events do not only occur in fictional texts – the location report in a news broadcast is a narrative convention of that genre, where the narrative is related to order and selection rather than plot. An audience will recognise the convention and be aware of its purpose in giving more immediate and 'on the spot' information about a news story. The same is true of the action replay in a football match where audiences expect that they will be given the chance to see action from a range of different viewpoints.

In fictional texts specific genres have their own predictable narrative events including the meeting in the incident room with the whiteboard in a police drama; the 'professional' argument in a hospital drama and the simple misunderstanding in a situation comedy. The audience have a sense of satisfaction when these events occur, as they confirm their understanding of the genre and their expectations of what will happen.

Texts such as magazines and newspapers have a narrative formula based on order and structure and readers anticipate what will appear in certain sections of the text – this too is a narrative event and readers are comfortable knowing where specific sections are to be found (for example, in a quality newspaper world news tends to follow domestic news).

Developed example: It can be the case that key narrative events are repeated in different versions of the same text. For example, in the vampire / horror genre, certain narrative events reappear in different examples of the genre over time. The original narrative came from the novel *Dracula* by Bram Stoker (1897) and several later film adaptations have been true to narrative events included within the novel even when 'up-dating' the content for a new audience.

Dracula: Prince of Darkness (far left); *Twighlight* (left)

TASK

Watch the following scenes in these films from the vampire / horror genre:

* *Dracula* (1931) starring Bela Lugosi – the opening sequence up to the point where Renfield cuts himself.

* *Dracula: Prince of Darkness* (1965) – the opening sequence up to the point Dracula claims his first victim.

* *Bram Stoker's Dracula* (1992) – the trailer and Scenes 2–4.

* *Twilight* (2008) – DVD Chapter 2, First Day at School, and Chapters 10 and 11, How Long Have You Been 17?

Now consider the following questions in relation to the extracts:

* What can be said about the iconography used in the film extracts? How typical is it of the genre?

* How important is the setting and how is it established?

* How do the audio and technical codes help to create the atmosphere?

* How have the character roles changed / remained similar across the films?

* What similar genre conventions are used in these films?

* How have the genre conventions been adapted to attract new audiences?

* How is the audience positioned in relation to the extracts?

Learning Point – Genre conventions including narrative events can be adapted and changed over time but the same narrative events can also recur regularly.

Iconography

This genre convention is related to the objects, costumes and backgrounds associated with a particular genre. These can help to define the genre and to raise an audience's expectations. The iconography of a genre is subject to sociological change as audiences expect more accurate and specific detail and as technology advances. Take, for example, the genre of the crime / forensics drama where the solving of the crime rests upon the team of forensic investigators and their range of technical and scientific devices. In programmes like *Waking The Dead* and *CSI Miami*, we see a range of technical equipment and understand its purpose and function. We also see it in use and audiences witness explicit views of injuries and operations involving blood and body parts and relevant forensic procedures. In both these programmes the iconography of the crime scene is very advanced. We, as audiences, are surrounded by the iconography of the laboratory and become involved in the action that takes place.

Relatively new genres have established their own iconography – for example, gaming and computer magazines have an iconography that includes graphic representations and recognisable logos, designs and backgrounds related to particular games. This iconography often excludes audiences who are unfamiliar with the genre and establishes exclusivity among users.

In programmes set in another time the iconography is used to establish realism. The attention to detail in the backgrounds and props in *Life on Mars* (2006–7) and *Ashes to Ashes* (2008-10) helped to establish these programmes securely in the 1970s and 1980s. This realism mainly relied on simple props and the audience recognition of them, for example, contemporary police cars and walkie talkies. Iconography can also establish the production values of the text. In high budget costume dramas, for example, *Cranford* (BBC 2007), the attention to detail in the setting, costume and props is essential in creating the realism of the period piece.

Costume and clothing are important in establishing genre and help producers of texts to communicate information quickly and effectively to audiences and to advance the narrative. In a hospital drama a character in a white coat wearing a stethoscope has a clear function that needs little explanation, as does the hierarchical distinction of the consultant in the suit. Audiences anticipate the role and behaviour of characters according to the clothing that they wear. Clothing can signify social standing, profession, income and values. It can also suggest conflicts within the narrative.

Props and objects can give information about cultural differences – the prevalence of guns and other weapons in American crime films is very different from those set in Britain.

TASK

Study the credit and **opening sequences** of *Waking The Dead* and *CSI: Miami*:

- How is iconography used to establish the genre?

- How is iconography used to highlight the cultural and procedural differences in the two programmes?

Mise-en-scène
– this French phrase literally means 'put-in-the-scene' and refers to everything that can be seen in the shot including characters, lighting, iconography.

CSI: Miami (far left); *Waking the Dead* (left)

Learning Point: Iconography is very important to rapidly establish the genre and the narrative and to give clues to the role and function of characters.

Setting

This is a further generic convention closely related to narrative events and characters, and can be genre and text specific. As with other conventions its link to genre is established through repetition which enables audiences to recognise settings and relate them to specific genres and programmes. The tracking shot through the Everglades in *CSI: Miami* is a feature of the opening credits and prepares the audience for the programme that follows. The establishing shot of the city skyline is used throughout the programme to remind audiences of where the programme is set and therefore the possible range of storylines. In this programme the narrative and crimes featured are often defined by the setting – the glamour of the wealthy areas set against the seedy underworld of drugs and border trespass. The inside settings where the key characters function are light and bright and the interview rooms are glass (suggesting transparency): the criminals will have nowhere to hide and the truth will always be uncovered. The mortuary and pathology labs are hi-tech and resemble sets from a science fiction film, thus emphasising the key role of science in crime solving.

In contrast, the settings in *Waking The Dead* are more realistic and urban, again representing the nature of the operations taken on by the team. They work in subterranean offices with no natural light. Theirs is an underground world suggesting that their role is to unearth the secrets of past crimes. Eve's laboratory is in stark contrast to the sunlit world of *CSI: Miami* although still very hi-tech. She works in isolation in a clinical, cold environment surrounded by the more stereotypical iconography of microscopes and test tubes.

Symbol – a sign with a symbolic link to what it represents. The understanding of the symbol is built up over years of habitual use. A symbolic sign is something that has taken on a meaning over and above what it actually is.

In soap operas characters are inextricably linked to setting in terms of areas of a specific country or individual streets and houses. The characters' houses are seen to be such an integral part of the audience's involvement with the programmes that the producers of *Emmerdale* and the late *Brookside* filmed in real locations specifically built for the programme. Take the characters out of the mise-en-scene and audiences would still recognise their domestic setting.

In non-fictional texts like news programmes, audiences become accustomed to location reports where the setting as a back drop is clearly established. The Political Editor for the BBC is conventionally filmed in front of either The Houses of Parliament or Number 10 Downing Street. This gives the impression of being at the heart of what is happening and therefore communicating up-to-the-minute news. Aspects of this setting, for example, Big Ben, become a symbol associated with the genre – they come to mean tradition, truth and the heart of news.

Technical codes

The way in which a text is filmed / edited and constructed, whether it be a moving image or print, communicates information to audiences regarding the genre. The producers of the text will also follow certain codes of layout, design and editing that allow audiences to recognise the form and style of its particular genre. This is established through the repetition of the format – audiences become familiar with this and have expectations of the text. The technical codes of a text also suggest the production values of that text. A 'high concept' action movie is recognisable through the filming and editing conventions it employs.

What is meant by technical codes and how do they relate to a study of genre?

Technical codes can be divided into the following areas:

1. Camera shots – including extreme close-ups, long shots and establishing shots.

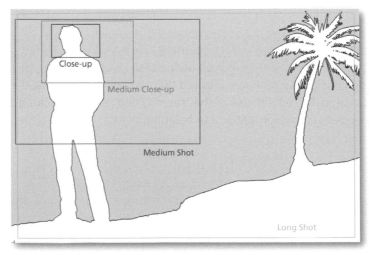

Certain shots are characteristic of specific genres. For example in a tense thriller, close-up shots will be used to build tension and to involve the audience. At emotional moments in soap operas the camera will zoom in to focus on a character's face for maximum impact. However, in wild life programmes in addition to close-ups we expect to see long shots of setting to give more information about where the filming is taking place. Point of view [POV] shots are used in computer games where the first person POV shot encourages users to play as if they themselves are part of the game. Through the POV shot, the user remains in control of the actions of the character as they move through the game. The player becomes the character. In the third person POV shot in gaming, the player controls a character but does not become them:

> 'the third-person point of view allows far greater freedom to tell a more traditional story. This is because the character on the screen is a separate entity and is dissociated from the player. This allows the designer to give characters their own personality and control how they behave.' (Stewart *et al.*, 2001: 126–7)

Tracking / reverse tracking shot
– the movement of the camera using a dolly or a steadicam to allow it to smoothly follow a character or the action. In a reverse track the camera moves backwards and the character / action moves smoothly towards the audience.

Third-person POV

POV

2. Camera angles – including high angle, low angle and aerial shot. The aerial shot of the car chase became a generic filming convention of the action drama. The repetition of this convention encouraged audiences to suspend their disbelief at being placed in this position. It also allowed them to feel more involved in the action. Hospital dramas make regular use of the tracking and reverse tracking shot, again to establish audience involvement and to heighten the pace of the action.

3. Editing – the way in which a text is actually constructed and put together can itself be an indicator of the text's genre. The fast paced car chase of an action film is a generic convention constructed to convey pace and dramatic action. The editing in the print format of teenage magazines is predictable and has a recognisable format with cover and sell lines placed around a central, usually close-up, image. This image will be brightly lit and airbrushed to suggest beauty and perfection. The front cover will be 'busy 'and colourful, and there will be a mixture of font styles and of upper and lower case lettering to attract the eye of the intended consumer.

Diegetic sound
– this refers to natural sound that is part of the *mise-en-scène* or 'sound you can see'. For example, the explosive sound as a gun is fired or the ambient sound of chatter and music in a restaurant scene. Non-diegetic sound is sound which is super-imposed upon the mise-en-scène or 'sound you can't see'. This may include the use of a voice over and music to establish a mood of tension or romance.

Audio codes

There is an expectation that certain audio codes will appear in specific genres:

- Sound effects – in action films we expect to hear explosions, gun fire, the screeching of tyres. The beeping of heart monitors and other ambient sounds may be conventions of a hospital drama.

- Non-diegetic sound may include a voice over in a documentary and mood music in a romantic film. Canned laughter is a generic convention of a situation comedy and serves to point the audience towards the humour in the narrative.

- Diegetic sound can refer to the style of the dialogue an audience will expect to hear in a particular genre. For example, a conversation in a heist movie like Ocean's Thirteen (2007) will include specific language related to the planning of the crime. In a hospital drama audiences become accustomed to technical language related to hospital procedures. The use of this specific language helps to establish realism.

Music is an effective indicator of genre. The music that accompanies the opening credits to *Match of the Day* or *EastEnders* has become familiar to audiences through repetition and for many people 'says' football and soap opera respectively. Music can be a clue to imminent action. The sound code in *Jaws* (1975) is recognisable to a range of audiences across generations. Contrapuntal music suggests action before there are any other clues on the screen and prepares the audience for what is to come.

Learning Point: A range of audio codes are employed by the producers of texts to indicate genre and narrative.

TASK

- Listen to the opening sequence of a film without looking at the screen.
- Write down what you think is happening using the audio codes you have heard, for example, sound effects, dialogue, music, etc.
- *Watch* the film and listen to the soundtrack.
- Watch the opening sequence of another film without listening to the sound.
- Make suggestions for possible music, sound effects, dialogue, etc. for this film.

How important are the audio codes to the understanding of the film?

Problems with Genre – hybrids and sub-genres

Life on Mars

We have talked at length about genres and how they are categorised and recognised through the repetition of a repertoire of shared elements. However, it is also true to say that some texts are more complex and difficult to categorise because they incorporate the conventions of more than one genre. When we consider the concept of genre from the industry and producers' perspective it is important to remember that here it has not been utilised as a tool for analysis – producers of media texts are constantly looking for new formats or to manipulate existing formats in order to maintain and attract audiences. These mutations are also closely related to how audiences respond to specific genres and their changing expectations linked to social and cultural change. At the moment there is an audience fascination with celebrity culture that manifests itself in the creation of new genres including gossip magazines and 'voyeuristic' television programmes like *I'm a Celebrity Get Me Out Of Here* (2002–) – a programme that incorporates conventions from more than one genre, including game / challenge shows and documentary. Consider also how older genres have transformed, for example, how the genre of the police drama has evolved from the early days of *Dixon of Dock Green* (1957–76) through to *The Sweeney* (1975–8), to the soap opera style of *The Bill* (1984–) and now to the fantasy hybrid format of *Life on Mars* (2006–7) and *Ashes to Ashes* (2008– 2010).

In the genre of documentary there has been a movement away from traditional informative documentaries to documentaries dealing with more 'popular' subject matter, to those exploiting the format through investigative reporting as in *MacIntyre Investigates* (2002), to the advent of the hybrid 'docu-soap'. This also then has links to the relatively new genre of reality TV, which combines conventions of documentary and game show whilst purporting to represent 'reality':

'It was presented in a way that the editors made the show. They had the capacity to make anyone look very good or very bad at the flick of a switch. One of the problems with the whole show was that the public thought it was real. They lost sight it was a game show and it became very personal to everyone watching it.' (Nick Bateman, 'Nasty Nick' contestant in the first British *Big Brother* house, speaking on *Panorama* 'Life on TV' BBC1 12th Nov 2000)

Detailed study: *Strictly Come Dancing*

This programme is a good example of a hybrid genre and also illustrates how the genre mix is communicated through a repertoire of key conventions that have grown, over time, to be easily recognised by audiences.

Strictly Come Dancing is a British television show based on a dance competition featuring celebrities paired with professional dance partners competing in a range of dances. The title of the show has links with the long-running series *Come Dancing* (1949–98), a more serious ballroom dancing televised competition whose aim was 'to teach the public about the joy of dancing' (BBC Cult TV) and alludes also to the film *Strictly Ballroom* (Baz Luhrmann, 1992) in which two mis-matched partners dance their way to success. These influences already suggest the programme's hybridity and the historical significance for some audiences.

The show began in 2004 and has traditionally taken the early Saturday evening 'family' slot and attracts a broad audience. To maintain audience interest there have also been five stand alone Christmas specials. During the series run there is a spin-off programme *It Takes Two* on BBC2 which gives up-dates on rehearsals and offers interviews, behind-the-scenes filming and gossip. This also serves to keep audience interest in between shows. *Strictly Come Dancing* is filmed in front of a live studio audience and the music is provided by a live orchestra. The show is broadcast from a specially constructed set at the BBC. However, in some series, shows were also filmed at the Tower Ballroom Blackpool where the original *Come Dancing* series was filmed in the 1970s.

The **genre** of the programme is a mix of sub-genres including a dance talent show and a reality TV programme, but it also includes conventions relating to a competitive programme for example, presenters, judges, contestants and challenges. The **iconography** suggests ballroom dancing with the glitter ball, glamorous costumes, a dance stage and a live audience. The lexis is also specific to the genre including language related to dance moves, music genres and dancing styles. This serves to engage the expert audience and those who are attracted to the programme for other reasons. The hybridity of the genre therefore attracts the audience range.

The **narrative** is very formulaic and the success of the programme ensures that it is repeated unchanged from series to series. This is a winning formula and one that has become a global export. A clear narrative structure is established that does not change from week to week, consequently, audiences have an expectation as to what will happen. The opening equilibrium introduces Bruce Forsyth and Tess Daley, the presenters, who come down the steps and have a chat and a dance. Bruce makes jokes usually incorporating some of his favourite catch phrases that some viewers will recognise and associate with his previous programmes. The judges are then introduced, the contestants come down the steps and the show progresses in an expected pattern. However, new narrative features have been introduced since the beginning of the series, for example, The Dance Off, which introduced tension when the couples with the lowest amount of votes had to dance again against each other at the end of the programme, in order to stay in the competition.

The '**characters**' in the programme are recognisable. They comprise celebrities from a range of sports and media who are partnered with now recognisable celebrities from the world of ballroom dancing. There are also judges who are the 'experts' and have established their own styles and this is reinforced, in each episode, by the programme-makers. The judges have almost become 'types' who react and respond in a stereotypical away and one that is now expected by an audience with previous knowledge of the programme. For example, Craig Revel Horwood is regularly grumpy and critical of the contestants while Len Goodman adopts a paternal and experienced approach. The replacing of Arlene Phillips with Alisha Dixon caused controversy and allegations of ageism were leveled at the BBC. This move happened at the same time that *Strictly Come Dancing* went head to head in the schedules with *The X Factor* – Alisha Dixon clearly was included in order to attract the younger audience to the programme.

The **technical and audio codes** help to establish the programme's genre. The close-up camera shots add to the narrative by showing the expressions on the faces of the judges and the contestants, and in editing there are continual cuts to the studio audience to show audience members and their reactions – these often include well-known celebrities. This also serves to make the viewers at home aware that the show is 'live' and to encourage interactivity with the studio audience. The opening credit sequence is highly stylised and is a fast-paced combination of images and music clearly establishing the hybridity of this programme.

Through the editing process there are also separate narratives constructed employing, for example, the footage of the contestants in rehearsal. We are encouraged to follow their highs and lows as they prepare for the range of challenges given to them through the series. Here a documentary style of filming is used – this is, at times, much more conventional of a reality TV programme whereby contestants speak directly to the camera articulating their worries and fears to

'Water cooler'
television
– phrase that
appeared with
the advent of
reality television,
it means that
the programme
is so popular
that viewers talk
about it around
the water cooler
the next morning
at work.

the audience at home. There is also 'fly-on-the-wall' footage of rehearsals where tension is introduced through emotional outbursts, possibly threatening injuries and confrontations. As in reality TV, the editing of one week's preparation is edited in order to construct a specific narrative and to gain the empathy or irritation of the audience. The audience feel as if they are in a privileged position having seen 'behind the scenes'. This again suggests a hybrid genre. The audio codes used include the noise of clapping and cheering, the distinctive theme tune and the dance music. This often comprises recognisable, popular tunes even when accompanying more traditional dances so as not to alienate the audience.

This programme is a reality television show and as such contains many of the conventions of this genre and also encourages the usual 'water cooler' moments for the audience. This is usually enhanced by the coverage in the tabloid press of the private and public lives of the show's stars.

TASK

- Watch an episode of *Strictly Come Dancing*.

- What repertoire of elements is used in the programme to suggest that it is an example of a hybrid genre?

- Consider how 'truth' and 'reality' are created through the genre conventions.

Learning Point: Relatively new programmes may use a mix of genre conventions to attract audiences.

FINAL TASK

Watch the opening sequences of texts from three different genres including a hybrid genre. Use the following table to help you to analyse how the text establishes the genre:

	GENRE	NARRATIVE	CHARACTERS	ICONOGRAPHY TECHNICAL / AUDIO
2ND VIEWING				
3RD VIEWING				
Effect				
Purpose				

Examination practice: In the examination you will be required to analyse a media text in detail employing relevant media vocabulary. Using a table like that above is good practice. For the first viewing you will just watch. For the second viewing you can make notes – use the table to help you to make useful and relevant notes about the text. Try to get as many examples as you can under each column. For the third and final viewing, consider what the effect and purpose of the specific technique is. This will develop your analysis further.

Digital storytelling – Daniel Meadows describes digital storytelling as 'short, personal, multi media tales told from the heart' (www.photobus. co.uk). It is a way of using the tools of the still camera, the computer and the internet to make stories. Images, music and voice come together to construct a narrative.

Narrative

Christine Bell

In this Section

• What do we mean by narrative?

• How narratives are constructed.

Narrative is a key concept employed to analyse a range of media texts – print and moving image, fiction and non-fiction. However, what we understand by narrative is undergoing a process of transition as textual formats advance and develop and audience responses change. Many texts now include audience involvement in the narrative – in computer games the player takes charge and makes decisions about where and how the narrative will progress. In sports programmes on television the viewer can select the desired narrative which will have a different outcome from the choice made by someone viewing the same text. When watching an event like Wimbledon, a viewer can select the game they want to watch and often the camera angles and shots. In this way, because of different viewing experiences, the audience can construct their own narrative and a process of selection occurs.

All media texts have narratives – fictional texts are concerned with a story and a series of plot events while in non-fiction texts the narrative can be analysed in terms of order, construction and genre conventions.

TASK

Construct a photostory or a digital storyboard of your day so far. Then consider:

• What aspects of the narrative you have selected and why.

• What you have omitted and why.

• Whether your 'story' is linear or moves about in time.

• What camera shots you have used and their effect.

What is essential is an understanding of how narratives are 'told' or 'shown' to an audience – what is omitted is as important as what is included. In the task above, a process of selection and construction has taken place to produce a version of your day. Non-fictional texts also have a narrative structure – a news programme is constructed to a clear and recognisable format starting with the headlines and ending with the weather. The same is true of a newspaper where audiences know what to expect in each section of the text and on the front and back pages.

Learning Point: All types of media text have narratives – a structure that is recognisable to audiences.

Narrative in still images and print texts

Photographs capture moments in time and documentary photographs are used time and again as historical artefacts that will tell the story of an event. They can often be more powerful than the moving image and when they are open texts the audience are left to speculate about what has happened before and after the photograph was taken. Audiences deconstruct the image by considering the type of shot, the angle, the composition of the photograph, the subjects and the gaze. Techniques may be employed, for example black and white and soft focus, to establish a particular effect.

Migrant Mother (far left); the aftermath of the Haiti earthquake in January 2010 (left)

Open texts – media texts that are not 'anchored' by a caption, copy or a voice over explaining their meaning. The decoding of the text is left to the audience. Once words appear with the image the meaning is established for the audience and the text becomes a closed text.

'Migrant Mother' is one of a series of photographs that the photographer Dorothea Lange made of Florence Owens Thompson and her children in February or March of 1936 in Nipomo, California. She was a migrant farm labourer. Dorothea Lange attempted to 'tell the story' of this woman through still photographs; this is just one of many taken.

TASK

Look closely at the two photographs above, one historical and one modern.

- What is the narrative behind these images?
- What do they 'tell' or 'show' the viewer?
- What clues are there in the photograph to help the viewer decode the narrative?

Narrative in print texts

Tzvetan Todorov [1939] is a Bulgarian theorist who published work relevant to a study of media texts. He suggested that the primary function of the narrative was to solve a problem and that characters pass through a series of stages following a linear narrative where events follow in chronological order.

Roland Barthes (1915–80) was a French writer who continues to influence the study of the ways in which meanings are produced by texts through signs and code systems (semiotics).

Printed media texts, for example, DVD and games covers, also have the task of communicating a narrative to the audience / user but as the medium is different from film so are the techniques used to 'tell the story'. The aim of such covers is to communicate the genre / theme and the story. This will be established through a combination of images and language and conveyed also through the colours, layout and design, and other aspects that produce visual impact. Hyperbolic language and imperatives are often used to attract attention teamed with screen shots from the game and the film to give a 'taste' of the narrative using codes of enigma and action to hook the potential audience. The 'blurb' on the back of the covers gives a brief overview of the narrative highlighting key plot situations and establishing the genre.

TASK

Study the covers for the DVD of the film *Bulletboy* and the game *Call of Duty: World at War*.

- How is the narrative conveyed through the text on the covers?

- How do the illustrations establish the narrative and the genre?

- What enigma and action codes are used?

- How can the images be analysed using visual codes?

- In what different ways is it suggested that the narrative can be accessed by the user in the XBox game?

Narrative structures

It is important to consider and to learn how apply traditional theories before we consider how they may have evolved and changed. Traditional theory as proposed by, for example, TzvetanTodorov suggests two narrative structures to be found in texts: linear and circular. These theories are important as they give a framework for analysing texts and for understanding the ways in which narratives are communicated to audiences. Todorov allows us to consider the structure of the narrative and how it is moved along through a series of narrative events from beginning to end, while Vladimir Propp considers the relevance of characters and their actions and responses within the narrative. Roland Barthes, through an understanding of semiotics, equips us with the specific language to allow a detailed study of all aspects of the text. However, not all theories can be applied to all texts and it is important to only use the most relevant one for the specific text to be analysed.

Todorov stated that narratives are led by events in a cause and effect format and suggested the following structure:

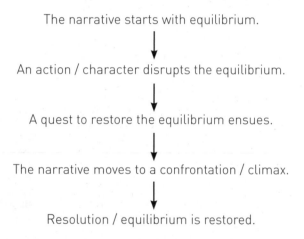

The narrative starts with equilibrium.

↓

An action / character disrupts the equilibrium.

↓

A quest to restore the equilibrium ensues.

↓

The narrative moves to a confrontation / climax.

↓

Resolution / equilibrium is restored.

This is a simple structure into which some texts will fit easily. However, we should already be considering the problem posed by the idea of a 'return to equilibrium' or the notion of a 'resolution'. Some texts that seek to challenge audiences offer open ended narratives leaving the audience to interpret what they understand by the ending. Other resolutions are far from a 'return to equilibrium', for example, the ending of the crime film *Se7en* (1995) which is bleak and desolate. In this text the audience eventually realises that the only resolution will be a tragic one and there will be no 'return to equilibrium' for the main characters.

Multi-stranded narratives

The narrative structure in many television programmes and some films does not always follow only one storyline. This is particularly the case in television with established series, for example, long-running dramas and soap operas. Here, audiences are familiar with characters and their history and therefore, some narratives will use links from previous episodes or will introduce another narrative strand that will run over a series of episodes. This strand does not conclude at the end of the episode and its function is to encourage viewers to watch the next, or subsequent, episodes to find out the resolution. In this way, the producers of the programme create narrative strands that will appeal to regular, loyal followers of the programme, but they will also include strands that start and end in one episode and therefore do not alienate first time or casual viewers.

Many television dramas, for example, *Casualty*, operate a 3-strand narrative structure. The strands will be introduced separately at the start of the programme and will then interweave as the programme progresses. In *Casualty* the linking factor of the narrative strands may be the setting, i.e. the hospital, or a particular character. One of the strands may be an ongoing storyline involving a relationship between two of the staff; another may be one centred around a patient in the hospital, and a third may be an accident that happens outside of the regular setting but involves the hospital staff and regular characters, for example, the paramedics.

Learning point: Narrative strands are important in attracting and maintaining audience interest.

TASK

Watch the opening of a television drama or soap opera that is long-running or runs over a set amount of episodes, for example, *Waking The Dead*, *Casualty* or *Hollyoaks*.

- What narrative strands are introduced in the opening of the episode?

- Are the strands driven by plot situations, setting or characters' relationships?

- How may these strands appeal to both regular and new audiences?

- Can you anticipate how the strands may interweave in this and future episodes?

However, not all texts conform to the linear structure. A key aspect of narrative is its ability to manipulate time and space and to involve the audience at an interactive level with the text. Many narratives are circular in their structure and move around within a time frame. In films like *Memento* (2000), *Eternal Sunshine of the Spotless Mind* (2004), *Crash* (2004) and *Vantage Point* (2008), the narrative is complicated and the audience challenged, due to the structure. In crime drama the narrative may start in the middle, work back to the crime and then forward to the resolution. Split-screen narrative techniques are used where the screen is split into two or three panels with a different narrative going on in each (for example, *Trial and Retribution*, ITV, January 2009) – the audience is more challenged in their viewing as they are asked to interpret what they are seeing at a more complex level through parallel narratives. As regards non-fiction, in sports programmes time and space are manipulated and we readily accept action replays and seeing the same event from a range of different camera angles, perhaps evoking different audience responses.

TASK

Look at the trailer for the film *Crash* (2004).

- How does this trailer challenge Todorov's suggestion that narratives are linear?

- What different narrative strands are introduced?

A study of the narrative of computer games raises some interesting questions. Some narratives are very simple because the world and the setting are more important than the plot. Some games conform to the three part structure of 'equilibrium – disruption – return to equilibrium', and other games experiment with more complex narrative structures, where there are a series of levels and movement through the levels is the domain of the player. Resolution may never be attained if certain narrative stages are not completed. There may be choices to be made which involve a forking path narrative where the storyline splits in different directions and therefore the narrative flow is not constant as it is related to the ability of the player to solve the puzzles. A player may also revisit the same narrative event several times and make different choices leading to different progressions through the game. The multi-player platforms, for example, the X-Box 360, introduce plot situations whereby the narrative is negotiated between the players. This will then change the direction of the narrative according to the choice of one of the players. This interactive nature of the narrative is a relatively new concept for analysis:

> 'the way that Lara Croft acts when one person plays her might vary a great deal from the ways that she moves or acts when another person is at the controls. This is why theories drawn from older media (film or literature, for example) can't fully describe digital games. Games also complicate old notions about the relationship between authors and readers, because players determine how the "hero" behaves.' (Burn *et al.*, 2003: 110)

Narrative techniques

As suggested earlier, the work of Roland Barthes continues to be useful to media students analysing narrative. He gives a clear set of codes which enable us to understand how media texts are communicated to and interpreted by audiences.

Barthes suggested that narrative was conveyed in texts through key codes including:

- Enigma codes – these are used by a range of media, fiction and non-fiction. These codes control the amount of information that is released to the audience in order to make them curious and to want to consume more of the text. Information is often undisclosed until further on in the text. Unexplained 'clues' in the form of enigmas are given early in the narrative. This may be a mysterious figure in the opening sequence, the headlines of a news report or the cover lines in a magazine. Trailers for new films and television programmes are an institutional device employing enigmas and designed to tease the audience and subsequently raise expectations.

- Action codes – these codes are a form of shorthand for advancing the narrative. They signal to the audience a narrative event that will take place, for example, the buckling of a gun belt in a Western or the packing of a suitcase.

Audience positioning in narrative

The privileged spectator position

This is where the camera places the audience within a superior position in the narrative. They are shown elements that the characters in the *mise-en-scène* cannot see. For example, a close-up shot shows the audience one character taking a gun out of her bag, which only the audience can see. In sports programmes this is a common narrative convention where the viewer, through action replay, sees the narrative more than once from a range of viewpoints. The function is to make the audience feel in a more powerful position in the narrative in that they can then discuss what has happened with increased knowledge and perhaps predict what is to follow.

Apparently impossible positions

Here, the camera gives the audience a view of the narrative from an unusual position, for example from the air or from behind a wall. The audience suspends its disbelief if the position increases its involvement in the scene. In the 'shower scene' from the film *Psycho* (1960) the audience witnesses the action in effect from *behind* the wall of the shower. This is effective because it allows the audience to see the victim and builds tension as a shadowy figure appears on the other side of the shower curtain. Similarly, a car chase can be viewed from an aerial tracking shot, which allows audiences to witness the ongoing action from an impossible position.

The Fast and the Furious

Psycho

Point of view shots [POV]

Here the audience sees the action from different points of view that will change their perception and involvement in the scene. The camera may show the point of view of the murderer or the victim or move between the two. This will obviously change the audience's positioning and their response. It is often the case that the audience may be placed in an uncomfortable position by the camera or one that positions the audience from a male or female perspective. POV shots also affect the way in which the audience relate to the characters. POV can also be established through voice overs where a character's thoughts are communicated to the audience; and direct address to camera in, for example, a news bulletin or documentary.

A flashback

Here the audience is given additional information about the narrative which enhances its understanding. Older media texts will use more contrived techniques to suggest movement back in time, for example, the hands of a clock moving backwards, pages of a calendar turning or misty filming. Today's audiences are assumed to be more sophisticated and able to decode signs in clothing and other iconography. In the film *Atonement* (2007) the narrative moves around in time and challenges the audience's perceptions with very few clues to what is happening.

Vladimir Propp (1895–1970) – researched the roles of characters in folklore and fairy stories. He wrote an influential book *The Morphology of the Folktale* (1928) which sets out his findings. This has been applied to media texts to discuss the important function of character in narrative.

TASK

Watch the opening sequence of the first episode of *Life On Mars*, a crime series where the main protagonist travels back in time to the 1970s after he is knocked down in an accident.

- What clues are the audience given to suggest that the character has travelled back in time?

- How does iconography help to establish this?

Learning Point: Narrative techniques work together to 'show' the audience the narrative.

Characters in narrative

Vladimir Propp, a Russian critic and folklorist, was concerned with the relationship between narrative and characters. Through his research, he argued that stories are character driven and that plots develop around the actions of characters. He looked at characters and their function within the story. He stated that it was possible to group characters and actions into roles and functions which move the story along.

While Propp's theory can be applied with relevance to some media texts, particularly those with narratives akin to folk stories like science fiction, Disney and fantasy, it is not possible to apply it effectively in its entirety to all texts. However, it is important to be aware of his work and its application, and his notion of character function still has relevance in some media texts, particularly with regard to the function of character types like the hero who has to accomplish or seek something and carries the events through the narrative and the villain who attempts to prevent the hero in his goal.

These roles can also be found in non-fiction texts – tabloid newspapers often make villains out of political leaders, particularly in narratives involving war.

Whether or not Propp is applicable, the function of characters in narratives is a useful focus of analysis. Certain texts have characters in them that we expect to see. This helps the narrative and communicates information as the audience understands their function and can anticipate how they will behave and even the type of narrative events in which they may be involved.

Learning Point: It is important to bear in mind that not all theories can be applied to all texts.

Technical codes in narrative

The camera 'shows' the audience the narrative through a range of camera shots, movements and angles that have been edited into a sequence. The editing process is where important decisions are made about how characters are represented and events told that will affect the response of the audience. Consider how the 24-hour filming of a reality TV programme such as *Big Brother* is edited into a one hour (with advertisement breaks – so really only about 45 minutes) nightly programme and the opportunities offered to the producers to manipulate 'characters' and storylines. Similarly, consider the 'fly on the wall' documentary footage used in *Strictly Come Dancing* (2009) to show the contestants in rehearsals is carefully selected in order to manipulate the audience. The short piece of filming can make an audience empathise with a particular celebrity or alternatively, make the celebrity appear foolish and irritating. Within the programme one extract where the celebrity is down and struggling will be followed with one which has been edited to produce an up-beat response in the audience.

In the same way, the soundtrack is a narrative device that communicates messages about the plot and what is to come. Tense music (often discordant and uncomfortable to listen to) is a signal of a particular narrative just as 'action' music (fast paced) signals pace and drama in the storyline.

TASK

Study extracts from three different texts, for example, a news programme, a web page and a computer game. Analyse the narrative construction using the following headings:

- Structure.

- Techniques.

- Characters.

- Technical and audio codes.

- Audience response.

TASK

Storyboard the opening sequence for a television drama or a film employing the following plot outlines and using a range of narrative devices:

- A murder.

- Establishing a setting.

- Establishing the feelings of a character.

- Creating an atmosphere.

- Creating suspense.

'Representation is the process by which members of a culture use language (broadly defined as any system which deploys signs, any signifying system) to produce meaning.'
Stuart Hall

Representations and Responses

Christine Bell

In this Section

- What is meant by representation?
- The role of selection, construction and anchorage in creating representations.
- How the media uses representations.
- The points of view, messages and values underlying those representations.

KEY TERMS TOOLKIT

Representation – the way in which the media constructs aspects of 'real life', including people, places, events, culture, ethnicity and issues.

Mediation – the process of editing and construction that the media text has been exposed to before it is presented to the audience.

Anchorage – the text, captions or voice-over that accompany a text and 'anchor' its meaning.

Denotation – the simple description of an image / sound without any meanings attached to it.

Connotation – the meaning that the audience give to the sign / image / sound according to its context and the cultural experiences of the audience.

When applied to a study of the media, representation is a complex concept through which we attempt to understand how the media constructs its messages and how audiences respond to that construction. The significant question, as dealt with by Wendy Helsby (2005), is whether the media constructs or reflects aspects of society. Are the media so powerful that they construct situations, opinions and beliefs that audiences accept as 'reality', or do they reflect the inherent opinions and beliefs that already exist?

Introductory Activities – Understanding representation

Before we start to study the concept of representation in any detail, it is important to examine how we look at things that are around us and how we interpret what we see according to our experiences, culture, gender and pre-conceived expectations.

TASK

Write a 50 word description of yourself.

Ask your friend to write a 50 word description of you.

- How do they differ?

These are two different representations of one person. If you had asked your boy / girlfriend or your mum or your grandad to do the same there would have been differences because of their positioning and relationship to the subject matter – in this case, you.

TASK

Take a photograph of yourself surrounded by objects that mean something to you. For example, clothes you like to wear, a CD of your favourite band, a cuddly toy, your iPod. Ask someone to annotate the photograph decoding the messages you have encoded.

- Were there any surprises? Did they interpret the codes differently from your intended meaning?

Encoding – the messages and ideas that are 'packaged' into a media text by the producers of that text.

Decoding – the ways in which any audience 'unpackages' or reads meaning into that text influenced by a range of factors.

Learning Point: The ways in which representations are understood and interpreted are affected by a range of factors including: relationships, context and cultural experience.

TASK
BROADSTROKE PORTRAITS

Someone from your class will stand at the front. Draw that person as accurately as you can. When you have done that annotate your drawing thinking about the following visual codes: clothing, gesture and expression.

What you have constructed here is a representation of the person. If everyone in the room holds up their drawing you will see how many representations of that person have been constructed in a short space of time.

- Compare the annotations – how do they differ? They will change according to the experience of the person constructing the image. They may be affected by how well they know the 'model', if they recognise the fashion brand they are wearing, if they like / recognise the band they have on their T-shirt, etc.

Before considering specific examples of representation in the media it is important to give some thought to what we are looking for and the questions we need to ask about the representations that are presented to us in a range of media texts (adapted from Stafford, 2001).

TASK

How do representations work in the media?

Look at the collage of images below. They are all 'representations' of gender that you would find in the media:

- Who or what is represented in the images?

- Where would you expect to find these images?

- Have the images been constructed in any way?

- Do any of the images contain a message – for example, what we are expected to think about the images?

- Choose two of the images – what questions would you ask about the texts?

Think about how you have interpreted the images. You will have looked at the images first and described them – this is called DENOTATION. You will then have tried to understand them and the messages they contain – this is the CONNOTATION of the image.

You will also have deconstructed the image using VISUAL CODES. The most common visual codes used to understand what we see are:

- Clothing – the clothing worn tells us something about the person, for example, a uniform, a football shirt, a 'fashion craze'.

- Gesture – body language communicates messages to others, for example, a wave, a salute.

- Expression – facial expressions are rapid communicators of information, for example, a smile, a frown.

- Technique – the way in which the image is presented carries meaning, for example, black and white, soft focus.

Key questions to consider about representations

1. What kind of world is being *constructed* by the media text?

What you need to know:

- That the world presented is constructed.

- That the reality presented by the text is constructed.

- That audiences deconstruct texts according to their knowledge of the world presented to them and their experience.

- That characters, locations and issues are presented in different ways.

2. How are *stereotypes* used as shorthand to represent certain groups of people?

What you need to know:

- That makers of media texts use audience recognition of types to transmit messages rapidly. Most media texts including films, magazine articles and television programmes have only a short time to establish characters and as a result offer limited representations. This is especially the case with advertisements (see Section 1 on Characters).

- Audiences often feel happier when a character stays within the limits of the stereotype because then they feel that they 'got it right'. They feel comfortable that they understand and can predict their behaviour and narrative function.

3. Who is in control of the text? Whose ideas and values are expressed through the representations?

What you need to know:

- Texts are constructed and manipulated by the producers of the text.

- A process of mediation occurs in the construction of a media text, for example, a news report.

4. How will audiences interpret / decode the representation in the text? At whom is the text aimed?

What you need to know:

- Representation is linked to the cultural experiences of the audience. The cultural competence will be different for different audiences.

- The ability to decode the representation will also be related to situation / race / gender / age.

- It is also affected by the audience relationship with the individual star / event / environment.

Stereotype
– stereotyping is a quick way for the producers of media texts to categorise people according to exaggerated features, behaviour, etc. Stereotypes can be both positive and negative. Some stereotypes can be based upon observable truths.

5. What ideology / message is contained within the representation?

What you need to know:

- You need to recognise, be aware of and at times, challenge the view being presented through the text.

- Particular interests / views of the world may be challenged or promoted.

- Texts may promote, challenge or judge the roles of gender, ethnicity or age.

Learning Point: Representations are constructions containing messages and their interpretation by audiences is influenced by a range of factors.

Construction and Mediation

By now, you will have learned that the 'reality' that we see on television screens and read in newspapers is constructed. Every time we watch or read a media text we are not seeing 'reality' but someone else's version of it. We rely upon receiving our information about a range of events from different sources as we cannot actually be there to witness what is happening first hand. However, what we finally see has gone through a process of mediation.

KEY TERMS TOOLKIT

Selection – for whatever ends up on the screen or in print, a lot more will have been left out. Someone will have made the decision about what will be included and what to omit. Think about how this might affect how the audience feels about what it sees.

Construction – the elements that go to make up the final text will have been constructed in a way that real life is not. When we witness an accident in real life we do not see it from three different camera angles and in slow motion. This is often the way we view an event in a hospital drama. In 'real life' arguments, we do not have the use of close-ups to show emotion – these are used regularly in films and on television

to heighten the experience for the audience. What we see when we watch a reality television programme, for example, *I'm a Celebrity, Get Me Out Of Here* is a selected construction of the hours of filming which have been edited often to show a particular viewpoint [whose?] about a storyline or character.

Focus – mediation encourages the audience to focus upon a particular aspect of the text to push us towards making assumptions and to draw conclusions. In a drama the camera may focus upon a particular character. Our eyes are drawn to the headlines and cover lines in newspapers and magazines.

Learning Point: Media texts are not 'windows on the world'. They present a version of reality.

Mediation and the representation of an event

Events around the world are represented daily on our screens in news bulletins and documentary programmes. The audience for these texts is more likely to believe what they see because they are seeing what they perceive as 'real' events played out before them. Consider the mediation process that takes place before a news report is shown on the television screen:

- The camera person has filmed the event. Mediation takes place immediately – they decide what to film and what to leave out.

- A voice over or 'to camera' report is filmed to accompany the footage as anchorage. This information will have been selected by the journalist, this therefore has now become a representation of the event. The language used by the journalist will be instrumental in constructing meaning and in offering the audience a representation of the parties involved in the event, for example, terrorists or illegal immigrants.

- The report is sent to a news agency who may edit this footage further.

- The report arrives at, for example, the BBC news room where decisions will be made about its place in the hierarchy of new stories that day – how newsworthy it is. This has implications for how the audience will view its importance – decisions are being made for us.

- When the report is finally aired it will be accompanied by a headline or an introduction by the news anchor. This can give a preferred meaning to the story. One that an audience may not challenge because it is presented with authority.

- The report may be preceded or followed by comments and opinions from a journalist or an 'expert' in that area who is a studio guest. They may be asked to speculate on future events or on the context of the report and may affect the audience response to what they see and hear.

- By the end of the report the audience may well have formed an opinion about the event because of the way in which it has been mediated through the different agencies.

It is important in a study of the role and function of the media, to consider how events are represented to an audience through media texts and how that representation may affect the way in which the event is viewed. The consideration of selection, construction and focus is essential when considering the representation of events in the media.

Examples of media events

- **Sporting events** – Wimbledon, The Olympic Games, football events. The way in which these events are represented may also lead to the consideration of representations of gender, for example, the portrayal of women tennis players in the tabloid press.

- **Pop festivals** – this could be linked to representations of youth.

- **Political events** – elections, visits of foreign politicians, scandals.

- **National events** – a royal wedding, a public funeral.

- **International events** – a war, the global recession.

- **Local events** – the promotion of the local football team, a local 'star'.

TASK

Study the front covers of the newspapers representing the event of the 2010 General Election. How has the event been represented in these media texts? Consider the following:

- The use of images.

- The use of language

- The point of view expressed.

- The differences in the way in which the event is represented.

- The effect the representation of the event may have upon an audience.

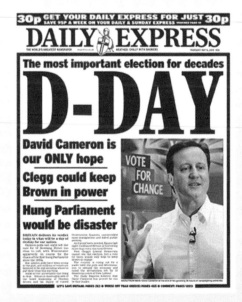

TASK

Choose an example of a current event, for example, a conflict in another country. Look at how that event has been presented in at least two different media texts, for example, a newspaper and a television programme. Consider the mediation process that the story has undergone and then answer the following questions:

- How has the chosen event been represented by the texts?

- Whose ideas and values are expressed through the representation of the event?

- In an event such as the one you have chosen, how easy is it for a particular point of view to be expressed – how are the audience encouraged to react?

- How might different audiences respond in different ways to the representation of the event?

Event – a 'happening' that is presented in the media and has significance for an audience. This may be a sporting event, for example, the 2012 Olympic Games; a local event, for example, the opening of a new factory; a national event, for example, The FA Cup Final or an international event like the volcanic dust cloud that grounded planes across the world in 2010.

Learning Point: Events are represented in a range of ways by different media texts. The representation is a construction that has undergone mediation. This will affect how an audience may respond to the event.

Anchorage

Images without words are open texts – the connotations of the image are left to the audience and the associations it might make. At this point, the texts can be said to be polysemic in that they can be interpreted in more than one way by different audiences. Once there are words in the form of a caption, a headline or a description, then the text becomes 'closed' and the meaning is clearly suggested to the audience. The decision regarding interpretation has been made for viewers / readers and they are, therefore, less likely to challenge or consider what they see.

Learning point: Anchorage – the words that accompany the image – affects the representation and how the audience respond to it.

TASK

Look at the image below.

For this image write two different headlines, captions and opening paragraphs for a news report that will change the way in which an audience views the image. How might different audiences interpret this image differently because of the anchorage?

TASK

Watch a news report with the sound off. Write two contrasting voice overs to anchor the piece and change the focus of the report.

- How have you changed the meaning of the images through the anchorage?

- What effect will the different representations you have constructed have upon audiences?

Dominant Ideology

Whose point of view is presented through the text?

This follows on from mediation and suggests the idea that those who are in positions of power use that position to communicate their opinions and beliefs. These people are usually called 'opinion leaders' and for the purposes of this study examples could include politicians as represented in the media, newspaper owners, editors and television producers. They present, repeat and reiterate a particular viewpoint that then appears to become the 'norm' for some elements of the audience.

How are young people represented in the media?

A good example of the way in which dominant ideology works in practice is the *Daily Express* and *Daily Mail*'s view of young people with headlines like:

'Out-of-control' British teens the worst behaved in Europe' (July 2007)

'THE HORRIFIC REALITY OF YOB RULE BRITAIN

'GANGS of hoodies are bringing terror to our streets, menacing communities, instilling fear and putting at risk the peaceful way most of us want to be allowed to live our lives.' (*Daily Express*, 18 Aug 2009)

These headlines written by 'opinion leaders' offer a very negative representation of young people using emotive and hyperbolic language. Language can therefore be seen to be a very powerful communicator of ideology. As many people already have a fear of young people engendered, in part by the media, they may accept the view given to them by the newspaper they choose to read. Many newspapers are less inclined to offer positive representations of young people and when they do they still use stereotypes as a way of defining them:

'We demonise all boys as feral ... then wonder why they turn into hoodies. A photograph of a boy in a hood is now the symbol of urban decay or the end of the world. Teenage boys – when not knifing each other or fathering children – are hanging around drinking and drugging. Or they are in their bedrooms playing violent games, which is anti-social. What the research commissioned by Women in Journalism highlighted was that there are very few good stories about teenage boys.' (Suzanne Moore, *Daily Mail*, 14 March 2009)

In this research it was found that the only positive representations of young people were to be found in reality television shows like *Britain's Got Talent* and *The X-Factor*, a good example being the recent success of teenager Joe McElderry and the young dance group Diversity.

'X-Factor winner Joe McElderry: small boy, big voice, great future

'Joe McElderry, the cherubic 18-year-old who has won X-Factor, has not always been the star of the show but those supporting him at home have always known his true potential.' (*The DailyTelegraph*, 14 December 2009)

Joe McElderry (far left); Diversity (left)

TASK

Look at a selection of newspapers OR visit the websites of some national and local newspapers:

- How are young people represented in the newspapers? Can you find examples of negative and positive representations?

- How do the images and language contribute to the representation? Is anchorage used to give an image a meaning?

- Is there a message contained within the story and images used?

The more that dominant ideas and beliefs appear in various forms in the media, the more they are accepted and therefore become the dominant ideology. One ideology and representation purveyed by current magazines is equating 'thin' with 'beautiful'. The popular magazines continue to use emaciated models as the true idea of what a woman should look like, although this is far from the 'reality' for many women. Other magazines like *Closer* and *Heat* produce paparazzi shots of 'celebrity cellulite' and 'bikini disasters' of those women over a size 10! They also castigate thin celebrities one week and then uphold their 'summer bodies' as an ideal the next, thus offering mixed messages to their audiences.

Learning Point: Those in positions of power who control the media messages received by audiences are also in control of how certain groups in society are represented, and indeed, whether some groups are represented at all.

Body Image – How does the media represent an issue?

As well as representing groups of people and events, the media, in all its forms, also influences the ways in which an audience responds to key issues relevant in our society. Body image and size is one of those issues. However, ideologies do change as society changes so there is hope for the death of the 'cult of thinness'. In September 2006 the Madrid Fashion week banned models with a BMI (body mass index) below 18 in an attempt to address the messages sent out to young people about how they should look. The organisers of London Fashion Week were urged to do the same. Tessa Jowell, the then Culture Secretary and the minister behind the 'body image' summit of 2000 which was set up to examine the effect of the fashion industry on young women, stated:

> 'It is, however, an issue of major concern for young girls who feel themselves inferior when compared to the stick thin young women on the catwalk. They all want to look as beautiful as that and see beauty in those terms...we shouldn't for one moment underestimate the power of fashion in shaping the attitude of young girls and their feelings about themselves.' (*Media Guardian*, 2000)

This was thought to be the start of the end of images of super skinny models that bear little resemblance to young people in real life. In their place emerged models with normal bodies. Kira Cochrane writing in *The Guardian* (15 March 2010) in an article headed 'Do I look Thin In This?' expressed her hope for a possible sea change:

> 'Hayley Morley, a size 12, took to the catwalk for knitwear designer Mark Fast. Lizzie Miller, a size 14, caused a furore when pictured naked with a role of stomach flesh in US Glamour magazine. And then there was the size 16 supermodel, Crystal Renn, who published her autobiography *Hungry*... Renn suggested that a new kind of model that might be emerging. "lush and sparkly with nary a jutting collarbone in sight".'

model Lizzie Miller (far left); Hungry (left)

Lizzie Miller appearing naked and looking like a normal woman caused a sensation in the magazine and fashion world. She had not been airbrushed like so many other models and appeared as she was. Hundreds of women responded to the image and supported the use of more realistic images in magazines. The model herself said about the frustrations of young women who do not conform to the ideal:

> 'I've been that girl, flipping through magazines trying to find just one person who looked a little bit like me. And when I didn't find it I would start to think there's something wrong with the way that I looked. When J. Lo and Beyoncé came out and were making curves sexy, I started to accept myself more. It's funny, but just seeing them look and feel sexy enabled me to do the same.' (*The Inquisitor*, 21 August 2009)

The *Daily Mail*'s headline read: 'The wobbly bits that shook the world: the joyous support created by one model's picture (flabby tummy and all).' (September 2009)

However, the 2010 round of fashion weeks brought about controversy and new claims that nothing has changed despite Beth Ditto sitting in the front row of one of the events:

> 'there were hollowed out necks striped with taut, rope-like tendons, straining to keep balloon-like heads aloft on childlike shoulders.... It would be a big leap forward if catwalk photographs didn't seem bound, instantly, for a pro-anorexia website. Surely that's not too much to ask?' (*The Guardian*, 15 March 2010)

One publication taking on this issue recently was *V* magazine. This magazine has been in circulation since 1999 and is an eclectic mix of fashion, art, music and film communicated largely through images. It describes itself as:

> '*V* is a place where uptown meets downtown, celebrities mingle with total unknowns, high art converses with underground culture. Chic, wacky, fun, fabulous...in a letter: *V*.' (*V* website)

It launched a special 'Size Issue' in February 2010 celebrating larger sized women and featured them in a series of fashion shoots and wearing clothes usually reserved for thinner models. The front cover pictured 250-pound *Precious* film star Gabourey Sidibe. The issue met with a range of responses, most of them positive. The criticisms centred on concerns that normal and larger sized women should appear regularly in fashion magazines and by confining them to a special 'Size Issue' the magazine industry was still saying that these women were unusual and not the norm.

In a further challenge to the size issue debate, Penelope Cruz guest-edited a recent edition of the French *Vogue* magazine. She chose as her models a range of 'plus size' women including Crystal Renn:

> '**Cruz's intervention comes at a key moment within the industry for models with body shapes more akin to those of the majority of women.'** (*The Guardian*, 24 April 2010)

However, the controversy surrounding this emotive issue continues with fashion blogger Garance Dore suggesting that the fashion world was not yet ready for 'normal' sized women and to include them on a catwalk was tokenism and that they were not 'flattering to fashion' (*The Guardian*, 2010). Dore's comments and those of Karl Lagerfeld who attacked larger women and branded them 'fat mummies' have ensured that this issue continues to be a relevant one within the media.

Theorists writing about the continued mis-representation of women in magazines offer a range of reasons. Winship (1997) asserts that women in magazines are created as men would like to see them, similar to the 'male gaze' theory in film, hence the size and perfection of the images seen. Women are encouraged to accept this aspirational and ideal version of themselves, despite their understanding of the difficulty in achieving a size 8 and the unreality of that representation where women are defined by their size and how they look! Althusser (1971) suggests that in accepting the images of women shown in the media women are engaging in 'mis-recognition of the self':

> '**The alternative is to challenge it, but students know from their experience that this is difficult. For Marxists, this is a form of "false consciousness". Put simply, the post-feminist backlash has served to "redistract women" – rather than continue to lobby for equal pay and positive representation in the media, they are reading *Hello* and commenting on the waistlines of their sisters.'** (McDougall, 2006: 156)

TASK

Research how the issues of 'body image' and 'size' are represented in a range of texts. These may include gossip magazines, fashion magazines, newspapers and television documentaries.

Learning Point: Media texts can contain a point of view that the creators of the text want audiences to accept.

Representations of Gender in Computer Games

TASK

In groups consider two computer games in terms of:

• Gender representations.

• Theme.

• Narrative, including, for example, aims and structure.

• User involvement.

• Technical aspects, for example, first / third person viewpoint, special effects.

One of the main criticisms of computer games is that although they are a relatively new media format, they continue to re-enforce traditional gender roles where men are seen as powerful and in control and women are there to be rescued, or are viewed as a reward or as a sex object. The themes of many games are also overtly male – racing cars, planning military operations or tracking down a target in a dimly lit intimidating setting. These 'narratives' (often there is no clear narrative construction) usually also involve violence and the use of weapons to some degree even if there are also interactivity and thought involved.

TASK

Look at the YouTube Top Ten Video Game Women and listen to the voice over which explains how they have been chosen: 'the ladies had to be hot and empowering – there are no bimbos here' [www.youtube.com/watch?v=cbua0yZYais].

• What representations of women are being suggested here?

At least boys get to see some action with a high level of exciting interactivity. Those games aimed specifically at girls tend to involve interest based activities or those concerned with fashion design and make-overs. These games reinforce representations of girls as only wanting to look beautiful and be popular and the animated versions of these games involving, for example, Barbie and Disney Princesses offer physically unreal representations of women in passive roles. Their main concerns are their appearance and their need to find a man of some description, be it Prince Charming or Ken! Events happen to them in the games and they rarely become pro-active themselves.

However, it could equally be argued that any games that encourage girls to engage with computers are acceptable and that some interest based games have complex narratives and involve skills such as decision making and have representations of girls as resourceful and active:

> 'Proponents of games designed for girls believe that any activity that encourages a girl to use a computer is a good thing, even if it might serve to reinforce stereotypical roles. Interest in computer games can lead to increased computer proficiency, an interest in well-paid technical careers and a general increase in the use of digital media by women.' (Stewart, Lavelle and Kowaltze, 2001: 133)

In the *Pippa Funnell* range of games which deal with the theme of running and managing a riding stable, the narrative is clear – you have inherited a run down stud farm and must work to make it successful again. The player moves from one stage to the next only when certain tasks are completed successfully. The rewards involve option choices: to acquire extra land, enter a competition or get a new horse. The mode of address is direct and at times Pippa Funnell (a real show jumper) intervenes to give advice and suggest moves. There are elements of enigma and suspense introduced into the storyline and the navigation around the village is complex.

In contrast, the *Imagine* series of games marketed specifically at girls offers an interesting range of questionable representations. These games were launched by Ubisoft in 2007 and the titles continue to expand along with their popularity. In the games girls can play at having a range of jobs including *Imagine: Wedding Designer*, *Imagine: Babies* and *Imagine: Doctor*. Whilst some of the professions are stereotypically those of girls, there are more challenging professions in the series including vets and doctors. However, the games' covers present girls in a typical way and the success suggested is usually linked to beauty and popularity rather that success within the job. *Imagine: Doctor* states that the player will 'become the favourite doctor in town' whilst also solving the mystery of the epidemic that is raging. The role assumed in *Imagine: Babies* is more traditional and domestic. The player is required to: 'keep the house clean: use fun mini-games to create a welcoming home for the babies: wash up, clean and vacuum, paint the walls, mow the grass, trim hedges and drive away spiders!' *Imagine: Detective* asks that the player uses their 'feminine sixth sense' to solve the crimes.

Interestingly, this series has had runaway success and is very popular with girls aged between six and fourteen, the target audience. A ten year old who played the games stated:

> 'the problem is it is so unrealistic – you never fail and you are never really challenged. I am sure that's not what it is really like being a vet or a doctor. A much better game is *Professor Layton and The Curious Village* which really makes you think. You can't move on until you have solved the puzzles.'

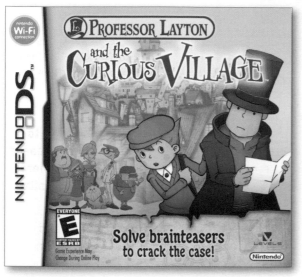

The game, *Professor Layton and The Curious Village*, is one played by boys and girls alike and indeed, also has an adult appeal. It is a challenging game working on different levels of difficulty – puzzles are set, some of these are essential and the player cannot move on without completing them, some are optional. The puzzles are complex and demanding and the more 'hints' the player uses the fewer 'picarats' (points) they win. 'Hint coins' are collected throughout the game to help in completing the puzzles. Some of the puzzles involve mathematics, others engage the player in lateral thinking and others are 'trick' questions. The gaining of picarats allows the player to access areas of the game at the end. It is a game involving thought and brain challenges rather than action.

Ubisoft launched a marketing campaign in 2008 for the *Imagine* series featuring popular television stars Fearne Cotton and Holly Willoughby, seen by the game's producers to be the right role models for the games' users:

> 'Mark Slaughter, marketing manager at Ubisoft, said the company has developed a marketing approach based around the aspirational concept of "Live your dreams". "Fearne and Holly were specifically chosen due to their complete fit with this territory and positioning," Slaughter added. "They are great friends, are fun, friendly and positive role models. They also exist in the area of aspirational media."' (*The Guardian*, August 2008)

TASK

Study the covers for the *Imagine* series of games aimed at young girls.
Consider how girls are represented in these games' covers commenting on:

- Use of images.

- Language.

- Use of colour.

- Game content / narrative.

Create a new game for the *Imagine* series and design a cover for the game
using the codes and conventions already established by the game's producers.

Or create a new game which challenges typical representations of young girls.
Design the cover for the game.

The Ambiguity that is Lara Croft

With regard to issues of representation in computer games, it is important to be aware that all games originated from technology that was originally used to create projects funded by the military and many computer game innovators were previously employed in roles related to warfare. This in part explains the prevalence of themes related to war and violence in computer games and plot situations involving hunting down and shooting enemies and targets.

The creation of Lara Croft was a major event in terms of the representation of women in this genre but she can be viewed as both a positive and negative role model. She is a stylised representation of a powerful woman existing in a virtual world which had been seen as the domain of the male. She is a post-modern woman who behaves like a man but, in appearance, is unmistakably a woman. She carries weapons and moves and acts like a soldier but is also openly exploited as a sex symbol. She is overtly sexual and her measurements are nothing less than unreal even if they are 'virtual'. It could be said that Lara Croft was designed by men to please men; yet the irony is that she is heralded as an icon symbolising female empowerment and the ability of a woman to exist and take control in a violent male world:

> 'the image of Lara has been employed in the promotion of female empowerment. Because she is born out of a male fantasy and so clearly caters to male desires, it is ironic that she has also become a poster girl for a new brand of feminism, recognised under the headings: 'cyberfeminism', 'cybergirlzz' and 'girrrlpower'. Women are supposed to ignore that the image was created neither by them nor for them.' (Herbst in Inness, 2004)

Lara is now internationally recognised and has been transposed into film played by a 'real' sex symbol in the form of Angelina Jolie.

'In a world ordered by sexual imbalance, pleasure in looking has been split between active / male and passive / female. The determining male gaze projects its fantasy onto the female figure, which is styled accordingly.' (Laura Mulvey, 1975)

In the computer game Lara Croft is seen as a dominant character. She is often filmed from below suggesting her power over the gamer. Her stance is aggressive with her gun mounted on her hips and wearing a determined and challenging expression. Her code of clothing is sexual and revealing which contrasts with her role, her behaviour and her involvement in overt violence. Her relationship with the gamer is also interesting. Although she is seen as a strong role model for a female, in the game she is viewed in the third person and, as such, is controlled by the gamer that is assumed to be male. The player follows her but controls her actions as she runs, jumps, meets dead ends, shoots at targets, etc. She actually has no control over her role in the narrative and in fact is controlled totally by the gamer which makes her translation into the active, resourceful heroine of the film an interesting one. For the male gamer, her representation is an ideal one – she is sexy, scantily clad, powerful, gun-toting, hyper-real and perfect. He does not have to deal with her imperfections as he would a 'real' woman – and he can control her without challenge!

Learning Point: Representations in media texts often contain polysemic messages that will be interpreted differently by different audiences:

> 'Once the player tires and the game is over, game and female alike conveniently disappear into electronic vapour. Lara offers a sexy identity void of demands and stipulations.' [Herbst in Inness, 2004]

This relatively new representation of women who are violent and are seen as indifferent to violence is also viewed as a worrying and unrealistic one.

TASK

Study the games' covers for *Lara Croft: Tomb Raider* and *Imagine: Dream Wedding*. Consider the gender representations created by these covers commenting on:

- Use of images.
- Language.
- Clothing / gesture and iconography.
- Design and layout.

TASK

Create a new female character for a computer game aimed at girls / women. Use the following headings to formulate your ideas:

- Description of appearance.

- Character traits.

- Game genre.

- Role within the narrative.

- Audience response / involvement / interactivity.

- Write a brief report comparing your character to the representations of a female character in an existing game.

The issue for media students is not only about the representation of women in computer games but also of men, ethnic minorities and the portrayal of violence. The main representation of men in computer games is as action heroes. These virtual images, like the ones of women, are physically unreal – good-looking, well-toned and white. They can fight dragons, drive fast cars and planes, plan a military campaign and never miss their target. The creators of these representations are also making assumptions, not necessarily correct, about what men want to see in computer games – action heroes and half naked women. It is necessary to challenge these assumptions and not fall into the trap of agreeing with the representations on offer.

The representation of violence in the game format is sometimes viewed as a worrying one because of the direct involvement of the player and because of the fact that is takes place in a virtual environment. The player is in control of the violence which, in some games, is extreme and unrealistic. When the player blows up somewhere or 'takes out' a target they do not have to account for their actions. There is no remorse and more worryingly, there may even be a sense of achievement. In some games violent behaviour is rewarded and is the only way in which the player can move onto the next level and complete the game. This is particularly true of games with less complex narratives whose main themes are violence and action.

The controversy surrounding this genre of games and their affect on the gamers was heightened in 2009 when *Call Of Duty: Modern Warfare 2* was launched with an 18 certification due to some of the violence contained within the game. Several reports assert that this game is being played by children as young as eight. The representation of men in this game is a worrying one for such a young audience. This game casts the player as several members of Task Force 141, a squad of heavily armed Rangers tasked with stopping a Russian terrorist named Makarov. Several critics of the game say that the game has sacrificed its narrative for Hollywood style technical effects and a high level of violence. The representation of men is a violent one and the interactive involvement includes the player inevitably in this role.

'*Modern Warfare 2*'s big attention-grabbing set piece is a terrorist atrocity in an airport in which the player (taking the role of an undercover agent) reluctantly takes part. It's upsetting, chilling and horrifying. You're supposed to be upset and chilled and horrified, of course – so on that level it succeeds.' (Charlie Brooker, *The Guardian*, November 2009)

The '*Sims2*' series

There are some interesting games that offer more positive representations of gender through the creation of a game that can appeal to boys and girls. In the '*Sims2*' series there is no complicated narrative – the objective is to create a family, choose a home and 'live with them'.

The representation of gender and 'race' or ethnicity is up to the player and not imposed upon them. The first stage is to create a family from a range of options including their name, the colour of skin and their body shape. The player can choose their clothes which are not all from a fashion show and can also choose their aspirations. There are certain restrictions in place, which unlike many computer games, aim to keep this one generally in the realms of reality – the family must include an adult (the player cannot create a family made up only of children), but the family need not be stereotypically 'nuclear'. The next stage is to choose a place to live that suits the family's needs. This can be aspirational or based in reality. The player is given a certain amount of money and if you can't afford it you can't have it! More money can be earned by, as in the real world, getting a job. The player can look for this job in the newspaper that is delivered to the house. There is also a moral code implied – children must go to school or the social worker pays a visit. The choices in this game are therefore life choices and are based in a 'virtual reality'. The viewing and gaming experience are third person and the player can choose to follow and be involved with different members of the created family. Other games in the series allow the player to become involved in going to university and setting up their own business. The game is interactive without being violent; it attempts to establish a 'real world' with real option choices and non-stereotypical gender representations and for this reason is popular with both genders.

TASK

Devise new ideas for a new computer game with a target audience of both genders.

Consider:

- Characters.
- Setting.
- Theme.
- Narrative.
- Representation issues.
- Audience response / involvement.

Produce the publicity material for the game.

Gender in Advertising – Selling beauty

The representation of gender in advertising has come a long way to the point where, as David Gauntlett suggests, men and women in adverts are treated equally and there are few overtly sexist stereotypes employed by the producers of advertisements:

> ' ... which presumably means that advertisers nowadays take their social role relatively seriously, or, to be more precise, have learned that it is not good business to offend any of their customers with sexist stereotypes.' (Gauntlett, 2002: 75)

We no longer expect to see the stereotypes of early advertising where the usual representation of a woman was a housewife who was judged by how white her husband's shirts were as she waved him off to the office.

Men, on the other hand, were often placed in the role of the expert or 'the voice of God' giving women information about changing their washing powder and getting their floors clean. The other representation was as macho men with burly friends in adverts for beer and cigarettes. However, despite the generally positive improvements in gender representations it was still found recently that:

> 'Women were twice as likely as men to be in commercials for domestic products and men were twice as likely as women to be seen in adverts for non-domestic products.' (Gauntlett, 2002: 76)

The postmodern representation of women that audiences expect to see is more likely to be of a confident, successful woman who owns her own car and can give the average man a run for his money – remember the 'Ask before you borrow it' advert for the Nissan Micra car where just retribution was given to the man who presumed to borrow the woman's car. There was also 'It's not make-up. It's ammunition' for Boots 17 where women were seen as dominant and in control.

Interestingly, the notion of 'equality' in advertising now extends to the fact that men as well as women use their bodies and looks to sell products to their own and the opposite gender. However, there is a difference. Men still appear natural and advertise fragrances, moisturisers and anti-wrinkle products but women seem to need to do more. They are involved in the selling of self-modification products like make-up which must be used to enhance and change their appearance – it is not enough to be natural, they have to look GOOD too:

> '...one could complain that women are being told that their natural beauty is not enough, and that make-up is required: that is an unequal message, since men aren't expected to go to so much trouble.' (ibid.)

Adverts create an idealised representation of beauty and perfection that women and now also men are asked to emulate and live up to. Men are shown to be perfect – well-toned, tanned and good-looking – and women have perfectly made-up faces and slender bodies.

This image is further exaggerated by the use of celebrity endorsement where an already beautiful and iconic celebrity is used to endorse the product. Was Claudia

Schiffer not already beautiful before she used *L'Oreal*?

Claudia Schiffer for L'Oréal Paris

For many women the use of celebrities to sell beauty products means that the attainment of the ideal becomes an even more impossible aspiration. We are persuaded to buy the products because we believe the representation of perfection that we see and suspend our disbelief at the air-brushed face even when the amazing eyelashes of Penelope Cruz are exposed as fake:

> '...the advertising of the beauty industry does go to a lot of effort to persuade women that they really need the latest skin, hair, nail and leg creams (containing the latest ingredients with complex scientific sounding names). And advertising regularly reinforces the desirability of particular physical looks.'
> (Gaunt, 2002: 81)

Learning Point: While representations in advertising have developed since the early days, it is still the case that images of perfection are used to sell products to men and women.

Maybe she was born with it?

TASK

Look at a range of adverts for *Maybelline* cosmetics. TV adverts can be easily searched for by product and brand on www.visit4info.com.

Consider the following:

* This is a long existing brand that has had its own make-over and has been re-invented to appeal to a new audience. How?

The slogan 'Maybe she was born with it. Maybe it's *Maybelline*' repeats the brand name, uses alliteration and is catchy. It is also enigmatic and suggests what *Maybelline* can do for you so that it appears like natural beauty.

The adverts usually include a close-up shot of a face, which has been technically manipulated to show perfection. This representation of perfection is directly linked with the product.

The mode of address is direct and challenging and in some adverts is also provocative and therefore appeals to both sexes in different ways. To women it offers empowerment and to men, it may suggest availability.

There is always a Unique Selling Point [USP] – something that no other product has (apparently) – for example, that will make your lashes longer or your lips shinier. The endorser demonstrates the effect of the product with a heightened focus on the key areas like lips, eyes and nails.

There is always iconic representation – the product is always clearly visible and often larger than life so that the buyer will recognise it.

TASK

Look at a range of adverts for beauty products that use celebrity endorsements. Consider how the representation of celebrity is used to sell the product. Look at the way age is represented with the use of Jane Fonda by *L'Oreal*, for example.

They're worth it too!

The concept of marketing cosmetics to men is relatively new. In the past the main product to be sold was after shave and the representation was always of very masculine role models (like boxer Henry Cooper and Brut aftershave). There was also no mention of the word 'fragrance' because of its feminine connotations. Now we have often more androgynous images and the representations have similar qualities to those used in advertising to women – good looks, sex appeal and a good body. These qualities are pushed to the limit in advertising for *Dolce and Gabbana* where sex is quite obviously used to sell and the models are photographed in provocative poses. The images are of glamour and luxury and the mode of address is direct.

The interesting element of this type of advertising is that the products are for men but many of the adverts are aimed at women as well as men and the responses may be different according to the gender. Take, for example, the advert for *L'Oreal Hydra Energetic* anti-fatigue moisturiser.

The slogan is 'He thinks he looks damn good. You think he looks damn tired'. The 'you' in the slogan is clearly the woman seeing this advert which was in a woman's magazine. The male model is stereotypically attractive and the average man would be quite happy to look like this. However, the advert suggests that a woman would have a different response and she is implored to 'help him', showing that the advert is targeted at her. However, there are clues that the producers of the advert are also targeting a male audience: the detail of the product includes information – 'non-greasy texture, non-sticky' – to provide reassurance to the male reader; 'apply in the morning and / or evening over the whole face' is information we assume a woman would not need; and 'use after shaving – to help sooth razor burn' is directly addressed to the male.

The logo is also interesting in that the supposed effects of the cream are represented as a re-charged battery – the analogies made are masculine as are the graphics and fonts. This is matched by the square, non-intimidating bottle shape and packaging and the fact that *L'Oreal* gives itself the title 'men expert'. This advert effectively demonstrates how one advert can be encoded to appeal to more than just one audience.

Dove for Men

Dove, who made such a success with using 'real women' in their advertising campaign, has recently launched a range of products aimed at men and at a particular type of man:

> **'In its TV ad, Dove Men +Care has tried to recreate the aura of fearless candidness that won its women's line so many fans. It's pitched at the mature man who's made it through marriage and fatherhood, rather than the mythical chick magnet of most campaigns.' (Times online, 20 March 2010)**

Its slogan says:

> **'MEN, you've reached a point where you're comfortable with who you are? Doesn't your skin deserve a little comfort?'**

The television advert takes the viewer through the stages in the life of an average man and uses some humour to suggest what is expected of him, for example, opening jars and mowing lawns. The stereotypes are still there. The print advertisements picture black and white images of the man with his children emphasising the idea of the 'new man' who is a hands-on dad. The suggestion – one that is usually used for beauty products aimed at women – is that now he needs a bit of 'me time' when he can indulge in a bit of pampering. Interestingly, *Dove* has introduced the word 'care' into their male products – again, normally a word that is the domain of female campaigns, for fear of lacking masculinity and suggesting it is less than manly to care for your skin. In male grooming products we are used to terms like 'face protectors', not 'moisturisers' to suggest the 'manly' nature of the product and to target men who are less comfortable buying grooming products. However, *Dove* suggests that the man who is their target audience is mature enough to see beyond this and is most definitely 'comfortable with who he is'.

The *Dove* campaign for real beauty

This campaign was launched by the makers of *Dove* cosmetics to attempt to raise awareness about what we now accept as normal images of men and women used by the cosmetics industry. They conducted a survey that came up with some startling, but not entirely surprising results:

> '97% or girls aged 15–17 globally believe that changing some aspects of themselves would make them feel better.' (www.dove.co.uk)

Dove has tried in its campaign to 'go beyond stereotypes' and to produce adverts using ordinary women of a normal shape and appearance and of a range of ages. These 'normal' representations included women with grey hair, with freckles and with curves:

> '...the interesting thing here is the risky bet *Dove* is making. Beauty-product marketing has almost always been aspirational: I wish I could look like her... perhaps if I buy this lip gloss, I will! But Dove takes a wildly different approach: that chick in the ad sort of looks like me, and yet she seems really happy and confident...perhaps if I buy this *Dove* Firming Cream, I'll stop hating myself!' (www.slate.com, 'When Tush Comes to *Dove* – Real women. Real curves. Really smart ad campaign' by Seth Stevenson')

In the Asda billboard campaign, *Dove* invited members of the public to nominate a woman they thought was 'beautiful' for whatever reason in order to re-define what we have come to think of as beauty. This reinforced their use of ordinary women in their advertising campaigns in order to present a more realistic representation of women.

TASK

Go to the *Dove* website and look more closely at its advertising campaign and its use of images:

- How do its representations differ from other cosmetic companies?
- How does it use representation to sell the product?
- What messages and values does the *Dove* campaign challenge and enforce?
- How may different audiences respond to this campaign?

Watch the moving image adverts produced by *Dove* including, *Amy*, *Evolution* and *Onslaught*.

What message is *Dove* communicating about the cosmetics industry and the representation of women through these films?

TASK

Create an advertising campaign for a new product, using representations which challenge the more stereotypical images of beauty in advertising today. Consider the following:

- The name of your product.
- The slogan.
- Images to be used.

Mock up the layout and design of your print advert.

Storyboard a television advert.

Write a brief report justifying your decisions.

Learning Point: Representation of some groups in the media is changing in order to mirror society and to challenge older, more traditional stereotypes.

Ethnicity – concerns nations or races and is defined by the identity, customs, dress, food, etc. of a particular racial group. For example, Beyonce's ethnicity also reflects her cultural identity, i.e. African American culture.

Race – the descendants of a common ancestor; those who belong to a certain race as defined by an inherited set of common characteristics.

Media representations of ethnicity

Stuart Hall referred to the representation in the media of people who are different from us as 'the secret fascination of "otherness" – in other words, the representation in the media of people who are different from us (Hall, 1997: 225). Hall also suggested that this representation of 'difference' continues to be problematic in the representation of ethnicity in the media. Black and Asian people are often represented as 'exotic' in some media texts, for example, fashion magazines, but this very representation also serves to highlight the fact that they are 'different': 'Difference signifies. It "speaks"' (Hall, 1997: 230). Difference can be used by media texts both positively and negatively – in order to celebrate and to divide. Over time 'difference' has been seen to be natural and therefore unchangeable.

TASK

Look closely at this image. In what different ways can this image be 'read'? For example:

- Is Kelly Holmes celebrating being British?
- Is she saying something about her black culture?
- Is the image saying something about being black **and** British?

Research some of the ways in which black sportsmen and women are represented in the media. What do your findings say about their cultural representation? You may find that sport is one of the areas of the media that offers positive representations of ethnicity.

Racial stereotypes have been used over time and across a range of media texts. The way in which ethnic groups are represented by the media still produces stereotypes – all stereotypes reduce groups of people to two dimensional constructions that lack individuality and complexity. With regard to ethnic minorities, the concern is that they become marginalised.

> '...the use of stereotypical representation can be seen to reflect the power relations within our society... Stereotypes work on audiences through repetition and recognition, the more we see negative or reductive images of ethnicity in the media, the more we accept this as the norm. (Dyer, 1993)

However, the representation of ethnicity in the media has changed considerably since earlier days when ethnic groups, particularly black people, tended to be defined by their cultural heritage and their relationship with Britain. Often, they were associated with inferiority, subservience and slavery. Later people from different ethnic groups hardly appeared in the media at all, or appeared solely as a butt of humour or as part of the criminal fraternity in crime dramas and the news. In the 1980s and 1990s the representations of people from different ethnic backgrounds reflected sociological changes:

> '...the expansion of the black ghettos, the growth of the black "under-class", with its endemic poverty, ill-health and criminalisation, and the slide of some black communities into a culture of guns, drugs and intra-black violence.' (Hall, 1997: 256)

However, there appeared alongside this a more positive representation of, particularly, black ethnicity through music and the emergence of a range of black artists and of the genre of 'rap' music.

 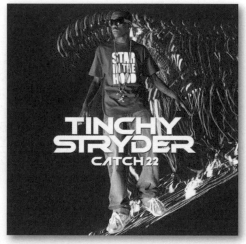

Andre 3000 (far left);
Tinchy Stryder (left)

The multicultural agenda of television has also helped in changing stereotypical perceptions, for example, C4's remit states that the channel must actively produce programmes for and featuring ethnic groups. There was also the advent of channels, for example, the Asian Network, created to cater for the needs of this cultural group. However, there is also criticism of this approach suggesting that it ghettoises ethnic groups by suggesting that they needed something different and away from the mainstream and therefore again emphasises their difference.

However, whilst there are now many more positive examples of ethnic groups across a range of media texts, the accusation of 'tokenism' is still levelled at some media areas including that of soap operas. This occurs when a particular family, for example the Masood's in *EastEnders*, is introduced into the storyline to suggest that this area of representation has been addressed. The family are seen to 'fit in' to the life of the street or the square, but often their cultural differences are inevitably suppressed or presented in a two dimensional way, for example, the Asian wedding in *EastEnders*:

> 'Watching Asian families on *EastEnders* is usually embarrassing. You know they are supposed to "represent" you, and with so few Asian actors on television it feels like a personal slur to see them shoehorned in, only to flail around without a plot (like the bland Ferreiras). Despite being supposedly set in the kind of east London borough where roughly 37% of the population is from an ethnic minority, *EastEnders* sticks rigidly to a limit of one black, one Asian family at a time.' (Homa Khaleeli, *Growing Up With EastEnders*, guardian.co.uk. February 2010)

However, Zaihab Masood (in *EastEnders*) is a strong female character who is a business woman within the community – an attempt by the programme to offer a more realistic and positive representation of Asian families.

In men's magazines it is still unusual to see a black or Asian man on the cover of, for example, *Men's Health*. Any articles featuring black men will typically focus on their 'stud' and 'cool' image and rely on stereotypes.

Despite the more prolific and realistic representations of ethnic groups in the media the use of black actors in certain roles can, worryingly, still cause controversy. This was certainly the case when it was announced that *The Wire*'s Idris Elba had been cast as the Norse God Heimdall in Kenneth Branagh's film *Thor* (2011), based on the Marvel comic character. Elba viewed this casting and his role in *Luther*, where he plays a black detective, as a positive step for the representation of ethnicity on television and in film, but that this should not be the key concern when casting an actor in a particular role. However, his opinion was not shared by fans of the comic who asserted in blogs that the 'whitest of the gods' should be played by

Heimdall / Idris Elba

someone of white skin. In his interview in the *TV Times* Elba countered the criticism: 'Hang about, Thor's mythical, right? Thor has a hammer that flies to him when he clicks his fingers. That's OK, but the colour of my skin is wrong?' (*The Guardian*, Wednesday, 28 April 2010)

He also suggested that as an actor he should not be defined by the colour of his skin, as is often the case with other black actors. Surely it should be how well the role is portrayed, not the skin colour of the actor? Anything else reinforces Stuart Hall's point that black and Asian people in media texts are frequently presented as either two dimensional characters or are characterised by their 'otherness'. This representation inevitably makes them appear different from the norm. There is, interestingly, not the same outcry when white actors from a different country with a different culture and accent are given 'English' roles, for example, Kevin Costner and now Russell Crowe as *Robin Hood*:

> **'I think we'll put ourselves in a corner if we just describe Luther as a black detective. There haven't been many in the past, but the fact that he's black is neither here nor there. We all know someone from a different ethnic background, we all mix, so it's great to have a character that happens to be black in the central position....He still bleeds, just like anyone else."** (*Daily Mirror*, 27 April 2010)

RESEARCH TASK

Find and analyse three representations of ethnicity from at least two different media texts, for example, film and magazines. Answer the following question:

* *How is ethnicity represented in the media today? Refer to the examples you researched in your answer.*

Consider the range of media representations of ethnicity:

- How has ethnicity been represented in these images?

- What messages are contained within these representations?

Learning Point: As society changes so do the representations of specific groups within society.

Audience Responses

Christine Bell

In this Section

- The ways in which audiences can be described.

- How audiences are constructed by the producers of media texts.

- How audiences are positioned.

- The ways in which different audiences respond to, use and interpret texts.

The main area of focus in a study of audience is the relationship between the text and audience. This is fluent and changing. In this post-modern, media saturated world it is no longer acceptable to suggest that there is only one way of interpreting a text and only one possible audience response. Audiences are not mass. They are complex and sophisticated in their responses. It is important also to consider the social and cultural experiences that affect audiences' responses to a range of texts. In this section, the initial focus will be on the range of possible responses and not necessarily upon audience theories. However, the analysis of the response may lead to an exploration of relevant audience response theories.

It is important to move on from the idea that the meaning within texts is already embedded and unchanging and that all audiences respond to messages encoded in the text in the same way. Audiences are made up of individuals who bring social and cultural experiences to their interpretation of any text which may alter the messages they receive from the text. Audiences are not unquestioning consumers as has been suggested by theories in the past:

> '...far from being turned into "zombies", it has grown increasingly clear that audiences are in fact capable of a high degree of self-determination in the nature of the responses that they make to the products offered to them.'
> [Stewart *et al.*, 2001: 25]

Audience Positioning

Stuart Hall, in his research (1973), suggested that texts were 'encoded' by the producers of the texts to contain certain meanings related to the social and cultural background of the creator of the text. However, once the reader of the text 'decoded' that text then the meanings intended by the producer may change.

Hall then went on to suggest three main perspectives involved in the way in which an audience responds to a particular text. This involves how the audience is positioned by the text and their subsequent response:

1. Preferred or dominant readings – this is where the audience interprets the text as closely to the way in which the producer of the text intended. If the social

and cultural experience of the reader of the text is close to that of the producer then there is little for the audience to challenge. A reader of *The Daily Mail* who shares that paper's political allegiance may agree entirely with their views on immigration and migrant workers:

'150,000 foreigners swell UK workforce: record numbers get permits as Britons lose job.' (headline in *The Daily Mail*, January 2009)

2. Negotiated readings – this is where the audience goes through some sort of negotiation with themselves to allow them to accept the way in which the text is presented. The audience may agree with some elements of the text and disagree with others. For example, in a magazine article where, because of the way it has been presented, they are asked to empathise with a situation they would not normally accept. They may need to adjust their viewpoint and their previous opinions in order to get the most out of the text.

3. Oppositional or resistant readings – this is where the user of the text finds themselves in conflict with the text itself due to their culture, beliefs or experiences. For example, a narrative in a soap opera that views a woman who is having an affair sympathetically will encourage a resistant reading in a person whose culture is against adultery.

Learning Point: Different audiences respond to media texts in different ways for different reasons.

TASK

Choose three different texts covering a range of media forms. For each text consider how they may produce dominant, negotiated and oppositional readings for different audiences.

Hypodermic needle effect – this is an example of a media effects theory. The suggestion is that the media text 'injects' ideas and opinions into the audience which, we are led to assume, are passive and unquestioning. An example of this theory would be the idea that violent media texts necessarily cause audiences to behave violently.

These perspectives allow you to begin to understand that one text cannot have a static meaning that is communicated in the same way to a mass audience. This concept should also allow us to challenge 'effects' theories that suggest that this is the case including the 'hypodermic needle' response which puts forward the idea that mass audiences are affected in a particular way by the contents of and messages within a specific text.

What affects the way in which an audience responds to a text?

Different audiences will respond to the same text differently according to:

• Gender – the relationships between the audience and text according to gender are complex. Men and women will respond to certain media texts in different ways. Certain research has shown that women prefer television programmes like soap operas that deal with narratives concerned with relationships and that have strong female characters. Men, on the other hand, apparently prefer more factual programmes related to news and current affairs. However, there are obvious problems with such research as it is generalised and the men / women asked may respond in a way they think their questioner expects, a response typical of that gender. It is commonly accepted that men too watch soap operas particularly those like *The Bill*. It is also easy to say that women would respond to 'lads' mags' like *Nuts* and *Zoo* in a disapproving way because of the way in which women are represented in the texts. How do you then account for the women who send in their photographs to be published in these magazines or on the website?

TASK

Study the front covers and an article from two magazines / magazine websites, one with a target audience of men and one with a target audience of women. How would men and women respond to both these texts? Consider the following:

- Layout and design.

- The mode of address.

- The 'gaze' of the central image.

- The cover and sell lines.

- Gender representation.

Discourse
– 'a way of talking about things within a particular group, culture or society; or a set of ideas within a culture which shapes how we perceive the world. So when I talk about "the discourse of women's magazines", for example, I am referring to the ways in which women's magazines typically talk about women and men and social life, and the assumptions that they commonly deploy.'
(Gauntlett, 2002: 16)

- Situated culture – this concerns how our 'situation' – our daily lives, routines and relationships – can affect how we respond to media texts; where we are and who we are with has an effect upon our media consumption. Watching a film surrounded by friends or family will be a different viewing experience to one where you view a film alone. This response will change again if you are watching the film at home or at the cinema.

- Cultural experience – this is how our culture – our upbringing, experiences and beliefs – affect our response to a text. This also relates to how our understanding and our view of the world are shaped by our media experience. We may have never visited New York but our media consumption of film and television programmes have constructed a view for us. We have an in depth knowledge of forensic procedures due to our viewing of programmes like *CSI* and *Waking The Dead*.

How texts construct and position audiences

Here we need take a more complex approach to texts which go beyond basic content analysis. Texts can be said to construct an idea of their viewer / reader. This can be applied to an analysis of magazines where the magazine constructs an idea of *Men's Health* man or *Glamour* woman. Here we can return to the work done on representation and consider the representations constructed by the magazines and the view of the world and related messages that they communicate to readers. Magazines offer discourses.

The discourses of magazines make their topics and subject matter appear normal and make assumptions about the lifestyles and interests of their readers – hence the construction. McDougall (2006) suggests that discourses contained within the pages of *Men's Health* include:

- Quick-fix problem solving.

- New male sensitivity.

- Male superiority / manipulation.

- Get a six-pack in six weeks.

- Male narcissism and society.

- How to look good.

- How to understand your girlfriend's needs.

- If you understand her needs you will get what you want.

Further evidence of the fact that magazines construct audiences can be found by looking at the media packs for magazines where reader profiles and information are set out, primarily for the use of advertisers. The reader information provided in the *Men's Health* Media Pack states:

> '*MH*'s readers recognise that health isn't just about physical concerns. It's about a lifestyle in its own right. *MH*'s readers see the big benefits in making small changes to their everyday life.' (*Men's Health* Presspack: http://www.menshealth.co.uk/tools/MP5c-media.pdf)

The *FHM* Media Pack gives a more elaborate idea of their readers and how they live their lives:

- *FHM* readers are MEN, plain and simple! Because a man knows his way to balance between gym, sex, career, health, sports, culture and is always up to date with everything that is new and useful to him!

- A female is not a retarded human specimen, nor just a partner for sex or an incomprehensible creature. A woman is a delightful and balancing companion for an *FHM* man.

- *FHM* readers are are not lads, studs, guys, blokes or gents but just MEN, 'because a man does just one thing but does it best: he lives his life at full!'

- The Media Pack also asserts: 'the *FHM* man has a genuine social mark of his identity as an intelligent, fashionable and attractive young man. That mark is the magazine itself.' (http://www.fhm-international.com/mediakits/D7F9562A176.pdf)

In this way it can be seen that the producers of the magazine construct an idea of their audience and the articles in their publication will mirror and attract this 'ideal man'. However, this may differ greatly from the actual reader of the magazine who may consume the magazine on an aspirational level and, by buying *FHM* or *Men's Health*, feels that he is buying into the world that the magazine has constructed.

Interestingly, in 2009 *Men's Health* took over from *FHM* as Britain's best selling men's title after thirteen years in the lead. The reason for the change may be the emergence of 'heteropolitan man' – a man who was no longer interested in magazines like *FHM*, *Nuts* and *Zoo* and their stories, for example: 'Eva's Big Boob Blowout!' (*Nuts* magazine, May 2010), 'Reader Zapped by 22.000 Volts, Shocking images inside!' (*Zoo* magazine, May 2010), and was more concerned with reading more thought-provoking articles and being healthy in mind and body. Reports suggested that modern men wanted the more realistic constructions of magazines like *Men's Health*.

Mike Shalcross, the deputy editor of Men's Health, said:

> 'What men want from magazines has changed. Lad mags haven't really evolved in the last ten years and it's difficult to persuade someone in that market to go to a newsagent and part with £3.90 for pictures of minor film stars or Page 3 Girls they can source for free on their laptop, without moving from their sofa, or even putting their crisps down.' (Patrick Foster, *Times* online, August 2009)

Learning Point: Sociological changes in audiences may affect the ways in which they consume and respond to media texts.

TASK

In small groups, look at two or three issues of the same magazine in print or on the internet:

- What do you think are the discourses of the magazine?

- What articles / features can you give as examples of these discourses?

- What idea of the reader is constructed by the magazine?

- See if the magazine has a press / media pack. How does it construct an idea of the reader for advertisers?

- How might different audiences respond to the magazine differently?

TASK

Looking at men in magazines

In small groups, look at two or three issues of a men's magazine. You are trying to discover the representation of gender constructed by the creators of the magazine and to consider audience responses to this creation.

Consider the following questions:

- What does the front cover suggest would be the concerns of the men who read this magazine?

- Look at the front covers of the magazines – how have audiences been positioned by mode of address, colour, use of images?

- Look at the images of men in the magazine – how could you describe them?

- How does the magazine represent men to men?

- How are women represented in the magazine through articles and images? How does this add to the discourse of the magazine?

- How might women respond to the representations in the magazine?

- What kind of world does the magazine create?

- Look at the press pack information for the magazine if it is available. How does this relate to the articles and content in the magazine? Does it reinforce the constructed representation?

- Does the magazine's construction relate to reality?

- Who would be the **different** audiences for this magazine?

TASK

Hot Seating

You should now really know your magazine. Be prepared to take on the role of the reader of the magazine and answer questions about yourself. The rest of the group will come up with questions to ask you about your interests, hobbies, lifestyle which you must answer in role as the consumer of the magazine you have been analysing. You will be put on the 'hot seat' and you will have to answer the questions in role using your research into the magazine to help you.

EXTENSION TASK

- Produce a treatment for a new magazine aimed at men.

- Design the mock-up for the front cover of the magazine.

- Produce the ideas for a web page for a reader profile of the magazine.

- Write a brief report demonstrating how your research findings informed the creation of your magazine, how you have attracted your target audience and evaluating what you have produced.

New Audiences – the interactive users

The focus so far has been upon how different audiences respond to texts and what affects that response. It has been clear that audiences are complex and changing. With the advent of new technologies and formats including computer games and websites, audiences have become interactive users of the media who are in control and active in their choices. In a video / computer game the user can view the action from the first or third person point of view and can make choices about the narrative and the actions of the characters. Often the domain of the male, as discussed earlier in this section, the computer game allows the male ambiguous control over female characters that have been created to be manipulated by him:

> '...the terrain of computer games has become the site of erotic spectacle; in it the virtual heroine, as Mulvey described, plays to the male, holds his gaze, and is utterly and completely in his control.' (Inness, 2004)

Some analysts say that games interact with the user on a range of levels because of the immersion in the artificial world created and therefore the messages encoded in the game are more powerful and elicit a more profound response than in other formats that involve the audience. The experience of 'gaming' is therefore a more heightened one.

The ideas of autonomy and control can also be applied to the users of internet websites. Here there is a wealth of information and experiences at your fingertips. However everyone will use the internet in a different way.

Learning Point: The ways in which audiences are offered opportunities to use texts and become active is changing *how* we analyse audience responses.

TASK

In groups discuss how you use the internet. Consider the following:

- Which websites you use regularly.

- What information / services you get from these sites.

- How much time you spend online.

- The different ways in which you and other members of your family use the internet.

- What does this research tell you about the internet and audiences?

The internet and web pages offer good examples of David Gauntlett's idea of the 'pick and mix' audience. Here the audience uses texts – it ignores some aspects of them and chooses the aspects that suit them at that time. The next time people play or search they may 'pick and mix' a different menu – the flexibility is there to enable the user of these formats to do this.

Having established the concept of using the media to satisfy the needs of the audience at that moment, it may be time to give some consideration to a particular audience effects theory that is relevant to this discussion – Uses and Gratifications. This is one of the more useful theories as it assumes an active (rather than passive) audience and emphasises what the audiences of media texts do *with* them rather than what the media *does to* the audience. However, the theory must be used with reservations as not all audiences have the needs suggested or use the media in this way. Blumler and Katz (1975) disagreed with earlier theories which placed the audience as a passive mass who could be influenced and would act upon messages communicated by the media. The Uses and Gratifications theory suggests that individuals and social groups use texts in *different* ways and the audience are no longer viewed as passive receivers.

The identified needs of the audience were later refined as:

- Entertainment and diversion – as a form of escape from the pressures of everyday life.

- Personal relationships / social interaction – identification with characters and being able to discuss media texts with others.

- Personal identity – the ability to compare your life with that of characters and situations presented in media texts.

- Information / education – to find out and learn about what is going on in the world.

The Uses and Gratifications theory – developed in 1975 by Blumler and Katz, it was an important study into the way in which audiences interacted with texts.

TASK

For each audience 'need' identified by the Uses and Gratifications theory, give an example of a specific media text that fulfills this 'need'. For example, an audience may watch the news or a television documentary for *information*.

However, you must consider that this theory can be now viewed as a simplistic way of looking at audiences that have become more diverse and complex as media formats themselves have become more fluid and changing. This theory assumes that the media itself has identified and catered for the needs of the audience when in fact it may well be the case that audiences respond to the texts on offer in this way as there is no other alternative. It may be that audiences have needs that are not being addressed by existing media texts:

'...in fact many of our "uses" and "pleasures" can be seen to be "making the best" of what is available and putting it to our [the audience's] use, which may be different from the one that the producer intended.' (Rayner *et al.*, 2003: 139)

SUMMARY TASK

Study any two media texts - for example, two web pages, magazines, film trailers or computer games:

1. Analyse them commenting on:

- Visual codes.

- Technical codes.

- Language and mode of address.

2. What representations are evident within the texts?

3. Suggest how different audiences may respond to the texts.

End Notes

In this opening section of the book, we have considered the concepts of genre, narrative and representation separately in relation to a range of diverse examples. We have posed questions about how texts are constructed, about the representations contained within them and about the ways in which different audiences may respond differently to those same texts. Finally here we consider how one text can offer a discussion of all of the above concepts and can provide a rich example for discussion.

SUMMARY TASK

ANALYSING *SLUMDOG MILLIONAIRE*

Focus one – Textual Analysis

Watch the trailer for *Slumdog Millionaire*. It introduces the key themes of the film and highlights the concepts of representation and narrative.

TASK

Analyse (through group discussion or as a written task) this text commenting on:

- Narrative codes.

- Genre conventions of a trailer.

- Technical and audio codes.

Focus two – Representation

Different areas of representation are contained within this text.

National Identity / place – representation of India

> '...what I really love about the film is it gives you what India really is now. It is rapaciously industrialising, everyone is on the mobile, traffic jams everywhere, smog, tower blocks going up like never before and that's modern India. And I don't think anyone's seen that on screen in Britain.' (Simon Beaufoy, BFI website)

During the film we see very contrasting images of India. Watch the following scenes which are useful for considering the different representations of India contained within the film:

- The Orphanage – here Latika, Jamal and Salim are witness to the deliberate blinding of a young boy to increase his earning potential as a beggar.

- The train journey (Scene 11) – here we are shown the contrasting fortunes of the passengers on the train and those of Jamal and Salim who travel on the roof and attempt to steal from those who are lucky enough to be inside. Here the different classes in Indian society are signified by the way in which they eat and travel.

- The home of Javed, the gangster character, where Latika is forced to live.

- The scene at the Taj Mahal. This is viewed by audiences as an icon of India and these scenes serve as a contrast to the slum scenes which is the part of India not normally used in films. One of Danny Boyle's aims in making the film was to show the 'real India'. Films set in the country previously tended to be:

> '...all big stars and they tend to shoot in studios now. They tend to be studio kind of pictures that don't reflect life. And they find people who have seen our film, find our film quite shocking. You know that it's so truthful you know about what the city is like.' (BFI website)

The German and American tourists that Jamal encounters in and around the Taj Mahal offer further representations of nationality more embedded in traditional stereotypes.

- The call centre is a further recognisable aspect of Indian life made more pertinent here by the additional references to western culture.

- The Bollywood style ending is more what an audience may expect from a film set in India and offers another example of this nation.

Representation of Issues – Poverty and wealth

The following scenes are useful to study for this area of representation:

- The scene near the opening of the film where the children are being chased through the slums by the police. Here, a range of camera shots and angles show the audience the slums and the living areas of those existing in extreme poverty. This is contrasted with the powerful man in his symbol of wealth – the big western car.

- The train scene again shows the contrast between wealth and poverty.

- The humorous 'toilet' scene which demonstrates the horrific reality of everyday life in the slums in a very memorable way.

- All the scenes in the film where the elements of poverty and life in the slum are highlighted.

Representation of Gender

- The men in the film are seen to be in control and powerful – Javed controls through fear and through turning the children against each other. The police initially use their power to control. The opening scene demonstrates how those in authority exert their power through violence directed at Jamal. However, the chief undergoes a process of transformation as he begins to believe Jamal's incredible story. Prem, the quizmaster tries to use his power to destroy Jamal's chances as he feels threatened by Jamal's knowledge and his success. The contrast is Jamal who is the sensitive, caring hero with a quest – to find and save Latika.

- The women in the film are in the minority and are presented as victims; Jamal witnesses the violent death of his mother early in the film. The representation of Latika is interesting – she is passive and is seen as a prize. She is the whole reason for Jamal being on the show *Who Wants To Be A Millionaire* and the shot of her at the train station comes into the mind of Jamal throughout the film and is an enigma for the audience. Here she is shot from above to appear vulnerable and is dressed in yellow, highlighting her role as a symbol of hope in the film. She has been abused as she is passed from one man to another and is waiting to be saved by Jamal. Her scar becomes symbolic of her journey. However, she also remains a classic beauty even after the life she has led.

TASK

Research two more examples of either gender or poverty / wealth in different media texts. Compare these to those in *Slumdog Millionaire*.

How does *Slumdog Millionaire* represent youth and age, and ethnicity? Back up your findings with key scenes from the film.

Focus three – Audience

'I think a lot of us particularly in Britain when the word India or Deli or Bombay is mentioned have still, despite how long ago it was, a slightly Raj like association in our heads. Of something rather noble or slightly old fashioned. I think that's our default position when someone mentions India.' (Simon Beaufoy, BFI website)

TASK

How might different audiences respond to this film?

What 'Uses and Gratifications' are offered by the film?

How have the producers of the film attempted to attract a range of different audiences?

BIBLIOGRAPHY

Books

Bell, A., Joyce, M., and Rivers, D. (1999), *Advanced Level Media*, Hodder and Stoughton: London

Dyer, R. (1993), *The Matter Of Images*, London and New York: Routledge

Gauntlett, D. (2002), *Media, Gender and Identity*, Routledge: London

Helsby, W. (2005), *Understanding Representation*, BFI Publishing: London

Inness, S. (2004), *Action Chicks: New I mages of Tough Women In Popular Culture*, Palgrave Macmillan: London

McDougall, J. (2006), *The Media Teacher's Book*, Hodder Arnold: London

Rayner. P, Wall. P, Kruger. S (2001), *Media Studies: The Essential Introduction*, Routledge: London

Stewart, C., Lavelle M. Kowaltzke A. (2001), *Media and Meaning, An Introduction*, BFI Publishing: London

Stafford, R., *Representation, An Introduction*, BFI Publishing/In the Picture: London/Bradford

Websites

www.frey.co.nz

www.slate.co.uk

www.dove.co.uk

www.menshealth.co.uk

MEDIA INDUSTRIES

Television

Colin Dear

To understand a media text fully you should consider how it has been produced, to whom it is targeted and how this audience will respond to it.

The way in which a text is edited and structured reflects the demands of the target audiences; this will then be represented in the marketing for the product. For example, Simon Cowell is represented as a villain in *X-Factor* (2004-) as audiences find the conflict between contestants and the judge entertaining. His persona is then used in tabloid newspapers to create publicity with mainstream audiences who are likely to watch the programme. These tabloid representations of the star feed back in the viewing of the programme as audiences believe they have gained added insight into Cowell's personality and his relationships with the other judges.

As a result of studying a text, its audiences and the industry which produced it, the distinction between these areas may begin to blur. A star persona such as Cowell's is created partly by the text, by its marketing and by the audiences themselves, so such a concept overlaps all three areas of text, industry and audience. That is not to say that dividing your studies into these elements isn't useful, but you should see them as a starting point rather than limits or restrictions to which you must adhere.

Choice of programmes

This section will explore case studies of three diverse programmes: an extract from the *BBC News 24* channel, E4's *skins* and HBO's *The Wire*.

Television comprises a vast amount of programmes spread across a multitude of channels, each watched by a smaller audience than ever before. New technology means that many TV viewers no longer only watch television sets, they use their computers to access BBC iPlayer, 4 on demand, Youtube, myspace and BitTorrent, or they buy box-sets of series on DVD. Other audiences increasingly reschedule programmes using services such as Sky+. At the same time genres are splintering and merging into an array of sub-genres and hybrids. All of this means that television is a complex, diverse and rapidly changing field of study.

This means there is no point in learning how TV works in theory. It is much more useful to look at how television works by exploring different programmes and you have a wide choice available to you. Choosing three programmes to study can be daunting, but remember you are not trying to 'sum up' the whole of television with those texts. Rather you are aiming to gain an understanding of how what we watch on television is structured in terms of narrative, genre and representation; of the different ways in which different audiences consume and use TV programmes, and of how an industry works to create and sell these texts.

Most studies of British television begin with developing an understanding of public service broadcasting and the BBC. Ever since television was first broadcast in the UK, the BBC's principles of informing, educating and entertaining have shaped discussion of what television should do and what should be broadcast. News is a good place to start as it fulfils very clear public service obligations which have to be balanced with the need to attract and keep audiences. *BBC News 24* is a BBC channel and must therefore conform to the corporation's identity and ethos. As a rolling news channel it needs to construct narratives that will serve the needs of an audience who may dip in and out of the programmes at various points in the day. It is also available via the BBC website showing the importance of new technology in allowing audiences to use the channel to meet their changing needs.

The programme *skins* is a useful choice as it is broadcast initially on E4 and then repeated on Channel 4. This scheduling reflects the impact of multichannel television and increased competition on terrestrial broadcasters who have created subsidiary digital channels to compete with their rivals. As *skins* is broadcast on both channels you can examine the ways in which the programme targets a niche demographic whilst fulfilling aspects of Channel 4's remit including demonstrating innovation and appealing to tastes and interests of a culturally diverse society (http://www.channel4.com/about4/overview.html). The show is also important in terms of channel identity, generating considerable publicity using a mixture of new technology and more traditional methods, such as good old fashioned controversy. In fact, *skins* is constructed more like a brand, with viewers invited to buy into a lifestyle, rather than simply watch the programme. Exploring this process of brand creation raises interesting issues about both audiences and industry.

To gain an understanding of television as a whole it is a good idea to study a programme broadcast on a digital channel. Small audiences generally entail low budgets so looking at cheaper programmes such as reality formats (*Four Weddings*, 2009–), imports (*Gossip Girl*, 2007–) or imported reality shows (*Jersey Shore*, 2010–) would be effective choices. *The Wire* is relatively cheap to import; however, its high quality makes it unlike most programmes broadcast on multichannel television but does mean the programme reflects BBC2's channel identity, the channel on which it was eventually broadcast. The reason *The Wire* is a useful text to study is that it reflects a number of trends within the TV industry including: America rather than Britain setting benchmarks for quality; the strategy of targeting small but affluent demographics, and the importance of the DVD buying market. Finally, using *The Wire* allows you to explore the reach of multinational corporations and the effects of globalisation.

Globalisation – a process where media ownership, production and consumption cross borders thereby enabling one culture to dominate another through the export of media products and with these products cultural ideologies.

BBC News 24

Rolling News

BBC News 24 broadcasts rolling news throughout the day and night. The 24-hour news channels use similar formats to traditional news programmes to structure their output, with the day broken up into hour long bulletins. Each hour on *BBC News 24* begins with headlines, which are repeated every fifteen minutes and regular time slots exist for weather and sport. This format is subject to change in the event of a breaking news story. The following hour will repeat this format and much of the previous content. However, items will be updated and expanded as events occur, in order to maintain audience interest. Text which summarises the headlines also scrolls along the bottom of the screen. This text, along with the repetition of headlines and familiar structure, enables audiences to use *BBC News 24* for quick updates rather than in depth analysis of stories.

BBC News 24 closely resembles the rest of the broadcaster's news output, both in terms of content and presentation. However, the fact that the channel is broadcasting 24 hours a day has two major effects on the construction of the news narrative. Firstly, the channel has much more time to fill, resulting in the use of a plethora of expert interviews and an added emphasis on showing the audience events as they happen. Secondly, there is a greater focus on 'breaking news'. This refers to the idea that events are occurring as the channel is broadcasting so stories may be pieced together over a period of hours as the programme is airing.

How do the logos represent the values of the BBC News and its role in the world?

Headlines

On Friday, 19 February 2010, at 9am the headline stories were:

- Economists support Gordon Brown (following a previous story in which other economists criticised the Prime Minister).

- The expected closure of the Corpus Plant steelworks on Teeside.

- A breaking news story about a nine-year-old boy stabbed to death in Bradford.

- Conflict between Labour and Conservatives about how to pay for care for the elderly.

- Build up to Tiger Woods' first press conference since the revelations about his private life.

- Prince William taking part in a charity photo-shoot.

TASK

Compile a list of the day's news stories using news websites such as the BBC, ITV, *The Guardian*, *The Sun*, *The Daily Mail*, CNN and Al Jazeera.

Select headline stories and place them in order of importance. Compare your choices with those of the BBC. What factors did you consider important in terms of newsworthiness? What do you think were important to the BBC's choice of stories?

Watch the news on the same evening. How did the BBC's choice of story differ from other channels? What do the BBC's choices tell you about their news values? What stories were ignored by British TV broadcasters? Why do you think these stories were not selected?

So what makes an item newsworthy? Researchers Galtung and Ruge (in Allan and Stuart, 1999: 62–3) suggested that a value is placed on an event to help determine whether or not it is newsworthy. News values focus on the properties of the events themselves and are typically classified into 'values', which include threshold (size); negativity (bad news is more interesting than good); and simplification (simple stories which have one interpretation).

However, you also need to consider other factors, such as:

- The needs of the target audience.
- The channel identity of the broadcaster.
- Balancing seriousness with entertainment.

The above selection of stories is typical of *BBC News 24*: the BBC frequently choose a political or economic story as their lead item as these stories reflect their traditional and formal identity. The economic recession and the forthcoming election also mean that stories about industry closures, unemployment and political conflict become part of larger, ongoing narratives. The audience have already been informed about similar stories so may be interested in how this larger narrative develops.

Serious crime is always placed near the top of the news agenda. If a story is shocking then it will be given more significance. Murders are often headline news but the killing of children has greater emotional impact for many audiences further raising the newsworthiness of the story.

Whilst seriousness is an important convention of news programmes, *BBC News 24* must also entertain viewers and compete with channels such as Sky News, as well as other news media forms. The use of tabloid style news stories featuring scandal and celebrity offers the audience entertainment and provides balance.

However, it is also a useful exercise to consider those stories that are not prioritised by the broadcaster. On screen text announced a UN appeal for further aid for Haiti but this story was not developed within the programme. You may want to consider how such a selection process constructs a representation of events and issues, as well as what this says about the *BBC News 24*'s agenda and audience.

Constructing the Narrative of Rolling News

Gordon Brown's speech

Despite not featuring as a headline, the main news item during the hour was a speech made by Gordon Brown to a conference hosted by the Policy Network. This item was heavily trailed throughout the morning. At various points the channel cut live to the conference room where audience members were sitting awaiting the arrival of the speakers. Whilst the camera panned the room the presenter listed guests at the conference and outlined the expected content of Brown's speech. Then, at 9.31, the channel interrupted the weather report to broadcast Brown live from the conference.

Constructing news narratives in this way is very different to the style of traditional bulletins. A fairly routine speech is given much greater emphasis due to the channel's need for live footage. Abruptly ending the weather report also gives an unmerited sense of drama. The audience is also shown the entire speech rather than selected sound-bites used by bulletins broadcast later in the day. The selection of key phrases from a speech is central to the construction of narratives in traditional news. *BBC News 24* uses captions to highlight sound-bites such as 'Brown attacks narrow nationalism of conservatives' to fulfil a similar purpose. In this case the caption helps anchor the representation of conflict between the two political parties which fits with the ongoing election coverage.

The speech ended at 9.56, in time to return to the weather. At 10am the headlines were repeated with actuality footage from the speech used to illustrate the top story about economists supporting Brown. This edited footage of the speech was combined with earlier interviews. These were then accompanied by graphics and a voice over from the reporter, thus forming a more structured item.

Breaking News

The term 'breaking news' has dramatic connotations; not only does it convey a sense of immediacy, but the audience associates the idea with the interruption of normal programmes for a story of great importance. Due to the nature of rolling news, most stories are reported as they are happening. In a sense, Gordon Brown's speech is 'breaking news'.

The story of the boy being stabbed to death illustrates the way news channels operate. The story is initially reported by the presenter and the audience is told simply that a nine-year-old boy in Bradford has been stabbed and is dead. At 9.23 there is a live link to a reporter in the BBC newsroom in Leeds. He has a few more details regarding time and place but little more is known. By 10.09 the reporter is on the phone, live at the scene and then by 10.46 *BBC News 24* shows pictures of him at the street which has been cordoned off. Each time the reporter adds details but information is still limited.

This item demonstrates the way rolling news constructs narratives differently to other news forms. A genuine immediacy exists. The story unfolds, or is constructed as the viewer watches. We learn that his older sister was also stabbed. That he was at her house. The story is put together piece by piece rather than being edited after the event for a more traditional bulletin. It also highlights the importance of actuality. Actuality refers to the added value of having footage live from the scene of an event. The reporter in the Leeds studio does not know anything that the main presenter could not tell us, but we cut to him anyway. Showing the cordoned off street does not reveal any newsworthy information but creates a sense of being closer to the news, that the audience might find out more. It is also more entertaining than simply watching the presenter in the studio.

TASK

Choose a breaking news story and make notes on how the story is constructed. Then watch a later bulletin. Compare and contrast the way the story is now being told. Pay attention to which elements of the story are prioritised and which have been left out. How do the processes of selection and construction change the representation of the event?

Genre Conventions

BBC News 24 conforms to key genre expectations such as seriousness and professionalism. Conventionally the mise-en-scéne, dramatic non-diegetic music and formal modes of address are used to create a sense of the importance of the news. However, news is increasingly shaped by the need to entertain audiences, evident in the tabloid style inclusion of celebrity stories featuring Prince William and Tiger Woods. The treatment of these stories also reflects the need to provide entertainment. Slow motion footage of Tiger Woods is mixed with still images of sensational headlines to create a visually stimulating item. Experts are invited to speculate about the forthcoming news conference gratifying the audience's desire for scandal.

TASK

Analyse an hour of *BBC News 24*. Identify features of the programme that are designed to represent seriousness and professionalism. Think about the following:

- *Mise-en-scène*.

- Technical, audio and written codes.

- The representation of presenters, reporters and experts.

Then, identify the stories which have been selected to entertain audiences. Analyse how the stories have been constructed to make them entertaining.

Finally, compare your extract from *BBC News 24* with a news bulletin from another channel. What features do they have in common which might be considered generic conventions? Does *BBC News 24* do anything differently, that might differentiate it from other programmes or channels?

Audiences

Like other rolling news channels, *BBC News 24* encourages audiences to interact with the programmes. Information for people wishing to text or email the channel is frequently displayed at the bottom of the screen. Audiences are often asked to contribute their responses to stories and at times to act as reporters, for example, sending in pictures of the disruptions caused by severe snow. This inclusive mode of address has become a convention of news programming and is indicative of a shift away from a more formal and serious tone.

Further interactive options are available to audiences thanks to digital technology. Pressing the red button allows viewers to select the items they want to watch, including opting for sports headlines, rather than having to watch the stories in the order proscribed by the channel. Empowering audiences in this way fundamentally changes the relationship between the viewer and broadcast news. Audiences can use *BBC News 24* to search for a particular story in the same way that newspaper readers can pick and choose the stories and sections that meet their needs. This interactivity is also similar to how people use the internet.

BBC News 24 is not only broadcast as a television channel but can be accessed online via the BBC's website. Thanks to the widespread availability of broadband, users can either watch a live stream or access video clips organised in sections including World, UK, Politics, Business and Entertainment. These clips range from brief actuality illustrating stories explained in accompanying text, through to entire features from *BBC News 24* such as *Your Money* and *Film 24*. To aid users browsing for interesting stories, the front page of the *BBC News 24* site provides links to both the most popular stories and those described as Editor's choice. The website also offers a forum – *Have your say* – providing users with the opportunity to use their content as the stimulus for social interaction. All of which means the behaviour of the users is far removed from the traditional view of television news audiences.

> ## TASK
>
> - Look at the website and identify different audiences who might use it. What can each of the audiences use the website to do?
>
> - Compare the behaviour of interactive users with the behaviour of traditional television viewers. How do the interactive features of the website change the way in which audiences use and respond to the news?

Industry

All eight of the BBC channels operate as **public service broadcasters**, which means they must do more than entertain audiences and generate revenue, they must fulfil a remit. The first Director General, John Reith, said the BBC should 'inform, educate and entertain'. This continues to be its mission statement, though now, all BBC content should be at least one of the following: high quality, challenging, original, innovative or engaging. The BBC also has a Royal Charter: a specific remit which is renewed every ten years and is paid for by the licence fee, a compulsory charge on all households with televisions which generates approximately £3 billion per year. When the Royal Charter is renewed, the cost of the licence fee is also set; therefore the BBC must show that it is fulfilling its remit (see http://www.bbc.co.uk/bbctrust/framework/charter.html for further information).

BBC News 24 can be said to play an important part in fulfilling a number of these key principles and in doing so represents the BBC's identity. For example, citizenship involves being well informed about social, political and economic issues whilst high quality, global news gathering fulfils the principle of bringing the world to the UK. The cross-platform structure of *BBC News 24* (digital television and the internet) also performs a significant role in building digital Britain. BBC News 24 encourages audiences to adopt new technology and to use it for information and education as well as entertainment. Audiences can even follow *BBC News 24* on Twitter, signing up to receive regular news updates via their computers or phones.

> ## TASK
>
> Explore the ways in which new technology has changed the way in which news is constructed.

Royal Charter 2006 (key principles):

- Sustaining citizenship and civil society.

- Promoting education.

- Stimulating creativity.

- Reflecting the identity of the UK's nations, regions and communities.

- Bringing the world to the UK and the UK to the world.

- Building digital Britain.

Channel 4 / E4 – *skins*

skins is a controversial teen drama which represents the lives of a group of teen-age friends. The second series (Feb–April 2008) consists of ten hour long episodes each focusing on a different character within a group of friends. This section will concentrate on episode five (10 March 2008) which focused on Chris, a lovable loser who has been deserted by his parents, slept with his psychology teacher and is primarily interested in taking drugs and having a good time. In this episode he is excluded from college, becomes an estate agent and begins a relationship with Jal, which is then jeopardised as he sleeps with his ex-girlfriend.

Narrative

Every character in the drama has their own narrative strand. Each has an episode devoted to their strand, however, storylines continue to develop and interlink with others as the series progresses. Throughout this episode the audience is positioned with Chris and events are seen from his point of view. A major disruption occurs when Cassie returns and reveals Sid and Michelle are having sex. However, the repercussions of this scene develop off screen as the audience are positioned with Chris, who is beginning a relationship with Jal.

Narrative models can be a useful tool for understanding the organisation and structure of stories. Labelling characters or stages in a narrative should not however be the end in itself, rather you should use the approach to highlight conventional or unconventional features of the story, identifying how the narrative attracts an audience's attention and keeps them interested.

Most narratives conform to a basic pattern: an equilibrium is disrupted then a hero overcomes a series of obstacles to restore happiness and balance, which is generally achieved by the end of the story. Such a structure is ideologically conservative; it supports the status quo. This is because stories that follow this model tell the audience that conflict and unhappiness are temporary, that individuals can save the world, that good triumphs over evil and that we will live happily ever after. Clearly, this does not always happen in life.

The programme does not fully conform to this pattern as each episode begins with a disruption; in this case Chris is expelled from college. Chris performs the function of the hero. He is, in this episode, the central protagonist. His quest is initially to take his life and future more seriously, then more specifically to get a job and somewhere to live. Chris completes his quest but at the point when he has everything – the girl, the job, the flat – meaning he has effectively reached a 'happy ending', his life is disrupted once more. Just as expulsion from college was his fault – his crimes denoted in CCTV footage, Chris makes another mistake, and has sex with his ex-girlfriend.

The lives of the characters in *skins* are represented as constantly being disrupted meaning that the characters conform to stereotypes of youth causing their own disruptions by acting irresponsibly. Not only does Chris lose his girlfriend, he also loses his job and his home because he moves into one of the flats he is supposed to be letting. This is where we leave Chris at the end of the episode, but it isn't a state of equilibrium as his life is in turmoil. Ideologically the programme challenges the belief that everything will turn out alright in the end, and characters are left facing new conflicts and problems. That said, Chris sets out once more to get a new job in the hope of saving his relationship. In doing so he is at least taking his life more seriously.

See notes on Mulvey's 'male gaze' theory at: http://www.aber.ac.uk/media/Documents/gaze/gaze09.html.

Representation

Where *skins* differs from many other teen dramas is that, despite the turmoil and the problems, the programme is also a celebration of youth, each episode featuring scenes set in gigs, clubs and house parties. The characters dress well without conforming to mainstream trends. Their lifestyles are exciting, soundtracked by a mixture of alternative music, and whilst not all the characters conform to the male or female gaze, the way they live and their group of friends make them desirable and aspirational.

Realism
– the portrayal of characters and issues as they appear in real life.

The characters' use of drugs is normalised without the characters being demonised. When attempting to sell his first house Chris paints an idealised picture of life in the house, finishing with 'imagine skinning up in the back garden...with the kids'. These customers are surprised rather than shocked, and buy the house.

The narrative of *skins* lacks the binary oppositions conventionally found in teen drama, for example:

- Children vs. parents.
- Youth vs. experience.
- Irresponsibility vs. responsibility.

The absence of these oppositions stems from the representation of the adults, who are as flawed as the young characters: Chris' ex-girlfriend was his teacher; his father and his mother desert him; even the principal is foul-mouthed and expels him because of the college's statistics. Characters are divided into those that are likeable and those that are not, regardless of age. The middle-aged estate agency manager bonds with and supports Chris whereas his young colleague is represented as annoying and aggressive.

It is often claimed that programmes like *skins* are more realistic than other teen programmes such as *Hollyoaks* (1995–) and *The OC* (2003–7). What those who say this mean is that the characters and narratives transcend simple stereotypes and the straightforward clash of opposites. Chris is a complex character; he is simultaneously likeable but cheats on his girlfriend, even while he genuinely wants the relationship to work. These complex representations of characters and their behaviour can be linked to discussions about realism, as this reflects our experiences more closely than less developed and more stereotypical characters.

Audience

The Uses and Gratifications model aims to explain how audiences use the media to fulfil their needs. McQuail (www.aber.ac.uk/media/Documents/short/usegrat.html) explained a number of uses which provide a useful starting point when explaining the appeal of media texts:

- Diversion – audiences will be entertained by the drama and comedy conventions used in the text.

- Value reinforcement – *skins* represents values such as enjoying life, friendships as an alternative to family which the viewers may share.

- Reality exploration – audiences might relate to Chris' relationship problems, evaluating their own behaviour as a result of viewing.

In appealing to its target audience *skins* predictably caused some controversy. *The Daily Mail* ran the headline 'Is this really what our teenagers get up to?' and asked 'if most teenagers don't stoop to the lengths of depravity depicted here, by putting the show's antics on TV are we encouraging them to do so?' However, academic discussions about media audiences have moved away from concerns about the straightforward effects of the media on the audience.

In *Media, Gender and Identity*, David Gauntlett (2002: 196–200) refers to the idea of a 'pick and mix' reader, in relation to women's magazines, but this concept might equally be applied to viewers of *skins*. His study found that women did not take these magazines literally, that many highly successful career women enjoyed the 'girly' interests in magazines due to the relaxing contrast they offered to their work lives, and that readers could choose the meanings and identities they liked, and ignore or discard the rest.

Similarly, *skins*' audiences might enjoy the representations of lifestyles involving music, fashion and excitement. They might also relate to some of the issues raised, or to the depiction of close friendships, dysfunctional families and adults who abuse their authority. In doing so the audience picks and chooses the meanings they like and discard the rest. For many audiences, what is discarded will include the celebration of drug culture and promiscuity which concerns newspapers like *The Daily Mail*. According to this version of audiences, teenage viewers under pressure to succeed in exams may enjoy the contrast Chris's character provides to their own lives, just as the career women in Gauntlett's study enjoyed the escapism of 'girly' content.

However, the 'pick and mix' viewer can do much more than simply watch *skins*. The programme encourages audiences to use interactive content across a range of media forms. Interactive media forms enable audiences to pick and mix the content they access, resulting in a truly active audience.

E4's demographic (16–34, predominantly ABC1s) are at the forefront of social networking and downloading content instead of watching television in the traditional sense. They are also quite likely to engage in fandom: *skins* exploits these factors, presenting an active audience with the opportunity to interact with other fans, as well as characters from the show.

E4's *skins* site allows fans to download exclusive material never broadcast on television including mini episodes and video blogs featuring the cast in character. The audience is able to gain greater insight into the characters and the direct mode of address encourages a greater sense of connection between character and viewer. This suspension of disbelief is reinforced through the user profiles and blogs written by each of the characters.

ABC1 – a social grade. It comes from a system which classifies audiences socially by the occupation of the head of the household. An ABC1 audience would be considered middle class and the C2DE audience is classified as working class.

Giving the characters' lives outside of the programme (even between series) may allow the audience to gratify their personal relationship needs. Many viewers do use social networking sites: Myspace, Facebook and Bebo to become part of a wider community, based on, but not limited to the TV programme. Viewers can become one of *skins'* 150,000 Myspace friends, join official and unofficial Facebook groups, including a 4,000 strong campaign to win a *skins'* party for Leeds.

The internet revolutionised and redefined fandom in the 1990s, enabling fans to communicate with each other, unrestricted by geography. Much attention has been paid to the phenomenon of fan fiction. Fans of programmes such as *Buffy the Vampire Slayer* (1997–2003) wrote stories, even novels, using TV programmes as source material: *skins* encourages similar, but more technologically focused (and socially acceptable) practises. Their site allows audience members to create their own related projects, including redesigning the logo, restyling the characters and producing party projections, used as backdrops for nights. These creative outlets for expression could allow the audience to gratify self-actualisation needs.

Audiences use skins as both an inspiration and outlet for their creativity.

TASK

Starting at E4's homepage, explore the interactive content and activities available to fans. Use both official and unofficial sites and then assess the interactivity of each text using the following questions:

- What can fans of the programme do?

- What is the relationship between the interactive content and the programme?

- Who are the target audiences for the interactive content?

- How does the interactive content gratify the audience needs? (Use McQuail's categories as a starting point but you can adapt them or create your own as well.)

Taking a further step away from the programme, *skins life*, an online magazine devoted to the lifestyle of *skins'* characters was launched by the production company, Company Pictures. This site enables users to upload artwork, video material and anything else deemed suitably creative. It also features magazine content focused on style and music, whilst promoting a live tour, which further extends the brand. There is even a competition offering bands or artists the chance to be support acts at these concerts.

Industry

E4 is a digital channel launched by Channel 4 in 2004 to specifically target 16–34 year-olds. This demographic is extremely important to advertisers as it is a group with a high disposable income but who are difficult to reach, as, contrary to popular opinion, they actually watch less TV than other audiences. This makes successfully targeting this audience difficult, but potentially highly profitable.

Channel 4 is a public service broadcaster but, unlike the BBC, is commercially funded. Its remit focuses on the following:

- Innovation.

- Risk-taking.

- Appealing to and representing minorities.

- Engaging young audiences.

E4 was launched as 'Channel 4 without the boring bits' (Kevin Lygo, Channel 4's Director of TV), presumably referring to those programmes not aimed specifically at youth audiences, such as Channel 4 *News and Dispatches*. It has been a relative success, regularly attracting hundreds of thousands of viewers and establishing a youthful channel identity. At the bottom line, it averages more than the 1% of the available audience share demanded by its parent channel.

Yet despite this success, E4 has an identity problem because the channel schedules few of its own programmes and relies heavily on previewing Channel 4 programmes, such as *Hollyoaks* (1995-), *Big Brother* spin-offs (2000-10) and repeats of *Friends* (1994–2004). *skins* offers E4 the edgy, distinctive identity the channel needs whilst delivering huge viewing figures: over 800,000 people watched the first episode of series 2.

The extensive marketing campaign made use of print adverts, expensive promos and internet banners. For the second series the cast also appeared widely, from *Friday Night with Jonathan Ross* on BBC1 to the cover of *Attitude* magazine, generating maximum publicity from their newfound celebrity status. Word of mouth has also made a major contribution to the promotion of *skins* partly as the result of its online presence outlined above.

TASK

Analyse this poster for *skins* and consider the following questions:

- How is youth represented?
- Explore the ways in which the poster contributes to E4's channel identity?
- In what ways does the poster appeal to the target audience?

The Wire

This section looks specifically at Episode One of Season Three (2006, UK).

Text

The Wire is a critically acclaimed American crime drama spanning five series (2002–8). Each series consists of thirteen one hour episodes which follow a wire-tap investigation into drug dealers in Baltimore. This investigation is the central thread of a sprawling narrative structure, featuring a large ensemble cast, which represents a dystopian America. Whilst never gaining spectacular viewing figures, like many HBO dramas, *The Wire* has a dedicated cult following.

Genre

Genre is best understood as a series of relationships between producers, texts and audiences. In order to keep audiences interested many texts challenge expectations, so you should pay attention to how texts challenge as well as conform to conventions. Crime drama in particular is a complex genre consisting of many sub-genres and hybrids and can traditionally be divided into three main sub-genres depending on audience positioning. The audience can be positioned with:

- The detectives.
- The criminals.
- The victims.

In *The Wire*, each of these strands has its own narrative. *The Wire* also uses conventions from various sub-genres and transgresses boundaries of them all, for example:

- Procedural crime dramas (programme examples include *NYPD Blue* and *Law and Order*) – although *The Wire* does not focus on a single, specific crime, one investigation (a wire-tap) develops across the five series. This allows the producers to extend the procedural crime drama format to include a surveillance unit, the homicide division and the Assistant State's Attorney, as well as the hierarchy of commissioners.

• Gangsters – the lives of criminals are represented. However, these narrative strands do not focus solely on the main criminals as is conventional. *The Wire* also includes narrative strands focusing on junior dealers, and even on Bubbles, a homeless drug addict who is introduced in this episode, trouser-less and attempting to sell scrap-metal.

• Buddy-cop sub-genre (which stems from the American dime novel tradition) –Detectives Ellis Carver and Thomas 'Herc' Hauk patrol the streets of Baltimore, chase criminals and use violence. This action based tradition is anchored by the use of the *Shaft* (1971) theme, played by Herc as they chase criminals. However, their violence is represented as brutality, they assault children involved in drug dealing, then charge them with loitering.

Narrative

The narrative of *The Wire* appears more complex than that of many other TV programmes. Some key features that contribute to this complexity include:

• No recap of previous episodes.

• Each programme features a pre-credit scene, which does nothing to progress the continuing narratives.

• No crime is committed to disrupt the equilibrium.

Yet, the whole of Episode One works to establish a state of equilibrium: the wire-tap team is failing; Jimmy's wife is seeing another man; the Barksdale organisation has lost territory; and Stringer is running the drug dealing business because Avon is in prison. Rather than representing disruptions this episode constructs enigmas: who is Proposition Joe? How can the police lower crime statistics? Why is the councilman undermining the Mayor? Each event develops the narrative structure, creating new enigmas, disrupting the previous disruptions and giving each character new priorities. Few, if any of these enigmas are resolved and consequently *The Wire* is difficult to analyse using any of the traditional narrative theories.

TASK

Watch an episode of *The Wire* and a more traditional crime drama like *Waking The Dead*. Construct a flow chart for each which outlines the main elements of the narrative:

• How do they compare?

• What does this tell you about the complexity of *The Wire*'s narrative?

There is no hero in *The Wire*. Each character has their own quest, although many are not clearly defined or cannot be achieved. In this episode Detective Jimmy McNulty's goal of charging Stringer Bell is not shared by the rest of his unit. It also seems highly unlikely to be achieved given that their surveillance operation is failing. Ellis and Herc have no quest beyond their day to day task of stopping drug dealing, which they are unable to complete, and the criminals sell drugs with no thought for the future.

However, the central binary opposition of police versus criminals is conventional and does help to structure the programme; yet within both sides there are a number of significant conflicts. The criminals are divided into two gangs with separate territories, and Series Three introduces a new gang led by Marlo. The police are divided according to hierarchy, Majors against the Commissioner, McNulty against Lieutenant Daniels. Each character has their own agenda which places them in opposition with colleagues and superiors. All these conflicts are given the same level of importance, including those that are personal, such as McNulty's jealousy of his ex-wife's new partner. Again, a complex set of relationships are presented to the audience.

The fact that episodes of *The Wire* do not conform to simple narrative models may help to explain why the programme feels so different to other TV crime dramas. Enigmas are rarely resolved, 'heroes' don't complete quests and the narrative is far more open than is conventional for the medium.

Audiences

According to Steven Johnson, 'some narratives force you to do work to make sense of them' (2005: 65); *The Wire* is part of a trend within American drama which asks audiences to make sense of information that has been deliberately withheld or left obscure. Johnson calls this process 'filling in' and controversially claims that this process is helping make audiences more intelligent, a trend clearly identified in IQ tests.

One of the distinctive features of *The Wire* is that it does require greater activity on the part of the audience than other more traditional crime dramas. In order to understand *The Wire*, it is necessary for the viewer to follow numerous, interconnected narratives involving a huge array of characters; more than twenty in this episode. No differentiation is made between returning characters and new faces like Councilman Tommy Carcetti; the audience is expected to pick up the storyline of political conflict without exposition. A single scene may refer to several storylines simultaneously. Audiences are also required to work out much of what is going on for themselves as information important to the plot is frequently withheld. Clearly, different audiences will respond to this text in different ways.

TASK

Select any episode of *The Wire*. List the characters, including information about them such as their occupation, quest and status. Then create a visualisation chart which identifies the main characters within the episode and highlights the links between them. Use your map to answer the following questions:

- How many narrative strands does the audience need to follow simultaneously?

- Identify the enigmas in the episode: what questions are raised by these?

- Which questions are left unanswered at the end of the episode?

Dystopia and audience pleasure

Usually, television is aspirational; representing glamorous, exciting worlds where good frequently triumphs over evil in new and dramatic ways. In contrast, *The Wire* depicts society in the bleakest possible terms. Characters are trapped in a decaying city, where crime and violence are rampant. *The Wire* represents Baltimore, and by implication the USA, as a dystopia.

It attempts to be realistic and thought-provoking, offering audiences insight into the decline of an American city, presenting them with complex moral questions and with characters more fully developed than those usually represented on TV. *The Wire* gives viewers an opportunity to experience situations they would never encounter, or wish to, in their real lives and therefore offers a different sort of escapism.

Texts which offer utopian pleasures represent lives which are not subject to the limits and problems experienced by viewers. *The Wire* is the opposite in that the characters' limits and problems are far weightier than those its audience are likely to encounter. Audiences may be able to relate to these features, but at the same time the characters' lives are sufficiently removed from and different to their own, so the audiences are entertained by them.

Utopian texts feature characters in possession of human power, meaning characters' actions can change the states in which they exist, whereas the characters in *The Wire* are pawns controlled by the systems in which they live. Everyone from drug-users, like Bubbles, to police commissioners experience powerlessness, denied the opportunity to take significant action by their roles within hierarchies, bureaucracy, addictions, laws, environments and their own flawed characters.

Perhaps more strikingly, there is a complete absence of transparency. Transparency refers to the clear differentiation between right and wrong, good and evil, but in *The Wire*, Stringer appears to be a criminal intent on pacifying the drug wars, whilst the police are corrupt and violent.

Contrasting the programme with Dyer's theory of Utopian Pleasures may help to explain how *The Wire* offers the audience a very different viewing experience. As the representation of dystopia denies the audience fantasy and familiar forms of escapism, *The Wire* is difficult to enjoy in the same ways as other mainstream television programmes. Complex and pessimistic it is a difficult watch, which may explain its critical acclaim but lack of viewing figures, at least initially.

Richard Dyer (1977) argues that some genre forms are 'utopian' because they allow a kind of fantasy escape.

Industry

The Wire was first broadcast in Britain on the digital channel FX, then later on BBC2. FX screens high quality US imports such as *Dexter* and *NCIS* in order to target 25–44 year olds, ABC1 males. Attracting a wealthy niche audience is a key strategy employed by some digital channels. Sometimes referred to as narrowcasting (rather than BROADcasting) this approach has proven successful, enabling a clear channel identity to be sold to audiences and advertisers.

Fragmented audiences and multi-channel TV

Success for digital channels – often defined as anything over 1% audience share (compared with ITV1's 18%) – is relatively small. FX's biggest ever hit, *Dexter*, topped 300,000 viewers (8 million regularly watch BBC1's *EastEnders*). Given the smaller audience share, digital channels have to survive on limited budgets. This is why multichannel TV is dominated by cheap television. A certain standard of content is required by advertisers, so some channels exist purely on the money generated by phone-ins. Otherwise, the cheapest programmes to broadcast are repeats and imports. Reality TV can be cheap to produce, but many channels buy in all their programmes. FX is a typical digital channel in that its schedule is made up exclusively of US imports.

What makes FX unusual is the high quality of its imports. This is partly because US television is enjoying a golden-age. The most significant cause for the increasing number of quality US dramas is the American cable channel HBO, which broadcast *The Sopranos* (1999–2007), *Six Feet Under* (2001–5), *Deadwood* (2004–6) and *The Wire*. HBO is funded by expensive subscriptions so it broadcasts these complex dramas to appeal to wealthy, highly-educated subscribers. The success of HBO had led to other US networks imitating complicated narratives and darker themes in their programmes. FX is able to acquire these programmes relatively cheaply, and in doing so create a distinctive channel identity. All channels, including digital channels, need a recognisable identity, especially now that audiences are overwhelmed with choice.

Monopoly
– where there is only one provider for certain goods or services.

> ### TASK
>
> Create a channel profile for FX and consider how *The Wire* has contributed to this identity.

In a monopoly, the market is controlled by one. In an **oligopoly**, the market is controlled by a select few.

FX is also able to afford more expensive, quality drama, even showing some first-run series in the UK, because it is part of the Fox network, which is a division of Rupert Murdoch's News Corporation. The world's media is dominated by a handful of multinational, converged companies including News Corporation and AOL Time Warner who own HBO. FX has the advantage of being able to broadcast programmes from the Fox network in the US. BSkyB is also part of News Corporation, so FX is distributed via another of Murdoch's companies. News Corporation's power over the British media has led to some critics accusing the company of creating a monopoly.

> ### TASK
>
> - Research ownership – use the internet to find out who owns the popular digital channels including Paramount, Trouble, Bravo, Living and MTV.
> - Explore the suggestion that multichannel TV is becoming an oligopoly.

BBC2

Influential TV critic Charlie Brooker championed the programme in his weekly *Guardian* column. The newspaper termed the programme '...the greatest TV series you've never seen...' (26 January 2008) and ran numerous articles on the show and in a world first, offered readers the opportunity to download the first episode, for free, from their website. This publicity succeeded in raising the public's awareness of the programme. Other critics and reviewers similarly praised the series and in March 2009, *The Wire* was finally broadcast on terrestrial television.

In keeping with their public service ethos, BBC2 broadcasts relatively few imported programmes. When the BBC2 bought *Heroes* (2006–) there was some discussion on whether that acquisition was appropriate use of the licence fee. Some argued that the money should be spent on original commissions; however, *The Wire* does conform to the BBC's remit to broadcast quality programmes and was relatively cheap to purchase.

BBC2 'stripped' the programme at 11.20pm or thereabouts most weeknights.

The aim was to make the audience familiar with the time slot so that watching the programme formed part of their daily routine. Stripping suits the complex structure and slow narrative development of *The Wire* as frequent viewing encourages audiences immersion in the programme. The programme had to be scheduled in the late evening due to television regulation. At 9pm, television channels can begin broadcasting increasingly adult content. This point in the schedules is called 'the watershed'. After 9pm, the schedules gradually become less suitable for children, but due to the violence and adult themes of *The Wire*, it would still not be appropriate immediately following the watershed. Due to the small number of people watching television at this time, only 600,000 viewers tuned in for the first episode. This was 8 per cent of the total television audience, which is fairly typical for BBC2. The scheduling also reflects the growing importance of 'time-shifting'. Time-shifting refers to the audience's ability to use new technology to record programmes and whole series, meaning that they effectively schedule their own viewing. Time-shifting presents the industry with significant challenges, not least how to fund programmes if audiences can avoid watching adverts. At the same time, this technology allows audiences to watch a programme such as *The Wire* despite BBC2 scheduling the programme in a way that is inconvenient for many viewers.

Stripping – refers to the scheduling of a programme at the same time every day.

FINAL TASK

With reference to *BBC News 24*, *skins* and *The Wire*, consider how important individual programmes are to broadcasters. You may wish to refer to:

- Attracting diverse audiences.
- Public service and channel remit obligations.
- Channel identity – scheduling, ratings, advertising and publicity.
- Programme content, representation and identification.

BIBLIOGRAPHY

Internet

The Guardian's online archive

http://www.guardian.co.uk/Archive/0,,,0.html?gusrc=gpd

What's this Channel 4?

http://www.channel4.com/culture/microsites/W/wtc4/

Books

Gauntlett, D. (2002) *Media, Gender and Identity*, 1st edition, Routledge: London.

Greber, G. (ed.) (2001) *The Television Genre Book*, BFI: London.

Johnson, S. (2005) *Everything Bad Is Good For You*, Penguin: London.

Rayner, P., Wall, P. and Kruger, S. Peter (2004) *AS Media Studies: The Essential Introduction*, 2nd edition, Routledge: London.

Rehahn, E. (2006) *Narrative in Film and TV*, Auteur: Leighton Buzzard.

Radio

Naomi Hodkinson

This section will explore three different radio programmes on three diverse radio stations: Planet Rock's *Breakfast with Alice Cooper*, broadcast on weekday mornings from 6–9am; Chris Evans' *Breakfast Show* on BBC Radio 2, weekdays 7–9.30am, and *Woman's Hour* on BBC Radio 4, weekdays 10–11am and Saturdays 4–5pm.

Radio has come a long way since it started in the 1920s. It was dominated in the UK by the BBC until the 1960s, when pirate radio stations paved the way for commercial radio. Today, radio is available in various formats:

- BBC Radio, which operates under a Royal Charter and doesn't carry adverts. There are sixty BBC radio stations: some national, some regional.

- Commercial and independent national radio stations like Classic FM and Absolute (formerly Virgin).

- Regional stations like Heart and Galaxy, which are owned by commercial company Global, or Kiss FM, which is owned by Bauer.

- DAB: digital audio broadcasting, comprising digital radio stations like Planet Rock.

- Community radio.

- Hospital and student radio.

Generally, BBC radio stations are still more popular nationally than commercial radio, although commercial stations dominate locally.

Radio programme formats differ, depending on their genre, from music to talk. A programme's overall style, format and content will be influenced by the station it airs on and the personality of its presenter. Each show has a structure which tends to follow a repeated formula and pattern. *Woman's Hour*, for instance, is a magazine show. It is broadcast live with a focus on the presenter and live guests and covers several different items. Some of these items may be pre-recorded. Chris Evans' *Breakfast Show* is a presenter-led music show, broadcast live. It has a focus on his personality and its expected conventions include music, chat, phone-ins and guests. Alice Cooper's breakfast show on Planet Rock is a pre-recorded classic rock music show with some talk.

Recent technological advances have helped radio's continuing growth and popularity. Internet radio uses streaming audio technology and most radio stations allow users to listen online. The use of studio webcams and instant messaging have changed the audience's relationship with radio – the link with the presenters is much more immediate and personal and popular presenters and shows have websites, blogs, forums, RSS feeds and podcasts. Podcasts, which feature each programme's highlights, can be downloaded free to a computer or an MP3 player and are usually published daily. Users can now listen to the radio on DAB, FM, LW,

MW, Freeview or Freesat channels, Sky or Virgin TV, online, on their mobile or on an MP3 player.

Digital Audio Broadcasting (DAB) was originally developed to allow more choice, better digital sound quality and easier station selection, for example by tuning into a station by its name or format, and extra features like MP3 playback and the ability to pause. However, only a third of UK homes have a DAB set (Rajar).

Nonetheless, it is growing steadily and digital platforms now account for just over 20 per cent of all radio listening.

Streaming audio – means that the audio starts playing as soon as the user triggers it, even if it hasn't downloaded yet.

Rajar

Owned by both the BBC and commercial radio, Rajar (Radio Joint Audience Research Limited) was established in 1992 to measure radio audiences using surveys and interviews of a representative cross section of about 130,000 adult listeners every year. It provides quarterly listening figures for about 340 individual stations, including sixty BBC stations. Listening figures from December 2009 indicate that BBC stations still have 55 per cent of the listening share and commercial radio 42.4 per cent. BBC Radio 2 is growing, with a 15.9 per cent listening share, Radio 4 has 12.4 per cent and Radio 1 has 9.9 per cent. Rajar figures indicate that more people listen to the radio today than ever before and that 89 per cent of over fifteens in the UK listened to the radio at least once a week in the final quarter of 2009 – more than forty-six million adults.

Chris Evans' *Breakfast Show* on BBC R2

The BBC, as a public service broadcaster operating under a Royal Charter, has a remit to inform, educate and entertain. (See the television chapter for further explanation of PSB.) It is regulated by the BBC Trust and Ofcom (the Office of Communications). As part of the BBC's wider public service broadcasting obligations, each of their radio stations has a distinct remit and identity. Radio 1 is pop and chart music, Radio 3 is classical and world music, Radio 4 is the talk station and 5 Live is for rolling news and sport. The BBC also broadcast the World Service and digital stations like 1Extra for street music and the Asian network. Radio 2 is generally more middle-of-the-road, supposedly targeting music listeners who are thirty-five years old and over.

Zoo format
– a genre of radio show, most often scheduled in the mornings, featuring two or three personalities and irreverent banter, skits and gags. It tends to focus more on entertainment than music. A current example is Chris Moyles' Radio 1 *Breakfast Show*.

Because of its mainstream appeal, Radio 2 has been dubbed 'the Tesco of the airwaves' (Plunkett, *The Guardian*, 5 January 2009). Under Bob Shennan, Radio 2 remains the UK's most popular radio station. Before Chris Evans took over the *Breakfast Show*, it had been presented by Terry Wogan and was the most popular programme on British radio, with more than eight million listeners (Rajar).

TASK

Go to: http://www.rajar.co.uk/listening/quarterly_listening.php and find out the current listening figures for the Chris Evans *Breakfast Show*. Compare these with the listening figures for BBC Radio 4 *Woman's Hour*.

Chris Evans replaced Terry Wogan on the BBC Radio 2 *Breakfast Show* in January 2010. With Evans as ringmaster, the team also includes Moira Stuart, who reads the news and weather, Jonny 'sports' Saunders and Lynn Bowles. All of them participate in the show's links and features and are part of the playful team relationship which has elements of zoo format. Bowles reads detailed travel news, meeting the station's PSB requirements to inform as well as to entertain.

Chris Evans

Although some traditional narrative theories cannot be applied in a straightforward way, Chris Evans' *Breakfast Show* does follow a consistent linear narrative structure with the same features every day at around the same time. Evans gives each show a theme by dedicating it to, for example, anyone who is feeling grumpy, has been ignoring the warning light in their car, or who had an early night last night. Many of the show's features encourage audience participation, for instance every Friday, after the 8 o'clock news, Evans plays Sammy Davies Jnr's 'Candyman' and encourages children to sing along.

On Wednesday, 10 March 2010, the show was dedicated 'to all the pot hole gangs out and about today'. Each narrative segment of the programme is framed and linked with jingles, chat and voice overs. The jingles consistently include a drum roll, a snatch of 'Oh What a Beautiful Mornin'' from a 1954 musical and 'Zippity doo-dah' from *Song of the South* a 1946 Disney film, sung by Bing Crosby. These set the style and tone of the programme. The show is punctuated with links and chat throughout, as well as approximately twenty-five music tracks over the two and a half hours.

Regular features are highlighted in italics:

7.00   *News and weather* with Moira Stuart.

7.05   Evans introduces the show and plays three tracks. He chats about today's sporting challenge and invites audience participation.

7.15   *Traffic news* with Lynne Bowles.

7.20   (Phone in) *Special day* feature gives listeners – usually children – the opportunity to call in and share what they are doing for the first time today.

7.30   *News and weather* with Moira, followed by *Moira's Golden Oldie*. This feature invites listeners to tell a story about the track that takes them back and hear it played.

7.35   *Wrong Bongs* allows listeners to phone in to correct the team's facts or pronunciation. Lynne reads out what they got wrong on the previous day.

7.45   *Sports news* with Jonny Saunders.

7.50   *Travel news* with Lynne.

8.00   *News and weather* with Moira.

8.12   *Mega phone call* (phone in) allows listeners to make an announcement through a real or improvised megaphone on air. In this show, a woman announces that she has finished knitting a tea cosy and is now starting work on a bobble hat.

8.20   *Head to headlines* where Moira and Jonny read out stories from the day's newspapers and Evans judges whose are more interesting. There is a running joke that he favours Moira, while Saunders is represented as the hapless sidekick who gets teased.

8.25   *Travel news* with Lynne.

8.30   *News and weather* with Moira.

8.36   *Mystery guest* where Evans has three minutes to interview a daily guest who he knows nothing about – today's guest is a woman who writes cookery books about one-pot dishes.

8.43   *Gob smackers* which features two records with a common link.

8.45   *Sport news* with Jonny.

8.50   *Travel news* with Lynne.

9.00   *News and weather* with Moira.

9.08   *Top tenuous* is when readers call in with inconsequential links to Cliff Richard.

9.15   *Pause for thought* is daily words of wisdom from guest contributors. Today's contributor, Reverend Reed, a vicar, explores the nature of bravery.

↓

9.25   *Travel news* with Lynne.

↓

9.30   *Hello goodbye* in which listeners call in to say hello and the team say goodbye in a similar voice.

The links between each segment create a seamless sense of flow and construct a narrative which is very similar every day.

TASK

Listen to any programme from Planet Rock's *Breakfast with Alice Cooper* and *Woman's Hour* on BBC Radio 4. Analyse their narrative structure by creating a flow chart like the one above. How does your selected programme construct a narrative?

Marketing

The marketing and promotion for the change in presenter of the *Breakfast Show* were highly visible from the day that Terry Wogan announced his departure in early September 2009. As well as detailed newspaper coverage, Evans joined Wogan on his penultimate *Breakfast Show* in December, appeared on *Friday Night with Jonathan Ross* in October and was interviewed in the January edition of *Esquire*.

A promotional television trailer for the show ran for one minute on BBC1, featuring Evans in the studio singing along to the Beatles' 'Twist and Shout' and the Rolling Stones' 'Get off my Cloud', then cut to listeners and to Terry Wogan singing along in a variety of places including in bed, in the shower and at work. Rival former Capital and Virgin Radio DJ Steve Penk argued that the 'sheer scale of this unfair cross-promotion' was 'excessive' and unfair on smaller and commercial businesses because it used licence money to give the show 'free' publicity and breached code (Plunkett, *The Guardian*, 13 January 2010). However, the BBC is entitled to promote its own programmes.

TASK

Watch the BBC advertisement for Chris Evans' *Breakfast Show* at the link below. How does it attract a range of audiences to the programme?

http://www.youtube.com/watch?v=5x_OHNM-i_w

Audience

The *Breakfast Show* is interactive and encourages audience participation with many of its regular features. This interactive relationship is reinforced by Evans' daily blog on the website, podcasts and a link to his Twitter account.

At the time of writing, there seems to be some debate about exactly who the target audience for the BBC Radio 2 *Breakfast Show* is. When Terry Wogan left, there was a vigorous media debate about Evans' suitability as his replacement. The majority of Wogan's traditional, and large audience were older listeners whilst Evans appears to be attracting a younger demographic. The BBC's commercial rivals complained that Evans is too similar to Chris Moyles on Radio 1. The Radio 1 target demographic is aged 15–34, while the Radio 2 charter remit is that it targets an older, 35+ audience.

There was concern that one segment of Wogan's audience may fall away when Evans took over in January 2010. It was argued that Evans would not suit or cater to the faithful Wogan audience known as TOGGS (Terry's Old Geezers or Gals). According to Rajar figures in early 2009, only 31 per cent of Sir Terry Wogan's *Breakfast Show* audience were forty-four or younger, compared with around 40 per cent of Evans' afternoon drive time show audience of 5.35 million. Nearly half of Wogan's audience were aged fifty-five or over, compared with just over a third of Evans's listeners.

Andrew Harrison, the chief executive of the Commercial Radio Trade Body, argues that the *Breakfast Show* play list has changed:

> 'Almost 40 per cent of its music comes from the last nine years, with a greater emphasis on new music than pre-1980 output and limited focus on its older listeners.' (Harrison, *Guardian*.co.uk, 4 December 2009)

On 10 March 2010, however, only eight of the twenty-three tracks played were released recently or currently in the top 40.

In the promotional lead up to the new show, *The Daily Mirror* quoted Evans as saying:

> 'I want kids and grannies. I want to play AC/DC and Matt Monro, Barbra Streisand and Pixie Lott. I don't want anybody to be marginalised' (Ellam, *Daily Mirror*, 27 December 2009).

The BBC Radio 2 web pages, however, say that 'the remit of Radio 2 is to be a distinctive, mixed music and speech service, targeted at a broad audience, appealing to all age groups over 35.' The *Breakfast Show* web pages, conversely, bill it as 'a fully interactive show for all the family'.

Play list
– a limited list of songs which must be played a certain number of times each week. It may be adjusted based on the time of day.

TASK

Listen to an extract of the Chris Evans' *Breakfast Show*. Write a detailed audience profile and apply Uses and Gratification theory. What different appeals and pleasures does it offer?

Look at the current Rajar figures for Chris Evans' *Breakfast Show*. Compare with the listening figures for other Breakfast programmes. What do these tell you about the success of Chris Evans' programme?

BBC Radio 4 *Woman's Hour*, weekdays 10–11am, Saturdays 4–5pm

Enjoying its recent sixtieth anniversary, *Woman's Hour* on Radio 4 is presented by Jenni Murray and Jane Garvey. Both presenters have a smooth, unflappable style and very upper middle-class voices and accents.

Woman's Hour is a magazine programme. This genre generally comprises a range of topics, reports, interviews and features. The programme focuses on news, politics and culture and plays no music. It is talk radio, combining interviews and discussions with a weekly drama. The mode of address is formal – for instance, while Radio 1 and Radio 2 are more likely to use jingles to frame the narrative, Radio 4's *Woman's Hour* tends to use a less informal mode of address, for example a continuity announcer saying 'this is Radio 4.'

Andrew Crisell explores the semiotic function of audio codes like words, voice, sounds, music and silence on the radio (1992). Because radio signs are auditory, they use time, not space, as the element for structuring meaning and narrative, for example by 'signposting' with utterances like 'later in the programme, we'll be talking to...'. Radio programmes also structure narrative with regular features in regular time slots.

Accent, stress, tone and emphasis are an index of the person speaking and have a semiotic function and effect. We can picture the presenter in the studio as we listen. So the well-modulated and formal tones of Jenni Murray and Jane Garvey are indexical of the Radio 4 house style – sedate, educated and mature.

Each hour long programme is made up of a varied mix of four to six items. The first forty minutes of the programme usually comprise interviews, discussions and debates and the final fifteen minutes is generally taken up by the current drama series. The Saturday afternoon show features highlights from the week.

Topics covered recently included the relationships women have with their clothes, young women and binge drinking, late abortions, 'empty nest syndrome' and how the Hollywood film industry was affected by the Communist scares of the 40s and 50s. Jenni Murray's show on 24 October 2009 included an interview with Patricia Cornwell about her new Kay Scarpetta novel, juries' expectations of rape victims, a 'celebration of suffragette voices' and a debate about the relative merits of hankies versus tissues! The website includes a 'food archive' as well as features on women's history in Britain since 1900 including information on women's rights, the equal pay and sex discrimination acts, women priests and Greenham Common.

House style – the consistent body of conventions employed by a publication or programme. House style refers to the 'personality' of a magazine, newspaper or radio programme and can be described in terms of its design style and mode of address, as well as the personality of its presenter.

TASK

Visit the *Woman's Hour* web page at bbc.co.uk/radio4/features/womans-hour.

Consider the different topics covered by the programme. To what extent do the discourses reinforce stereotypical notions of femininity?

Representations of Women

Jenni Murray (far left); Jane Garvey (left)

The programme treats women's position in society very seriously and its discourses are generally educated, sometimes even elitist. For instance, on the website in March 2009, there was an image of Delaroche's painting *Execution of Lady Jane Grey* to support Jane Garvey's visit to the National Gallery to discuss the painting and Lady Jane Grey's life and death with a historian and the curator of the gallery. However, the programme does also touch upon lighter topics: what sets it apart from some women's magazines is its willingness to inform intelligently. It may position its audience as a woman of a certain age, but it also assumes that women are academically able and well informed. They may be interested in cooking, but they are also interested in politics and current affairs.

Edwina Currie, reviewing Jenni Murray's 2006 book *Woman's Hour from Joyce Grenfell to Sharon Osbourne: Celebrating Sixty Years of Women's Lives*, compares *Woman's Hour* to the Women's Institute:

> 'Like the Women's Institute, *Woman's Hour* may seem fluffy and inconsequential to non-believers, but in reality both are seriously subversive. Put women together and they will tackle controversial subjects with a ferocity to make masculine hearts quail.' (Currie, *The Times*, 9 September 2006)

She argues that the programme offers a window onto British women's lives over the last sixty years.

TASK

Listen to an episode of *Woman's Hour*. How far do you agree with Edwina Currie's statement?

Industry

The BBC website explains that the remit of Radio 4 is to be a mixed speech service, offering in depth news and current affairs and a wide range of other speech output including drama, readings, comedy, factual and magazine programmes. The service should appeal to listeners seeking intelligent programmes in many genres which inform, educate and entertain (bbc.co.uk). *Woman's Hour* meets all three aspects of the BBC's public service broadcasting remit.

The BBC are responding to new technologies with web pages as well as podcasts. BBC Radio is broadcast on DAB, FM, MW, LW, Freeview, cable and satellite, online and on your mobile or MP3 player. The *Woman's Hour* web pages allow users to listen online and to archive programmes under the headings the arts, relationships and family, fashion and beauty, food and cooking, health, history and science, home and garden, international news, leading women, politics and law, society, sport and leisure, and work. This may suggest a more active and technologically able audience than might traditionally be assumed.

TASK

Look at the homepage for the *Woman's Hour* programme. What is its house style?

Audience

Woman's Hour has an average weekly audience of 3.06 million (Rajar). While the main target demographic appears to be educated women in their mid fifties and the topics they cover appear to favour 'women's concerns', they are of general interest and although the web page's tagline is celebrating, informing and entertaining women, the BBC claim that 40 per cent of *Woman's Hour*'s listeners are male. They do feature discussions on more male oriented topics like men's friendships or infertility and often have prominent male guests like Benjamin Zephaniah, David Cameron or Tony Parsons.

Crisell (1992: 212) draws a distinction between the way people may listen to a programme like W*oman's Hour* compared to how they might experience music radio. An inattentive listener may have a music show on in the background or just use it to frame daily routines. He or she may be doing something else while the programme is on. Talk radio, he suggests, is more likely to invite active engaged listening.

Reach – the number of people aged 15+ who tune into a radio station for more than five minutes in one week (Rajar).

TASK

Listen to an episode of *Woman's Hour*. How might different audiences respond to *Woman's Hour*? Refer to the programme in your answer.

Planet Rock's *Breakfast with Alice Cooper*

With a weekly reach of 708,000 listeners, Planet Rock is a national, DAB, multiple award-winning independent classic rock station. It directly involves, and has been supported by, rock artists from bands like Queen, Black Sabbath, Jethro Tull, Marillion and Thin Lizzy, who helped its owner Malcolm Bluemel to save it when it was threatened with closure. The station prides itself on authenticity and being passionate about rock music. Presenters include old timer rock stars like Alice Cooper and Rick Wakeman. Planet Rock can be heard on DAB, online and on cable and satellite TV.

Syndication
– refers to the way a radio station may buy a programme or news feature from outside its network, which will also be broadcast on other networks.

MediaSpan
– the MediaSpan Network works mostly in the US (www.media spannetwork. com) and offers local and regional advertisers the ability to deliver their message with co-ordinated display ads, audio streaming, email and video marketing options through a single point of contact for sales, management, tracking and delivery.

Planet Rock was going to be closed down in 2008 by its previous owner, GCAP Media. They pulled out of DAB, arguing that it isn't commercially viable in the UK and that growth in digital radio is likely to come from FM and internet radio. Global, UK commercial radio's biggest commercial radio company and owners of Classic FM and Heart took over GCAP while Bluemel, millionaire boss of a visa and passport applications business, entrepreneur and rock fan, bought Planet Rock in 2008.

Broadcasting since July 2006, *Breakfast with Alice Cooper* is a globally syndicated talk show and uses pre-recorded voice-tracking technology to produce the illusion that Alice Cooper is broadcasting live from here in the UK, when the show is actually from Phoenix, Arizona. The show is syndicated by United Stations Radio Networks as *Nights with Alice Cooper* and is available globally in various forms at more than one hundred stations across North America, Europe, Australia and New Zealand. British news, traffic and travel from Sky are edited in with the advertising, which explains why he doesn't talk to the woman who reads the news and travel. Planet Rock is also part of the MediaSpan network, which provides online marketing and advertising solutions for over 4,000 local and independent media properties.

Text

Alice Cooper's breakfast show is music radio, playing about eight classic rock music tracks every half hour in comparison to the three or four you might hear on Radio 2. It has a consistent narrative structure and format, anchored by news on the hour and traffic and travel reports every half hour. Cooper's voice links the different narrative segments and advertisement breaks. There are no jingles, but segments like news and music are linked instead with a very deep male voice over saying things like 'If god was a DJ, he'd rock! Planet Rock…'. Cooper's talk sounds very spontaneous and unscripted, as if he is chatting with a friend. If he refers to a news story, it is to crack jokes about it, for instance during his show on 8 March 2010, he poked fun at young people in the wake of a report about the negative effects of Facebook.

Cooper's show also features interviews with his celebrity friends from the world of rock music, funny stories, trivia and bizarre news (Planet Rock website). *This Day in Rock* explores what happened on that particular day in rock history. On March 8, he celebrated the anniversary of the first *Beavis and Butthead* show. Other features include *Cooper's Covers*, *Alice's Freaky Facts* and *Cooper's Closet Classic*.

Industry

As an independent commercial radio station, Planet Rock generates revenue by carrying advertising. Advertisements on *Breakfast with Alice Cooper* on 16 February 2010 were for Lloyds TSB, Vauxhall commercial vehicles, the High Voltage rock festival, business advice, internship vacancies in the graduate talent pool, and for help with stopping smoking, suggesting an older, solvent, male target audience. Planet Rock teamed up with Absolute Radio in 2009 to sell its sponsorship and promotions assets and airtime and online advertising. Absolute was formerly Virgin and is one of the UK's three independent national radio stations. Absolute and Planet Rock are both male-targeted national brands and tend to feature similar advertising.

Nights with Alice, an extension of the breakfast show, runs on Saturday nights, featuring 'the bits we couldn't air in the morning' (Planet Rock website), suggesting some self-regulation to protect younger listeners. Radio is regulated by Ofcom (ofcom.org.uk) and is subject to their regulations about radio broadcasting content, which cover issues like protecting the under eighteens. While a Planet Rock profile on the TV Performance Channel received complaints in 2006 for the use of bad language pre-watershed, Alice Cooper's programme has not received any complaints to date.

'App' – applications, specifically for the iPhone. As well as music, these include recipes, games and news.

TASK

Read the Ofcom Broadcasting code which was revised in December 2009. This can be downloaded as a pdf at: http://www.ofcom.org.uk/tv/ifi/codes/bcode/bcode.pdf. Summarise its key principles. How might it affect the content of a show like *Alice Cooper's Breakfast Show*?

Planet Rock's website demonstrates the convergent possibilities of new media. The stereotypical passive listener has become the active 'user'. Not only can users listen live or again online but the website features news, games, dating and a 'vault' of top 40s for things like driving songs or greatest albums, with links to iTunes or Amazon so that listeners can buy the music. There are gig guides, links to bands' websites, a ticket search function, magazine subscription deals with Future publishing (another edgy British company which publishes *Guitar World* and *Classic Rock*, as well as film and gaming titles) and classic rock merchandise. It also offers a free iPhone 'app' downloadable from the website which enables users to tune to Planet Rock on the move and to bookmark songs they like which they can download later from iTunes.

TASK

With reference to the three radio programmes you have studied, explore the extent of their global reach.

Audience

The target demographic for *Breakfast with Alice Cooper* is mainly male rock music fans aged 30–54. The programme's music genre, the advertising it carries and the fact that only one of Planet Rock's ten or so presenters is female, appear to reinforce the assumption that Cooper's listeners are a niche audience of mostly older male rock fans.

Planet Rock has a strong relationship with its listeners, perhaps because it targets a niche audience by sticking to one music genre and a specialised format. The website targets classic rock fans by offering listeners access to rock aristocracy through live interviews, features and concerts (Planet Rock website). There was an online campaign to *Save Planet Rock* when GCAP threatened to close it. Users are part of a wider community, invited to e-mail Alice Cooper and the station has profiles on Facebook and MySpace. The independence, authenticity and spontaneity of the show are part of its appeal.

TASK

How might other listeners who are not the target demographic respond to *Breakfast with Alice Cooper*?

End Note – Presenters as personalities

Stars are constructed representations with a persona which carries meaning and which their target audience will find appealing. Presenters, like stars in film, will attract audiences to their programmes and are a factor in its commercial success. According to Graeme Burton, star characters are constructed representations with 'larger than life qualities' (1990: 89). Most programmes 'rely on the presenter as a point of contact' and their personalities influence the style of each show.

Crisell explores why radio presenters often disguise reading (from a script) as spontaneous talk. He argues that 'the act of reading implies absence – the separation of addresser and addressee'. This may explain why the presenters' talk, while it is in fact scripted, 'is delivered as if it were unscripted and impromptu' (Crisell, 1992: 59), making the relationship with the audience seem more genuine and personal. The presenter / audience relationship is one of the crucial appeals offered by radio programmes, so that listeners may trust and relate to their favourite presenter and use the friendly voices on the radio to gratify their need for company.

Alice Cooper is not someone you might expect to be a DJ. His public star persona may appear shocking to some audiences, but to anyone who likes rock, he is a god. He pioneered a particularly theatrical and heavy sub-genre of rock music in the early 1970s and was famous for his heavy make-up, his outrageous showmanship and live performances which used stage props influenced by horror film iconography. Now in his sixties, he is also" known for his social and witty persona offstage" (*NME*). [This is taken from the NME website at www.nme.com/artitists/alice-cooper] He appeared in *Wayne's World* and *The Simpsons*, is a successful business man, publicly Christian, an ex-alcoholic, a devoted husband and passionate about golf!

Chris Evans' personality creates the atmosphere of the Radio 2 *Breakfast Show* but Moira Stuart is also an important and popular presenter. She may keep the TOGs listening because of her long standing status as a BBC news reader.

Evans used to have a maverick reputation. Already well known from Channel 4's *Big Breakfast* and *TFI Friday*, Evans has caused controversy in the past for unreliable and erratic behaviour at Radio 1 and when he was sacked from the Scottish Media Group, to whom he sold his companies Virgin Radio and Ginger Media. Now that he is back with the BBC, his reputation is more mature and mainstream. For instance, he makes frequent reference to his wife and child and his fondness for golf. As with Alice Cooper, this establishes a more hegemonic masculine persona and suggests that both are more mainstream and establishment personalities than used to be the case.

Jenni Murray and Jane Garvey, the presenters of *Woman's Hour*, are both well established and experienced BBC presenters: Garvey came from 5 Live and Murray used to present *Newsnight* on BBC2 and the *Today Programme* on R4. *The Daily Telegraph* (Pile and Reynolds, Telegraph.co.uk, 12 December 2008) says that they offer a 'perfect balance of questing irreverence and serious clout'.

All of these programmes' presenters conform to hegemonic notions of gender in their presentational style and with their star personas.

TASK

How important is an established star persona to the success of radio programmes? Refer to three programmes in your answer.

EXTENSION TASK

- Explore how men and women are represented in three radio programmes. To what extent do they challenge stereotypical notions of gender?

- How are three radio programmes marketed and promoted?

- Explore how your chosen texts offer a range of appeals and pleasures to their target audiences.

References and further reading

Books

Burton, Graeme (1990) *More than Meets the Eye*, London: Edward Arnold.

Crisell, Andrew (1992) *Understanding Radio*, London: Routledge.

Websites

BBC Trust review: http://www.bbc.co.uk/bbctrust/our_work/service_reviews/service_licences/reviews_r2_6music.shtml Accessed 15th February 2010

Breakfast with Alice: http://www.planetrock.com/article.asp?id=234601 http://www.nme.com/artists/alice-cooper, accessed 10/6/10

Chris Evans' *Breakfast Show*: http://www.bbc.co.uk/radio2/shows/chris-evans/

Woman's Hour: http://www.bbc.co.uk/radio4/womanshour/

radioandtelly.co.uk: http://www.radioandtelly.co.uk/radio.html, accessed August 2009

Rajar listening figures: http://www.rajar.co.uk/listening/quarterly_listening.php

Ofcom Broadcasting code: http://www.ofcom.org.uk/tv/ifi/codes/bcode/bcode.pdf

Media Guardian: John Plunkett, *Second acts for DAB and Douglas*, 5 January 2009: http://www.guardian.co.uk/media/2009/jan/05/radio-dab-commercial-bbc-lesley-douglas accessed August 2009

Media Guardian: John Plunkett, *Rajars: More than a third of UK is now listening to digital radio*, 7 May 2009: http://www.guardian.co.uk/media/2009/may/07/rajars-digital-radio, accessed October 2009

Media Guardian: John Plunkett, *Rajars: UK radio audience at new high*, 6 August 2009: http://www.guardian.co.uk/media/2009/aug/06/rajars-radio-audience-record, accessed October 2009

Media Guardian: Mark Lawson, *Swapping Terry Wogan for Chris Evans makes sense*, 7 September 2009: http://www.guardian.co.uk/media/2009/sep/07/wogan-evans-swap-mark-lawson, accessed December 2009

Media Guardian: John Plunkett, *Radio 2 must do more to appeal to older listeners, says BBC Trust*, 15 February 2010: http://www.guardian.co.uk/media/2010/feb/15/radio-2-older-listeners, accessed February 2010

The Guardian: John Plunkett, *BBC TV promotion of Chris Evans's show 'excessive', claims rival DJ*, 13 January 2010: http://www.guardian.co.uk/media/2010/jan/13/chris-evans-radio-2-steve-penk, accessed February 2010

Telegraph.co.uk: Stephen Pile and Gillian Reynolds, *The Year in Lists: TV and Radio 2008*, 12 December 2008: http://www.telegraph.co.uk/culture/culturecritics/gillianreynolds/3725964/THE-YEAR-IN-LISTS-TV-and-radio-2008.html, accessed December 2009

Mirror.co.uk: Dennis Ellam, *Chris Evans: I want kids and Grannies to listen to new Radio 2 show*, 27 December 2009: http://www.mirror.co.uk/celebs/news/2009/12/27/chris-evans-i-want-kids-and-grannies-to-listen-to-new-radio-2-show-115875-21924589/, accessed December 2009

Organ Grinder blog, *Radio 2's audience is getting younger – at last the BBC Trust is poised to act*, posted by Andrew Harrison, Friday, 4 December 2009: http://www.guardian.co.uk/media/organgrinder/2009/dec/04/radio-2-bbc-trust, accessed 19 February 2010

Edwina Currie, *A Woman's Proper Place*, *The Times*, 9 September 2006: http://entertainment.timesonline.co.uk/tol/arts_and_entertainment/books/non-fiction/article631779.ece, accessed 19 February 2010

Production
– The technical production of the film as well as the finance required to produce it.

Distribution –
release strategies, production of prints and DVDs, marketing and promotion of films.

Exhibition
– opportunities created to view films, at different cinemas, multiplex, art house and increasingly on the internet.

Independent cinema – this refers to films that have not been produced by one of the major Hollywood studios.

Blockbuster
– also termed a high concept film, it is a studio produced film which has a high budget.

Film

Deborah Jones

This chapter begins with a brief exploration of industry trends in relation to high concept films and then focuses on three texts – *The Dark Knight* (Christopher Nolan, USA/UK, 2008), *Shifty* (Eran Creevy, UK, 2008) and *This is England* (Shane Meadows, UK, 2006) – as a way of exploring films, their audiences and the industries that produce, distribute and exhibit them.

The films in this section have been produced in very different ways: the first being a studio production and the other two being examples of independent cinema. Therefore key aspects of the industry will be considered in terms of the context of production in order to understand how this impacts on the types of film created, the distribution strategies employed and the ways in which audiences can view these films.

When you study any film you will be concentrating on genre, narrative and representation – the key concept areas that are important to an understanding of any media product. In this section these areas are covered across the three films while the concluding tasks encourage you to further your understanding through considering the links between the media texts and the industry contexts. You will also be looking at the pleasures offered by the different texts, how audiences are targeted, and the different ways in which audiences may respond to these texts. For the purpose of study these areas are generally considered separately but you will see how they overlap as your understanding of the links between text, industry and audience develop.

The Dark Knight – The high concept blockbuster film

The blockbuster budget allows for stars, fast moving scenes, spectacular sets and special effects. These films tend to foreground visual and escapist pleasures above all else as cinema's potential to provide spectacle is fully utilised. The strong visual appeal of the films enhances their ability to attract global audiences as lavish sets and fast action scenes tend to translate universally. As a result of this emphasis on the visual, the plot of a high concept film tends to be simplified in order for a mass, global audience to understand it. Todorov's narrative structure is easy to apply to these films and Propp's archetypes are plentiful (as Propp's theory attempts to identify universal patterns in texts). Although blockbuster movies are generally star driven, genre products many also engage with contemporary themes and issues that can account for some aspects of audience appeal.

Big budget mainstream films relying on mass audiences employ state of the art technologies to create their wide appeal. Therefore they have traditionally been at the forefront of technological innovation, which is often part of a film's unique selling point, while also advancing the technical capabilities of the industry. Part of *The Dark Knight*'s success can be attributed to it being the first mainstream film to employ IMAX technologies during the filming process, making technological innovations in film production an interesting area for further investigation in order to explore the interrelated links between the industry, the texts created and audience appeal.

Industry Trends – Superhero films

The film industry has a long history of comic book adaptation but it was 1978's *Superman* in particular that proved to be a turning point for the industry as film conglomerates realised that comic books were a potentially lucrative store of material to be delved into. Comic book films became profitable brands that were sold through huge marketing campaigns, were given wide theatrical releases, often internationally, and were able to bring in enough profits for companies to reinvest in other ventures. Licensing deals were made that ensured that all avenues for revenue could be exploited to maximise profits.

The 2000s saw a proliferation of 'superhero' movies. These texts can be seen as examples of the cinema of spectacle – movies that impress with CGI enhanced visual imagery. They also have high levels of action and fast paced sequences that fuel excitement as impossible scenarios are effectively realised. Culturally these superhero films can be read as US 'wish fulfilment' texts for post 9/11 audiences. Some theorists argue that in the years following this devastating event the 'American psyche' was fractured. In the superhero genre, the protagonists are invincible, supreme American 'saviours', and heroes Spider-Man and Superman both wear the red, white and blue colours of the flag (in *Spider-Man* [2002] and *Superman Returns* [2006]). These films often feature the motif of people falling from buildings to be rescued by the hero before they hit the ground; for example, Mary Jane and Gwen Stacy in the Spider-Man films, and Rachel from Bruce's apartment in *The Dark Knight*. Superman even grabs a plane hurtling towards a baseball game and eases it safely to the ground, while *Iron Man* [2008] is a cheerful reassurance of US military might. The superhero films therefore, while proving to be successful commercial commodities for the industry, at the same time answer audiences' needs on an ideological level as reassurance is sought – and given.

As well as exploiting a potential psychological audience need, studios are interested in adapting these comic book sources for financial gain. Superheroes have pre-

IMAX – motion picture film format that has the capacity to record and display images of greater size and resolution than conventional 35mm film format by using a larger film size 70mm.

Merchandise – a range of products linked to the release of a film. The sale of these products adds to a film's commercial success.

Fan base – comic books have an exceptionally loyal audience. There is a strong online community where fans will debate the merits of artists, writers and characters, and cinematic adaptations of their icons.

Media conglomerate
– an international company with a wide range of different commercial interests.

DC Comics
– an American comic publishing company that is responsible for Superman, Swamp Thing and Wonder Woman. It is now part of the Time Warner multinational conglomerate.

sold qualities: a loyal, obsessive fan base which can guarantee a profitable opening weekend; a nostalgic appeal for an adult audience already familiar with icons that echo from childhood, and a ready appeal to contemporary young audiences who are attracted to bright, larger than life characters and swaggering special effects. Plotlines can draw from decades of comics that have established iconic characters with their costumes and gadgets which also allow for brightly coloured merchandise opportunities.

Production Context

The Dark Knight was produced by Warner Brothers (part of Time Warner, one of the world's biggest conglomerates). Warner Brothers decided to reboot the Batman franchise with *Batman Begins* (2005) which was to be a Batman rooted in the 'real world', mirroring the procedural concerns of the phenomenally successful CSI, and exploring key themes of masculinity and responsibility which are developed further in the sequel, *The Dark Knight*. Christopher Nolan, the director, co-writing with his brother Jonathan and working with a budget of approximately $185 million, created a spectacular film that offers audiences a film *experience*.

Like other superhero films *The Dark Knight* originates from a comic book source. The first Batman story was published in the comic *Detective Comics* (Number 27) in 1939. As the title suggests, the Batman comics of the thirties / early forties were primarily crime fictions, rather than superhero texts. The Batman character solved the petty felonies committed within the murky frames of these pulp issues, relying solely on his detective skills and rudimentary gadgets. The success of Batman ensured that the character became a key feature in *Detective Comics* and soon had his own title (*Batman 1*, 1940).

The DC Comics Logo

The first appearance of 'The Bat Man'

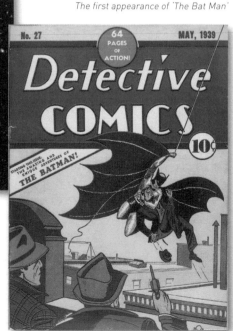

Transposed across multi-media platforms, the Batman brand has become malleable to the gratifications of multiple audiences, yet resolute enough to retain core values and appeal. Like all enduring brands, it has adapted to modern social contexts and developed to suit more sophisticated audiences. Today the brand appeals to a wide range of audiences and takes on many different forms: there is *Batman: The Brave and the Bold*, a cartoon series for younger audiences (along with respective merchandise); the publication of at least six monthly Batman comics for fans, and the movie, *The Dark Knight*, for the mainstream audience.

Genre

The film industry uses genre as a means of minimising the risk of failure as it produces the kinds of film it thinks audiences will like, predicting future success based on what has already been commercially successful. *The Dark Knight* is a hybrid genre as it utilises the conventions of the superhero film and transposes them within the conventions of the police procedural. Consider the costumed avenger, his tragic story origin, tortured alter ego, the gadgets, spectacular action and the world that Batman inhabits. It's a world of police stations, noirish back rooms, clubs, docks – the emphasis is on detective work, clues and forensics, with gangsters, police commissioners and district attorneys serving as Gotham's populace. So while genre offers audiences the pleasures of familiarity and reassurance, hybridity offers enough difference to generate fresh audience appeal.

TASK

Watch the opening sequence of the *The Dark Knight*. Consider the following questions:

- What genre expectations are established?
- How typical is it of other superhero films you have seen?

The standard IMAX screen is 22m x 16.1m, approximately eight stories high. Films are usually exhibited in purpose built cinemas.

The opening sequence also serves to showcase the film's production values and establishes it as not only a big budget summer blockbuster but a cinematic achievement. The heist scene, one of the six sequences in *The Dark Knight* filmed using IMAX technologies, clearly demonstrates the film's ability to plunge an audience directly into the depths of an imagined world rendered with the quality of heightened reality. In terms of genre this technology allows for a comic book film that uses the cinematic language of crime thrillers as the hyper realism that the IMAX format affords; the film is a world away from the inky dayglo of most superhero films.

The second IMAX sequence takes place later in Hong Kong and presents the audience with spectacular visuals that maximise the full potential of the IMAX format. Having followed the Chinese crime boss Lau to Hong Kong Batman's intention is to take him back to Gotham's jurisdiction. Filmed from above Batman perches at the pinnacle of a skyscraper, a small figure against the impressive scale of the city, from which he then plunges. The audience experiencing the film on the giant screen looks down the frame also seemingly from a great height and can enjoy the visceral pleasures offered. The advantage of IMAX technology is fully exploited for cinematic effect as Batman majestically swoops through the cityscape before smashing through the office building to claim his prey. Nolan achieves this visual feat through a combination of effects where stunts are filmed for real in order to create an overall sense of realism not usually found in the greenscreen superhero genre. Here the technology used actually becomes integral to the representation of Batman as he is the most real of all the superheroes having no superpowers at all and therefore serves to make the hero credible.

Representation and Narrative

Bruce Wayne / *Batman* – Representation of masculinity

Crucially, Batman is not superhuman, but merely human. His mentor Alfred warns him, 'Know your limits'. He was not bitten by a radioactive spider (Spider-Man), propelled to our earth from another star system (Superman), nor is he even a mutant who has been subjected to government tests (Wolverine). He is a character who is steadfastly within the aspirational grasp of the audience. There is something unquestionably adolescent about the character noticeable through his choice of disguise and endless 'toys'. The defining image of Batman's humanity is the bereaved child at the scene of his parents' death; the point where Bruce Wayne also 'died' and Batman was 'born'. The adolescent Bruce, bequeathed by his father a considerable fortune, trains his body and mind to superhuman perfection and then dons the dark cape to become the Batman.

The persona of Bruce Wayne is interesting – he is Batman's disguise, an artificial representation, constructed to 'fit in' to society. The role of Bruce Wayne is 'acted'; he is a stereotypically arrogant, wealthy playboy, a deliberately exaggerated 'representation'. His apartment is appealingly modern; we see Bruce on a sun blessed yacht surrounded by beautiful women. He is attractive and well dressed. However, the audience knows that these trappings of wealth are to him artificial and trivial.

TASK

Explore the following:

- In what ways does Bruce Wayne offer points of identification for a young male audience?

- How is Batman presented as an aspiration figure?

The world of *The Dark Knight* is almost exclusively male. There is a lack of strong, developed female representations and although Bruce is fixated upon 'winning' the girl Rachel, she functions as a reward for the hero, reinforcing typical representations of gender in these kinds of film

TASK

Watch the scenes found on the DVD Chapters 5 and 6 (restaurant scene) and Chapters 11 and 12 (fundraising evening):

- What do we learn about the relationship between Batman and Rachel?

- In what ways can Batman be considered a stereotypical hero?

- How stereotypical are Batman and Rachel in terms of gender representation?

Narrative theory, such as Propp's, can provide a useful starting point when studying a text like *The Dark Knight* which uses patterns of storytelling that help to create and maintain mainstream appeal. Batman is the hero in almost every respect; he completes a 'journey' of understanding, defeats the antagonist and attempts, although ultimately fails, to rescue a princess. While the character type provides recognisable spheres of action in terms of the superhero genre there are differences provided through the layers of storytelling complexity. The darker tones belong to the realms of a crime film where reassuring resolutions are not always guaranteed. But, while narrative theories can be a useful starting point for your analysis of this film, you also need to challenge them – Batman is also presented as a complex, flawed hero. He is driven by vengeance and employs brutal methods. He is truly a 'dark' knight, who is decisive, strong and capable of extreme physical feats. In his first scene we see him contrasted with the false Batmen who have taken up the vigilante mantle. When Batman emerges from the shadows his first action is to bend the barrel of a vigilante's gun. This is evidence of his moral code but also displays his physical abilities. As Batman defeats the adversaries the music score is dominated by a fanfare and heroic crescendos, and the camera focuses exclusively on him with close-ups of his determined expression as threats come from off screen. The sound design and visuals present Batman as a heroic presence.

So, while the masked Batman fulfils the narrative role of a hero, the film itself discusses the 'brand' values and archetypal benefits of Batman as an icon of hope to the beleaguered residents of Gotham, 'Gotham is proud of an ordinary citizen that stands up for his rights.' With the escalating debate in Gotham around the vigilante Batman's role, a TV title poses the question, 'Batman: crusader or menace?' Harvey Dent, Gotham's white knight, pointedly comments on the Batman's difficult position: 'You either die a hero or live long enough to see yourself become the villain.' It is from the gulf and tension between the Batman persona and the human behind the mask where the film finds a lot of its thematic substance; Batman has put on hold his personal need, a relationship with Rachel, until the day Gotham no longer needs a Batman. In answer to Batman's frustrations his mentor tells him, 'Endure. They'll hate you for it but that's the point of Batman.' This hero, with blood on his hands, offers a very different incarnation of Batman from previous ones. The film itself:

> '...refuses to trade on fannish affection for the long history of the franchise... (this Batman is)...willing to become a monster and sacrifice his civilian life in order to continue his campaign.' (Newman *Sight and Sound* vol 18 issue 10:59, Oct 08)

TASK

Apply Lévi-Strauss's theory of binary oppositions to your analysis of *The Dark Knight*.

Representation of the Joker

'Just as the Batman has earned his name from his garb, so did another figure gain his...a figure suggesting a ghastly, deliberate mockery, like death haunting life...that mirthful menace known as the Joker!' (intro to *Batman 4*, 1940)

With his bright clothes, scruffy demeanour, verbosity and dark humour, the Joker is a binary opposite to the metallic, sleek Batman. The two have enjoyed a symbiotic relationship for over half a century in comics but it is their relationship within *The Dark Knight* around which the action escalates and their relationship develops. When Batman asks him, 'Why do you want to kill me?' The Joker replies, 'What would I do without you...you complete me.'

The film's opening scenes introduce the character in broad daylight. The iconography of safes, robbers, money and guns suggests the crime genre, while the music score with its unnerving strings is designed to unsettle. As the Joker's gang invades the bank, the camera oscillates between glides and hard close-ups creating a sense of unease. The bursts of merciless violence and pointed enigma codes serve to build anticipation. The film plays its own 'joke' on the audience who are positioned with the Joker from the hunched reverse shot (the third in the film), but we are unaware of this until his final, leering close-up fills the screen: 'What doesn't kill you makes you stronger.'

The Joker's violent and unpredictable character is reinforced though his preference for knives – he chillingly explains, 'Guns are too quick you can't saviour all the little emotions'. This together, with the way he is referred to as a terrorist, taps directly into societies' anxieties (knife crime and terrorism).

TASK

Watch the interrogation scene (DVD Chapter 23)

- What do you learn about the relationship between Batman and the Joker?

- How does the scene challenge typical representations of the hero and the villain?

- In what ways does the camera work, lighting / editing / mise-en- scène / dialogue / music add to these representations?

There was a great deal of hype and excitement surrounding the *look* of the new Joker and real interest in Heath Ledger's performance as the representation of the Joker formed a central part of the film's promotional campaign. Ledger faced a real challenge in creating a Joker that was true to the mythology but unique to the film. The character had to appeal to the established fan base and to a mainstream audience, Ledger identified his Joker as 'a cold blooded, mass murdering clown':

'I ended up landing more in the realm of a psychopath, someone with very little to no conscience towards his acts'

Many of the performance codes employed make this Joker distinctive to *The Dark Knight* and to Heath Ledger: the hunched shoulders, the tick of the tongue and, in the dress codes, the iconic purple suit that is scruffy and worn in appearance. Much of the film's advanced publicity reported that Ledger's preparation for the role involved shutting himself away and *inhabiting* the Joker from within. The Joker was the feature article in *Empire* magazine (January 2008) and was the first full revelation of the Joker's appearance, featuring an interview with Heath Ledger entitled 'Fear has a Face'.

TASK

How does *The Dark Knight* represent masculinity? Consider the ways in which Batman, Bruce Wayne and the Joker are presented to the audience through, for example, their dress codes, body language, action and dialogue.

Marketing and Promotion

In keeping with the blockbuster marketing model *The Dark Knight* was hyped as an event release where the publicity and advertising that led up to the date of its release employed cross platform strategies that were fully utilised to appeal to the full range of potential audiences. The methods of marketing included:

- Official website.

- Viral campaign.

- Print media (magazine feature articles).

- Press releases.

- Teaser and full theatrical trailers.

- Television spots.

- Merchandise (Mattel produced toys and games).

These avenues of marketing are employed by the industry to secure box office and further commercial success and aim to maximise the film's audience appeal and so profits. The promotional websites featured puzzles and clues that led to a gradual revealing of aspects of the Joker's 'look' and provided challenging activities that encouraged active audience engagement. Some of the clues led to other linked sites ensuring continued interaction and a fictional edition of 'The Gotham Times' created a virtual world that users could become a part of. The teaser trailer featured the iconic voices of the main characters juxtaposed against a black screen, setting in motion the conflict between the Joker and Batman. The numerous posters featured alternatively either Batman or the Joker but the main promotional poster interestingly did not use the conventional modes of appeal which are stars and genre signifiers. The associated merchandise, an important area of revenue, appealed to the young male audience.

TASK

Watch the main promotional trailer for *The Dark Knight* and study the promotional poster.

- List the features which would create audience appeal and consider the range of possible audiences that this trailer attempts to appeal to.

TASK

Research other marketing strategies used by *The Dark Knight*, for example, different posters, their website, articles and magazine covers promoting the film.

- To what extent do you think the marketing strategies employed contributed to the film's global success?

Regulation

The British Board of Film Classification (BBFC) is the independent regulator of the film and video industry in the UK. It is responsible for classifying films that have a cinema and DVD release and also video games. When classifying films it operates according to a set of basic principles. In general terms the BBFC tries to ensure that films reach the widest audience possible, allowing adults to view films as freely as possible while protecting children from any 'moral harm'. (BBFC guidelines booklet can be downloaded from their website www.bbfc.co.uk.) The categories that help to determine classification cover the areas of theme, language, nudity, sex, violence, imitable techniques, horror and drugs.

Whilst the specific details for every criterion are outlined for each certificate, there are inevitably issues that arise in relation to individual films which could fall between two categories and in these cases the board takes into account – the intentions of the film-maker, the expectations of the general public and the film's intended audience as well as a film's special merits. *The Dark Knight* was one such film. It was issued with a 12A certificate and served to refuel the long running debate about the relationship between viewing violent scenes and the potential effects of this viewing on audiences, particularly younger audiences.

While the film's promotional campaign was successfully generating anticipation in audiences, some areas of the press focused on the film's reputed violent scenes and overall dark tone. Some journalists argued that the film was entirely unsuitable for family viewing and even urged parents not to take their children to see it. Many articles focused on details of scenes and, in highly charged language, expressed fears that the film could 'taint' children's 'fundamental vision of the world and adult norms of behaviour' (*Daily Telegraph*, 26 July 2008).

Assertions of the link between screen violence, potentially imitable scenes and the possible effects on children's behaviour, were articulated with links drawn to society's current concerns with violent crime, particularly knife crime. The coverage prompted high profile people to join in the debate and to express their concerns. The suitability of the 12A certificate for *The Dark Knight* was brought into question as was the legitimacy and desirability of a 12A category as a whole.

The debate surrounding *The Dark Knight* and the 12A certificate raises important issues for the BBFC with regard to managing the balance between film-makers and their right to freedom of expression, the industry's financial desire to reach the widest audience possible and the need to keep up with the shifting nature of society's moral barometer. For the media student these issues and debates are interesting areas to explore as they help to make the links between the way in which the industry is regulated and the impact this regulation has on media texts and their audiences.

TASK

Read closely the criteria for a 12A certificate regarding violence and imitable techniques (BBFC website).

Read *The Dark Knight* case study on the BBFC student website.

Outline the key points of the BBFC's justification of the film's 12A certificate.

Now review three key scenes from *The Dark Knight* that caused some of the controversy:

* Chapter 13: The Joker's gate crashing of fundraising gathering.

* Chapter 6: The disappearing pencil.

* Chapter 23: Batman and the Joker in the interview room, good cop / bad cop routine.

Do you think the BBFC came to the right decision in awarding a 12A certificate?

TASK

Explore how different audiences might respond differently to *The Dark Knight*.

How far do you think the production values of the film can account for the film's appeal?

For students there is a specifically designed site, www.sbbfc.co.uk, giving information about the history of the BBFC, categories notable case studies and resources.

Further information on films aimed at a younger audience is available on a linked site for parents: www.pbbfc.co.uk.

Shifty

Production Context

Shifty provides a sharp contrast to *The Dark Knight* in terms of its production which raises pertinent points in terms of what is a viable commercial film; does cinema always have to be the big blockbuster at the expense of smaller film project? As *Shifty* is a very low budget independent film, its study offers an insight into the film-making process and the ways in which budget can affect the type of film created, its methods of marketing and the ways in which audiences are able to view the film.

Shifty is the debut film feature of Eran Creevy who both directed and wrote the original screenplay. The film was made with the support of the Film London Microwave Scheme. Launched in 2006 this scheme, supported by BBC Films, encourages film-makers to shoot a feature film for under £100,000. The scheme challenges new creative talent to propose a feature film which can compete in the commercial market. *Shifty* premiered at the 2008 London Film Festival before being released on 24 April 2009 across fifty UK screens. It received a BAFTA nomination for Outstanding Debut film by a British Director, Writer or Producer and sparked industry interest and debate concerning future approaches to film-making in Britain.

TASK

- In what ways might a low budget influence the style of film made?

- Watch the interview about the filming of *Shifty* on www.bbc.co.uk/filmnetwork/features/shiftyinterview.

- What particular challenges did the director face?

- Watch the titles and opening sequence of *Shifty*. What do they reveal about the film's production values?

- Compare this opening sequence to that of *The Dark Knight* or another big budget Hollywood film. How do they differ?

Narrative

The plot of *Shifty* revolves around the life of a young Muslim crack dealer, Shifty (Riz Ahmed), operating in the suburbs of London. Creevy wrote the screenplay from his own experiences growing up in the suburbs of Essex and condenses these into a tight twenty-four hour structure which gives the film its shape. Shifty's daily routine involves supplying drugs to an array of different local inhabitants whilst keeping ahead of his rival dealer. This routine is interrupted by the unexpected return of an old school friend, Chris (Daniel Mays) who wants to rebuild their friendship after an absence of four years. The film starts therefore with a disruption suggesting that something has already happened within the film's diegesis. The audience have to play an active part in piecing together the narrative cues that are given through dialogue rather than through the use of other possible narrative devices such as flashbacks.

Diegesis – the fictional world of the film in which events occur.

Three dimensional characters drive the narrative as Shifty goes about the mundane business of supplying drugs to an array of often desperate characters whose existence is anything but glamorous and often quite desolate. Trevor, a drug addict, is a character whose aggression escalates as pressures of work and domestic responsibilities mount which leads to a violent confrontation between him and Shifty. This then causes recriminations between Shifty and Chris that force underlying tensions between the friends to the surface. They are forced to eventually confront the reasons for Chris' leaving four years previously as narrative enigmas embedded within the story are resolved. A rival supplier, Glen is a tangible threat throughout the course of the narrative as Shifty tries to keep one step ahead of him. Glen becomes the narrative catalyst which forces Shifty to revaluate his chosen career path in the film's climax. Shifty has to make a decision: either to stay and continue to live his chosen life as a drug dealer, or to leave with Chris. The narrative is quite conventional therefore in its structure as the protagonist Shifty faces a set of problems that need to be overcome and this leads to a closing denouement (resolution). However as the events take place, the relationship between the two main characters also unfolds which gives the film an emotional reality and a sense of truth. It is through identification with character and the universal theme of friendship that audiences can relate to the story.

TASK

Watch the trailer of *Shifty*.

- What narrative expectations are set up?

- What do we learn about the relationship between the characters?

Genre

Shifty has been referred to as alternately a gangster thriller, urban drama and crime thriller but it defies neat categorisation. While it shares on some levels similarities to other urban dramas in its subject matter such as *Bullet Boy* (2004) and *Kidulthood* (2006) – films which also offer a representation of street life in Britain – *Shifty* is set in suburbia and the drug dealing protagonist is not forced into this lifestyle through circumstance but through choice. Its filmic style is pared down, without the stylistic flourishes of Guy Richie's *Lock, Stock...* (1998) or *Snatch* (2000). Equally it does not glamorise the seedy underworld of drug dealing explored in traditional gangster films. Instead the film offers an observational slice of life, using location shooting and an unobtrusive filmic style to give the story a sense of realism.

TASK

After viewing the film, consider how far it reinforces or challenges typical genre conventions.

Compare how genre is used in the three films you have studied.

Marketing and Promotion

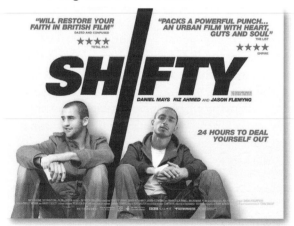

The distribution of *Shifty* was managed by the UK company, Metrodome, which was responsible for considering the commercial prospects of the film and devising appropriate strategies that would target all possible interested audiences. As small distribution companies do not have big budgets, the marketing campaigns need to be creative and direct. Distributors often start by looking at aspects of genre that can be foregrounded to generate audience appeal. The distinctive features of genre are aspects of narrative, characterisation, settings, iconography as well as filmic techniques or stylistic conventions. Genre is a useful promotional device as audiences can easily recognise genre conventions and can therefore make active choices about their genre preferences. For the industry, genre can help to generate interest and therefore profit as audiences it is argued like the reassurance and familiarity of genre mixed with the promise of variation or difference as part of a film's unique selling point.

Shifty is ultimately a story about the friendship between Shifty and his old school friend Chris and it is this key theme of friendship that Metrodome decided to highlight in their marketing campaign. As the film is devoid of spectacle, with low key filming style, realistic settings, an emphasis on dialogue and relationships, different pleasures are offered by the film compared to those of a Hollywood blockbuster. It is these different pleasures that are highlighted in the promotional materials. Marketing strategies included: a trailer, main poster, fly- posting, pirate radio adverts, a web page that allowed for free downloading of the official *Shifty* remix track, links to social networking sites and press interviews.

Metrodome submitted the film for classification making a request for a 15 certificate which would allow for a wider target audience. This was issued after cuts were made. The BBFC had considered the film's realistic portrayal of violence, the subject matter and its treatment, as well as the strong language in making its decision. Ultimately The BBFC decided that the film acted as a cautionary tale about drugs which was in keeping with its guidelines for a 15 certificate. (Further details on this decision can be researched on the BBFC website.)

TASK

Explore how the different marketing strategies employed by Metrodome attract its audience.

What different pleasures does the film offer audiences?

This is England

Representation

This is England is an independent film directed by Shane Meadows released in April 2007. The plot revolves around the experiences of a troubled young boy, Shaun, growing up in England in the 1980s, which was a time of great unease in society due to mass unemployment, social and political dissatisfaction, the aftermath of the Falkland's War and a rise in racism. As an independent film, it offers points of contrast with *The Dark Knight* and points of similarity and difference with *Shifty*. It deals with challenging subject matter –particularly the issues of racism and violence – and explores masculinity as one of its key themes. The film also opens up interesting debates with regard to audiences and how they are positioned in relation to the film as well as their possible different responses.

Films, like any media, don't simply provide a window on reality; they provide representations of it – versions of reality. At their simplest, representations are images plus points of view about them. Representations therefore incorporate points of view about the 'reality' they represent. They are therefore ideological and have the power to reinforce the way the majority of people think by constantly reflecting and reinforcing the dominant ideologies. However, representations can also challenge dominant ideologies by presenting alternative points of view.

Representations and events

Opening and title sequences are useful for the study of representations as they not only establish central characters, but place them within a social context. This is particularly significant when social, cultural and historical settings are important to the themes and narrative of the film. The central narrative of *This is England* is set against the back drop of the events of the time.

The opening title sequence of *This is England* is a montage of archive footage from 1980s TV – hence its deliberately grainy quality. It is edited to Toots and the Maytals' ska track '54–46 (What's my Number?)'. The track was originally released in 1968, then remixed and reissued in 1979 and suggests the early days of skinhead culture (pre-National Front and British National Party associations) to which the film later refers. The fonts of the titles are produced in a stencil-like typeface, recalling army stencils and dog tags. In his DVD commentary, the director Shane Meadows says that the numbers which scroll up under the cast and crew's names are real numbers from the dog tags of deceased British soldiers in the Falklands War, a creative decision which hints at the challenging ideological stance of the film.

The opening montage sequence superficially looks like a 'history' of the major events and popular cultural trends of the early 1980s. It moves from the trivial and absurd (including *Roland Rat*, an icon of Saturday morning kids' TV, *Space Invaders*, Rubik's cube and *Duran Duran*'s New Romantic hairstyles and make-up) to the increasingly serious (national and political events such as the wedding of Prince Charles and 'Lady Di', anti-US air base protests, the miners' strike, a National Front march down Whitehall and race riots). Throughout the sequence, the Prime Minister of the time, Margaret Thatcher, appears in various contexts as an all-pervading influence. The sequence ends with footage from the Falklands War, with a shocking image of a British soldier being rushed to safety on a stretcher, holding up the bloodied stump of one leg. The final image from the Falklands War reminds audiences of a war that many have forgotten and links them to the back story of the main character Shaun, whose father was killed there.

This is England's title sequence

Margaret Thatcher
– conservative Prime Minister from 1979 to 1990. She took Britain to war against Argentina over sovereignty of the Falkland Islands in 1982 and presided over the collapse of the mining industry and a time of mass unemployment. She also introduced a kind of popular capitalism, which provided economic benefits for some.

The images of course are not a simple 'history': they are a highly selective representation of that era and serve to point to the challenging ideologies the film conveys. Indeed, the representation of the 1980s contained in the film suggests that the impact of the social and political changes made by Margaret Thatcher and her government pervaded all aspects of life, personal and social, national and international. The construction of the title sequence provides a good example of how a director, through his or her choices, constructs a point of view about reality and the representation of a sequence of events – in this case Britain in the 1980s.

Representation – Youth and masculinity

The sequence that follows the opening titles introduces audiences to the central character of *This is England*: Shaun, a twelve year old who is growing up on a Nottingham council estate in the 1980s and who is befriended by a tribe of skinheads. The scene begins with Shaun waking up in bed. His room, clothes and later the surrounding streets clearly represent the poverty that Shaun's family live in. Shaun's life is also characterised by conflict: he argues with a shop-owner; is bullied by other boys and ends up in a fight. In the playground the pupils are grouped in clearly defined tribes each with recognisable identities evident in their clothes and haircuts. Shaun stands out from everyone else on the non-uniform day held on the last day at school, as his flared jeans, tan boots and stripy jacket collar are conspicuously out of fashion. He is alone and does not belong to any of the groups of pupils. Most significantly the joke which provokes the fight makes the audience aware that Shaun's father is dead, increasing his sense of isolation. Shane Meadows constructs the character of Shaun sympathetically. His miserable facial expressions, tatty clothes and small size (especially relative to those he confronts) encourage the audience to feel sorry for him, so they hope that he will find the acceptance and friendship he desperately needs The sympathy for Shaun is essential for the audience to follow the character as he falls under the influence of the Nazi skin-head Combo.

Combo

Shaun

TASK

- How does Shaun develop as a character throughout the film? Select three key moments to highlight the ways he is represented.

- Explore the different representations of youth in the film.

- How is social class represented? What role do social issues such as poverty and unemployment play in the film?

- Explore the different representations of masculinity as presented through the characters of Woody and Combo.

- With reference to the three films you have studied, how are traditional representations of masculinity reinforced or challenged?

Audiences – Differential readings

This is England provides a good example of the different ways different audiences can respond to a film text. Texts generally construct preferred meanings but these are not the only interpretations available to audiences. Various factors influence how audiences decode texts, not least the demographic and psychometric profiles of the audience. For example consider how your ethnic background could influence the way you respond to Combo or how someone's social background might determine the way they interpret the class issues in the film. An audience member's political beliefs may also impact on their interpretations of the film given the representations of social issues and Thatcher's influence on 1980s society.

TASK

- Suggest three different audiences for *This is England*.

- How do you think those different audiences will respond to (a) Shaun and (b) Combo?

- In what ways does the film appeal to a teenage audience?

- How might a contemporary audience relate to the issues raised in the film?

- How far does the film allow for different audience readings?

Industry and Regulation

Representation is also central to the regulation of film. No theme or issue automatically receives an 18 certificate; rather the BBFC considers the treatment of the subject in terms of its context and the sensitivity of its presentation. *This is England* received an 18 certificate from the BBFC due to the inclusion of racist violence and language even though the film aims to examine this behaviour and its causes. The decision was extremely controversial with the director Shane Meadows who argued that compared with the violence depicted in other films *This is England* should receive a 15 certificate especially given the important themes the film tackles (http://blogs.guardian.co.uk/film/2007/04/an_18_for_this_is_england_this.html). Bristol council agreed with Meadows and rejected the BBFC's certificate allowing younger audiences to see the film (http://news.bbc.co.uk/1/hi/england/bristol/6601559.stm).

TASK

- Why do you think the film was awarded an 18 certificate?

- Do you think the BBFC's decision was justifiable?

- Is fifteen too young to understand the themes represented within the film?

- Compare the regulation issues raised by *The Dark Knight*, *Shifty* and *This is England*.

End Notes – Production, distribution and exhibition

All three of the films discussed in this section suggest important issues about the industry which can be researched further. The grid below offers some starting points.

What does the table suggest about the production, distribution and exhibition of each film and the differences between them?

	The Dark Knight	Shifty	This is England
Country or origin – according to production funding	USA / UK	UK	UK
Certificate	12A	15	18
Production companies	Warner Brothers Legendary Pictures DC Comics Syncopy	BBC Films Between The Eyes Film London	Big Arty Productions EM Media Film4 Optimum Releasing Screen Yorkshire UK Film Council Warp Films
Distribution company (UK & USA)	Warner Brothers	Metrodome Distribution (UK) (all media)	Optimum Releasing (theatrical)
Budget – millions (estimated)	$185,000,000 (estimated) (approx) £100,000,000	£100,000	£1.5m
Opening weekend USA and UK only / (Number of screens)	$158,411,483 (USA) (20 July 2008) (4,366 Screens) (£900,000,00) £11,191,824 (UK) (27 July 2008) (502 Screens) Saturation release	£50,000 (UK) (26 April 2009) (51 Screens) Narrow Release	$18,430 – USA (29/7/07 – 1 Screen) Narrow release £207,676 - UK (29/4/07 – 62 screens) Narrow release
Website	www.thedarkknight.warnerbros.com	www.shiftyfilm.com	www.thisisenglandmovie.co.uk
Awards won	Oscars 2009: 8 nominations Won – Best Performance by an Actor in a Supporting Role (Heath Ledger, posthumous award) Won – Best Achievement in Sound Editing BAFTAs 2009: 9 nominations Won – Best Supporting Actor	Oscars 2009: No nominations 5 British Independent Film Awards nominations[2008] BAFTA s 2010: 1 nomination (for Outstanding Debut by a British Writer, Director or Producer)	Oscars 2008: No nominations 7 British Independent Film Awards nominations (2006) Won – Best British Independent Film Won – Most Promising Newcomer (Thomas Turgoose) BAFTAs 2008: 2 nominations Won – Best British Film

TASK

Text

Consider all three films in terms of their genre, their narrative structures and their key areas of representation. Summarise, briefly, their similarities and differences.

- How significant are locations to the narratives of the films?

- Compare and contrast the representations of masculinity in each of the films.

- Explore the different roles women have in the films.

- Do the representations within the films reinforce or challenge typical representations of gender?

TASK

Audience

Use evidence from each of these three films to support your answers to the following:

- Suggest the different audiences for each of the films. In what ways do they offer audiences different pleasures?

- Explore the ways in which the films create audience appeal.

- Explore the different ways audiences might respond to these three films?

TASK

Consider the key themes, marketing campaigns, distribution and audience appeal of your three films.

To what extent are they global?

TASK

Industry – Film promotion

Analyse each of these posters to consider the following:

- Design and layout.

- Images.

- Use of colour.

- Typography.

- Language and mode of address.

- Persuasive strategies, e.g. star, genre or anything else.

What expectations does each poster set up in terms of the type of film that is being promoted?

In what ways are the posters similar or different to each other and to others that you have studied? How can you account for these differences?

TASK

Technology

Consider the ways in which the film industry uses new digital technologies. Begin by exploring the official websites of each film. Then consider the use of lightweight digital cameras, digital editing techniques and the use of special effects. Finally, research how the films have used social networking sites.

- Explore the impact of digital technologies on these three films.

Biography

Internet

www.bbc.co.uk/filmnetwork/features/shifty

www.bbfc.co.uk – British Board of Film Classification

www.bleedingcool.com – British site foregrounding chat, criticism, reviews on current comic book developments

www.boxofficemojo.com

www.dccomics.com

www.filmeducation.org/shifty

www.filmeducation.org/slumdogmillionaire

www.guardian.co.uk/film/2009/apr/24/shifty-filmreview

www.imdb.com

www.mediamagazine.org

http://microwave.filmlondon.org.uk

www.millarworld.tv – discussion forum for comic book aficionados

www.pbbc.co.uk – British Board of Film Classification parental guidance site

www.sbbfc.co.uk – British Board of Film Classification student site

www.thedarkknight.warnerbros.com

Books/articles

Hamilton, E. *et al*, *Batman: Black Casebook*, London: Titan, 2009

Moore, A. and Bolland, B., *Batman: Greatest Stories Ever Told*, London: Titan, 2005

Moore, A. and Bolland, B., *Batman: The Killing Joke*, New York: DC Comics, 1988

Newman, K., review of *The Dark Knight, Sight and Sound*, October 2008, volume 18, issue 10

Richardson, S., 'Playing with Personas: Heath Ledger, Joaquin Phoenix and "Real Life"' in *MediaMagazine*, December 2009

Sabin, R., 'The Perils of Strip Mining' in *Sight and Sound*, August 2008, volume 18, issue 8

Computer Games

Sam Williams

The computer and video games industry continues to be one of the most rapidly expanding cultural industries. Gaming has become big business and the market is expanding at a dramatic rate: in 2008 worldwide software sales reached $11.7 billion. This year on year growth is proof that the games are no longer part of an 'interesting little industry' but as the chief economist at the Los Angeles Economic Development Corporation says, 'serious money' (www.theesa.com).

In the UK, in 2009, more money was spent on video games than on films – including trips to the cinema and sales of films on DVD. In the twelve months to the end of September 2009, £1.73 billion was spent on games in the UK according to data company GFK Chart Track (www.chart-track.co.uk) whereas £1 billion was taken at the British box office with a further £198 million on DVD and Blu ray releases. This means that £500 million more was spent on games than on films during this period. The year 2009 saw Nintendo's DS become the best-selling console with sales of over 10.5 million. The most popular game of 2009, *Modern Warfare 2*, owed part of its success to its cross platform availability and as a result sold more than 15 million copies globally. It has now exceeded sales of £615 million – a similar figure to the fastest grossing movie of all time, James Cameron's *Avatar* (2010). Other top sellers included *Wii Sports Resort* and *Wii Fit* plus each selling more than a million copies in the UK in 2009.

Choices of consoles have also rapidly increased and expanded and gamers can now choose from several hand-held and console based devices such as the Xbox, Playstation, DS, PSP and the so called 'next generation' systems like the Xbox360, Playstation 3 and Wii. Many games are also played on PCs. Games themselves have become more diverse, more complex and often require users to be active constructors of meaning. According to Newman and Oram, they are 'an important part of an emergent "new media"' (2006:37). A new media whose popularity can be attributed to the convergent nature of the media form itself and its ability to utilise other forms of the media such as magazines, adverts, films and the internet.

Until recently, the study of computer and video games as media forms was one that was largely neglected and perhaps the idea of playing and studying games was seen as something a little 'childish'. However, the average gamer according to the ESA is thirty-five and has been playing for at least eleven years; 25 per cent of gamers are over fifty and the gender gap continues to narrow with 40 per cent of gamers being female. Perhaps our notion of computer games and gaming is one that needs addressing and updating?

Another impact of this growth in games and games culture is the need to regulate and control the industry. The BBFC regulate and classify games and since 2008 have worked with PEGI (Pan European Games Information) to provide consumers with appropriate information about the content and nature of games. The use (and over use) of computer games and the content of some of them have proved controversial, especially when content is deemed inappropriate or violent. Games like *Manhunt*

The Entertainment Software Association (ESA) – the US association exclusively dedicated to serving the business and public affairs needs of companies that publish video and computer games for video game consoles, personal computers and the internet.

and *Grand Theft Auto* are often cited as harmful and the possible effects of games like these on young people have become a concern of both parents and official bodies. In 2008 the Government asked Dr Tanya Byron to review the impact of digital technologies such as the internet and computer games on young people. A review of progress and an action plan was compiled in January 2010 (http://www.dcsf.gov.uk/byronreview/).

The impact of this report on the computer games industry is twofold. Firstly, it clearly gives some status and validity to an industry which has all too often been treated in a reactionary manner. The Byron report does not condemn all games and does not see them all as being harmful or detrimental – unlike many previous governmental responses to computer games. Instead it seeks to look at the effects that developing technologies can have on audiences and users. Secondly, it addresses a need for regulation of a rapidly growing area of the media. Whilst it does not condemn outright violence within computer games, it does recognise the need for appropriate guidelines and advice in order to regulate computer games which are now viewed as texts to be blamed in media generated panics but texts worthy of study.

The growth in the games market means that there is vast choice of games for you to study. This section will consider three different texts:

- *World of Warcraft*.

- *DJ Hero*.

- *Tomb Raider*.

It will approach them from the areas of text (genre, narrative and representation), industry and audiences / users.

World of Warcraft

Genre and context

The growth in the games market can clearly be seen in the success of *World of Warcraft*. Developed by Blizzard, it was the top selling computer game of 2008. Outselling its competitors *Final Fantasy XI* and *Everquest*, it is currently the world's largest online role-playing game (or MMORPG) and, according to Blizzard, has over 10,000,000 monthly subscribers and has generated an estimated revenue of more than $500 million.

World of Warcraft is part of the ever growing genre of online computer role-playing games in which a large number of players interact with one another in a virtual world. In this fantasy world, players assume the role of a fictional character and take control over many of that character's actions. A player can choose how the character looks, behaves, what they do, what they say and when. MMORPGs are distinguished from single player or small multi-player CRPGs by the number of players, and by the game's persistent world.

These role-playing games were inspired by early games such as *Dungeons and Dragons* and are structured in similar ways. The central stories usually involve a group of characters (a party) who have joined forces to accomplish a mission or 'quest'. Along the way the adventurers must face a great number of challenges and enemies (usually monsters inspired by fantasy, and, to a lesser extent, science fiction and classic mythology).

Each character has a range of skills, attributes and possessions that a player is able to track on screen. These include energy levels, skill levels in a particular area and items a character has in his / her bag. These are traditionally displayed to the player on a status screen as a numeric value, instead of a simpler abstract graphical representation such as the bars and meters favoured by other computer games. In this way a player can instantly see how 'healthy' their character is and also when they are about to die!

Blizzard Entertainment – a division of Vivendi Games, an American computer game developer and publisher.

MMORPG – a Massively Multi-player Online Role-Playing Game.

CRPG – a Computer Role-Playing Game.

Persistent world – a world that continues to exist and evolve while the player is away from the game. In this sense it is similar to the real world where events continue to happen whether a person is asleep or absent from the action.

Avatar – a computer user's representation of himself or herself. This could be a three dimensional character or just a two dimensional icon or picture

Class – the game has nine character classes that a player can choose from. Each class has a set of unique abilities and talents..

Note the range of skills, etc. represented on screen.

Who are you? The representation of Self

The use of an avatar is a key feature of the MMORPG and so one of the first decisions you will have to make playing *World of Warcraft* is to choose your character. A player can choose from ten different races living in one of two factions. Will you be 'good' and part of the Alliance or part of the slightly more sinister Horde?

These avatars are, in many ways, similar to the representations people construct via social networking sites like My Space or Facebook, where a persona is created through the images people choose to upload and the information they include in their profiles. You might like to consider whether these multi-user social networking sites like these are also MMORPGs?

In *World of Warcraft* the characteristics and personality traits of each race and class are something to consider before making your choice.

The official *World of Warcraft* strategy guide offers clear advice about choosing your character because the avatar you adopt says something about yourself. According to the guide you should consider whether 'you want to get up close and personal?' or 'Is ranged combat more your style?' or 'Is magic a way of life?' (*World of Warcraft* Official Strategy Guide, 2004: 25).

There is a clear implication that the game expects that your avatar will be a representation of yourself. You can focus on your personality traits and highlight the aspects of yourself that you choose. In some ways you create your own star image. Mark Stephen Meadows defines an avatar as 'a social creature dancing on the border between fiction and fact', a kind of online virtual body (2008: 14). Within the fantasy world of *World of Warcraft* this difference may appear to be more obvious, as you are clearly not a Night Elf, Gnome or an Orc. However, it is not always quite this straightforward because in *World of Warcraft* you may stress or change aspects of your personality through your avatar. You could become the warrior that you are not brave enough to be in real life or highlight your intelligence by becoming a warlock or shaman. This can be taken to extremes in other MMORPGs where you can completely re-create yourself. The highly popular and controversial *Second Life* is an alternate world where you can be someone else just by setting foot there. Unlike *World of Warcraft*, in *Second Life* you have complete control over your choices from skin colour to hair style to breast size.

Second Life – an internet based virtual world that was launched in 2003. Residents can interact with one another via avatars in a complex social network.

Second Life

TASK

Compare MMORPGs like *World of Warcraft* and *Second Life*. What similarities and differences can you see? Consider the following:

- Genre conventions.

- Narrative structure.

- Representational issues.

- Audience / user profile.

The following sites may be useful:

www.secondlife.com

http://www.guardian.co.uk/technology/secondlife

Part of *World of Warcraft*'s advertising strategy uses the idea of character identification and used actor Mr T in a recent television advertising campaign to explain their Warcraft avatars.

NPC (Non Player Characters)
– these are the various people of Azeroth who give quests, offer services and exist to provide the 'back story' of the game.

Mr T insists that he is 'Night Elf Mohawk'. The director responds by reminding him there is no Mohawk class. Mr T is adamant that he can be a Mohawk as well as a Night Elf. It is clear that he has invested personally in his avatar and sees it as a representation of himself. His final comment is to tell the director to 'Shut up, fool!' This reminds us that the representations of characters in these MMORPGs are clearly linked to representations of who you are and what class you are. It is more personal than taking on the role of a prescribed avatar such as Mario or Lara Croft.

The success of this campaign now means that you can now see Night Elf Mohawks as part of the gameplay. You can claim the Mowhawk Grenade from these NPCs and as Blizzard's official site tells us:

> 'The Mohawk Grenade is Mr T's latest invention: an in-game item that, when hurled at another character, gives everyone within the blast radius an instant T-riffic haircut. Don't worry, you and your friends will look gooooood.' (http://www.worldofwarcraft.com/info/faq/mohawkgrenade.xml)

TASK

Create a new avatar for *World of Warcraft* under the following headings:

- Appearance/dress.
- Personality.
- Special powers and weaknesses.

Consider how colours, costume and accessories help you to create your avatar. What are the connotations of your choices?

Explore the ways in which your character reinforces or challenges typical representations of gender/ethnicity within games.

Narrative, Ludology and Play

The structure of games is another feature for us to examine as they are generally split into levels, worlds, laps, rounds and areas of play. In *World of Warcraft*, the concept of narrative is complex. On the one hand the game has a clear narrative structure, a detailed story and a range of character types and seems to fit conventional narrative analysis. However, it has been suggested that computer games do not sit comfortably within traditional narrative frameworks because the narrative is fluid, not fixed. Different users will construct their own narratives as they play. Instead we should approach them through the analysis of play or 'ludology'.

When starting to play *World of Warcraft*, the immediate or 'birthing' world is one where a new player may explore with little fear of running into much trouble. There are very few hostile characters and a player is unlikely to be challenged or attacked by other players. As an inexperienced level one Night Elf you may learn about your character, build your hunting skills by attacking the relatively harmless wild boar and eventually work out how to accept quests from the NPC characters.

There is of course the possibility that you may wish to leave this world immediately and aim for Lordaeron or Central Kalimdor. However, this is not to be advised as you are almost certain to be attacked by Orcs or Trolls or the much more complex (higher level) creatures you are not yet equipped to fight. You are certain to die and have to start all over again. The structure of the game then, whilst allowing some narrative freedom, clearly directs and guides the player in these early stages. There are clearly defined rules of play in both PVP and PVE options and these rules are discovered through play.

Games are also spatial and when analysing them you need to consider how this space is created and used. *World of Warcraft* is set in the fictional world of Azeroth, but this virtual space is also under attack from others, or is forever being contested. The space is changed when moving from PVE to PVP modes and the nature of the contest is prioritised.

Space is a part of all games and narrative spaces are often selling points of games because the emphasis may fall on how many levels or screens a game may have. The game world is constantly growing and two dimensional spaces are rapidly being overtaken by three dimensional spaces which exist in a persistent space.

Games in general are considered narrative because they possess some narrative traits, a narrative structure of sorts and some form of back story. Academics such as Henry Jenkins and Janet Murray see computer games as 'spatial stories' and sites full of 'narrative potential' (2006). Although the game does not require that a player know the history or lore of *Warcraft*, it has a very detailed narrative back story as well as a variety of cut scenes with NPCs. By looking at the community website we can establish the origins of their universe and how the lands that the characters move through were established:

> 'The Titans explored the newborn universe and set to work on the worlds they encountered. They shaped the worlds by raising mighty mountains and dredging out vast seas. They breathed skies and raging atmospheres into being. It was all part of their unfathomable, far-sighted plan to create order out of chaos. They even empowered primitive races to tend to their works and maintain the integrity of their respective worlds.' (http://www.worldofwarcraft.com/info/story/chapter1.html)

Ludology – from the Latin word Ludus meaning 'to game'. This means the study of games and play. This term was first used by Gonzalo Frasca in 1999.

PVE mode (Player versus environment) – PVE mode is where the player concentrates on solving quests or battling monsters.

PVP mode (Player versus player) – PVP mode is where duels and battles are played out against other online users.

So detailed is this narrative that you can read about events like the exile of the High Elves which took place 7,300 years before the world of the first *Warcraft* game existed.

TASK

Look at http://www.worldofwarcraft.com/index.xml:

- Research the history of *The World of Warcraft* and create a timeline tracing key events in your character's story.

- How does the narrative progress / flow in *World of Warcraft*?

- Consider the movement between levels, what is required to progress, what challenges or problems you may meet along the way and when and where the narrative ends.

- To what extent can we apply conventional narrative theories to *World of Warcraft*?

However as suggested earlier, there are also some theorists who do not feel that the term 'narrative' is adequate when analysing the structure of games. Clearly it cannot be denied that the term narrative brings with it some problems. Computer games are a relatively new discipline for study and are interactive in a way that many other media forms are not. It has been suggested that terms such as 'narrative' and even 'audience' have been applied to the study of computer games without critical thought and that conventional theories can not always be made to fit them.

It is true that there are some definite differences between the structure of games and narratives despite there being a recognisable overlap. Ludologists suggest that computer games are not narrative forms because they are played – the player actively constructs their own path through the game implying that the game itself does not have a narrative of its own. One of these ludologists, Espen Aarseth, discusses a need for a new term of reference to allow students to analyse the structure of games (http://www.ludology.org/articles/ludology.htm) hence the term ludology.

Professor Jesper Juul of the New York University Game Center argues that the three main reasons why computer games are non-narrative are:

'1) Games are not part of the narrative ecology formed by movies and novels.

2) Time in games works differently than in narratives.

3) The relation between the reader / viewer and the story world is different than the relation between the player and the game world.'

(http://gamestudies.org/0101/juul-gts/)

However, a clear aspect of narrative in relation to computer gaming can be explored when you look at the link between films and games raising the question of whether the narrative of one media form be transferred into another. Initially it would seem that the answer to this is 'yes' because most current blockbuster films are also released as games. We have only to think about *Harry Potter*, *Star Wars* and *Transformers* as recent examples.

Equally more and more games are being repackaged in movie format, some more successfully than others. Whereas this would seem proof that of the narrative basis for most games, Juul sees it as overriding evidence that narrative theory is entirely inadequate. In a dynamic game or system like *Warcraft*, a player's experience and journey through the game are quite personal with individual outcomes. In a film, only a very small part of this story can be told – some names and characters may be similar but it can only be a selective and limited part of the experience:

> **'The fairly non-descript game characters and open player positions become more detailed movie characters; the simulation is converted into specific events.' (Jesper Juul, http://gamestudies.org/0101/juul-gts/J Juul)**

The film reduces the game to a specific number of set action sequences and limits the number of characters. This is removed from the experience of the games player who cannot predict which other characters may become part of their game or what the result of their meetings will be.

It would seem then that the transfer of narrative from game to film is not as straightforward as it is from film to game. The story is not the same story in the way that we could recognise the narrative of *Harry Potter* within the video game. This problem can be seen by the delayed release of *The World of Warcraft* film. Its director, Sam Raimi, discusses this problem on the *Warcraft* web site. He comments that:

> **'We want to be really faithful to the game. We would have our writer, Robert Rodat, really craft an original story within that world that feels like a World of Warcraft adventure. Only obviously it's very different 'cause it's expanded and translated into the world of a motion picture.' (http://warcraft. moviechronicles.com/)**

The problem, it would seem is tension between interactivity and narrative. Juul sums it up by saying that there:

> **'is a conflict between the now of the interaction and the past or prior of the narrative. The relations between the reader/viewer are different to those of gamer/player.' (Jesper Juul, http://gamestudies.org/0101/juul-gts/J Juul.)**

Users and the MMORPG

Media texts are considered to be polysemic and can be read / used in many different ways by different audiences. If we consider how games texts are constructed we could apply Stuart Hall's theory of preferred reading (1980) to the ways users may respond. Although the narrative of the text has been designed in order to encourage a certain expected response, there is no doubt that the makers of *Warcraft*, Blizzard, desire their game to be read / played in a certain way and for audience / users to conform to certain rules. In a world where your character has a degree of free will there is always the potential to ignore the encoded meaning or expected mode of behaviour. In *Warcraft* this form of aberrant behaviour is known as 'ganking' or going after inexperienced or lower level players. Whilst this is not entirely illegal, it is not a way to earn respect. 'Griefing' is another aberrant form of play. This is where a player ignores the objectives defined by the game world and instead seeks to harass or cause grief to other players. An episode of *South Park* deals with just such negative play. 'Make Love, Not *Warcraft*' shows the boys being killed in PVP mode by a griefer. Makers Blizzard are forced to become involved in a desperate attempt to save the World (of Warcraft) by passing on a secret sword.

South Park: Make Love, Not Warcraft

TASK

- Look at the 'Player Interaction' section of *The World of Warcraft* website. How do Blizzard use these rules to regulate play within the World?

- Explore 'griefing' and other rogue forms of play by using internet sites, games chatrooms and blogs. How might different audiences respond to this behaviour?

Often the typical perception of a gamer is male, usually a lone teenager who spends endless hours alone in his bedroom blasting his way through alien worlds, gunning down innocent bystanders or driving recklessly and with great speed. Gamers are often represented as being anti-social and isolated. It has been suggested that the dangers of excessive gaming could be anything from demonstrating a lack of social skills to actually being influenced to behave in a mindlessly violent way.

However, the nature of gaming itself is changing and the whole idea of the lone gamer hidden away in their room is one that no longer appears credible. Firstly, many more girls are now also playing games. Games like *The SIMS* and MMORPG's like *World of Warcraft* are making sure of this. Secondly, more and more people are coming online and playing games across the world together. You are now likely to be part of a huge online community where you can interact with a variety of other global users. In *World of Warcraft*, PVP mode allows you to test your character against another player in another part of the virtual (and real) world. Players also use forums and chatrooms to communicate about the game, about specific characters and quests or the latest upgrades and patches. Surrounding *World of Warcraft* is a very large virtual community and users can enhance their enjoyment of the game with a range of post game activities or experiences such as fan art, comic strips and storytelling.

The *Warcraft* Industry

Like many popular games, *World of Warcraft* has expanded into other markets such as film, board games and comics and has been promoted by Blizzard. *The South Park* episode, 'Make Love Not *Warcraft*', gives an indication of the effect of the game on popular culture. Games are often marketed via celebrities such as Mr T. Despite some teething problems, a film version of the game with a £100 million budget behind it is earmarked for release. Games are big business and appear to have a thriving life beyond the game itself. Action figures, trading cards, board games, t-shirts and a whole range of other merchandise can be bought by fans.

TASK

Explore the impact of changing technologies on gaming. Consider how this has affected:

- The production of *World of Warcraft*.

- The impact of convergence and how the internet, satellite and mobile communications have affected production, distribution and marketing.

- How audiences / users are positioned.

- The need for regulation and control.

How has *World of Warcraft* (and subsequent expansion packs) been marketed? Consider how and where they were publicised (TV adverts, cinema, specialist magazine, the internet).

Discuss *World of Warcraft*'s global impact.

DJ Hero

Genre and Music Games

Whilst music in games has always been an important part of the experience, the development of the genre of music games has been one of the success stories of the industry. A music game is one where the game is almost entirely orientated around the player's interaction with music or a specific song. Early examples mixed music and game-play and, as early as 1997 the Sony Playstation game *Pa Rappa the Rapper*, featuring the rapping puppy dog, emerged as one of the first rhythmic games with the need to master a kind of hip-hop singing and rapping in order to impress the girl puppy in the game; whilst *The Legend of Zelda Returns* (1998) featured music making and a musical puzzle as a part of the game-play.

Pa Rappa the Rapper

Within the music game genre there are different sub-genres. One of the most popular is the rhythm game where a player is required to press the button or activate the game's controller at the correct time and in sync with the game's music. Games such as *DJ Hero* and *Guitar Hero* are examples of this. Equally popular are tonal games such as *SingStar* which have a relatively simple rhythm and prioritise the tone or pitch of the delivery as a marker of success.

Guitar Hero was first launched in 2005 with subsequent further editions and speciality versions such as *Guitar Hero: Metallica* and *Guitar Hero: Van Halen*. In 2009 both *Band Hero* and *DJ Hero* were launched, clear proof of the popularity of this genre of game in the developing games industry.

DJ Hero was developed by Freestyle Games, is published by Activision and is available for the Playstation3, XBox and Nintendo Wii .The game is played on a wireless deck and movable turntable and is based on 'turntablism' which is the art of using pre-recorded songs and sound effects to create remixes. The player takes on the role of DJ and once they have progressed through the training sessions there are a range of set lists and play lists that can be accessed.

There are three tracks which appear on the screen and which correspond to the buttons on the turntable controller. The player has to insert beats and adjust the cross fader as the levels become more complex. To score points, the player must press buttons to activate certain beats, move their cross-fade between the two songs, and 'scratch' the turntable on the game's custom controller in time to the beat and in the correct direction to marks that scroll on the screen in order to score points and perform well for the virtual crowd. The game features a single player career mode, where your career progresses as you successfully complete tasks, as well as co-operative and competitive multi-player modes. The game also features a mode for selected songs for the DJ to play alongside another player using a *Guitar Hero* guitar controller.

TASK

List the main genre conventions of a music game. How typical is *DJ Hero* of the genre?

Within *DJ Hero* you have the opportunity to choose which DJ you play. You are also able to customise your outfit and the decks you are playing with. Representations of gender within the game seem to be hegemonic and reinforce stereotypes. The dancers in the club space are all female and are dressed in crop tops and hot pants. While most of the DJs are male, there are a few female examples, such as Candy Nova. However, she also wears hot pants and a midriff-revealing top. There are many shots of Candy which focus on her flat stomach, her tattoo, her long legs and various other parts of her body. These shots are not so evident when Cleetus Cuts or DJ Kid Itch (both male) are on the decks. It may not surprise us that the world of the Club DJ is notoriously difficult to succeed in if you are female, but perhaps games do not need to reinforce and encourage these prejudices. What do you think?

TASK

Explore the different DJ profiles on *DJ Hero*. Explore the ways *DJ Hero* reinforces or challenges representations of gender and ethnicity.

Arcade play – an amusement arcade where versions of computer games are available to play. Popular in the 1980s gamers could choose from cabinet or tabletop versions of games like *Pac Man* or *Donkey Kong* amongst others.

Audience and Social Play

All too often computer games research has ignored the presence of other players and the possibility of simultaneous collaborative play as well as the social contexts that surround and support computer games. However, it has always been the case that games have had multi-player options or have allowed players the opportunity to play against a friend and even the early days of arcade play made computer gaming a social pastime.

Recent technology means that most games are now feature social interaction as part of the experience – for example, games which use multiple input devices (like *Guitar Hero*) and Massive Multi-player Online games (MMOs) and Massively Multi-player Online Role Playing Games (MMORGs). Multi-player games tend to encourage teamwork and friendships develop between thousands of gamers all over the world as they are online simultaneously and take part in global gaming sessions. Being a games player does not mean you are a loner. In fact Henry Jenkins states that:

> '60% of frequent gamers play with friends, 33% play with siblings and 25% play with spouses or parents.' (http://www.pbs.org/kcts/videogamerevolution/impact/myths.html)

Games like *DJ Hero* and *Guitar Hero* are often played as community games where players assist and comment upon one another's progress. Whilst games such as *Band Hero* actively require more than one player, games such as *Guitar Hero* and *DJ Hero* encourage social play not only through their structure but through the marketing of the product. The idea of being a DJ is to play for a crowd and to show off your mixing skills. The promotional trailers for *DJ Hero* actively encourage social play from the early teaser trailers featuring the Daft Punk duo to the full cinematic trailer which shows multiple DJs working together to unite a crowd of would be party goers. The suggestion throughout *DJ Hero*'s marketing is that this game is to be enjoyed with others, that there is pleasure to be derived from not only being part of the active play but also being part of the audience. The ability to be able to appreciate and enjoy the music and the remixes of the DJ is also a feature and aspect of the game itself.

TASK

Look at the official website www.djhero.com:

- What does the website suggest about the target audience for this game?

- What pleasures can users derive from social play?

Industry and Global Networks

Some of the most popular games for social play come from Activision and their Hero franchise. Activision are a leading publisher of computer games. The company was founded in 1979 as an independent developer and distributor of software.

Over the years Activision have created, licensed and acquired a group of hugely recognisable brands such as, *Call of Duty*, *Guitar Hero*, *Tony Hawks* and *X Men: The Official Game*. According to their official site, Activision products cover a range of genres and platforms and their target consumers range from:

> **'...casual players to games enthusiasts, children to adults mass market consumers to value buyers.'** (www.activision.com)

Activision also have links to DreamWorks and have publishing agreements with MGM and EON productions making them an important player in the computer games industry. Although they started as developers and distributors of games, Activision have now expanded into all areas of the gaming industry and they have grown into a market dominator – recently merging with Vivendi to form Activision Blizzard. When we consider that some of the biggest selling games of recent years – *Modern Warfare 2*, *Call of Duty* and *World of Warcraft* – are now under this one company, we can see the global importance of Activison Blizzard.

TASK

Look at Activison's website.

- Draw up a list of the companies they are affiliated to. How extensive is their global reach?

Convergence, Music and Marketing

A game like *DJ Hero* allows for two of the most powerful industries to work together. In a recent promotional interview for the game hip-hop star Jay-Z called this convergence a 'natural phenomena' (http://www.gametrailers.com/game/dj-hero/6217). *DJ Hero* used some of the biggest names in hip-hop and r&b to support the launch of the game. Grandmaster Flash takes on the role of the in-house DJ and the game has been marketed by Jazzy Jeff, David Guetta, Daft Punk, DJ Z-Trip and DJ AM, whose sudden death prior to the release of the game did not affect this strategy. Artists Eminem and Jay-Z have also served as consultants for the game; a special edition of *DJ Hero*, titled the *Renegade Edition* has been branded with their names and includes a limited edition of the controller, a music CD of their songs, a DJ stand, and a travel case for the units. These music stars not only contributed to the remixes available in the game but also provide some additional downloadable content for the game as well as appearing as playable avatars. Videos of some of these music artists playing the game as well as a whole range of fan video can be found on both the official website and You Tube. The contributions of current and successful recording artists to games such as *DJ Hero* and *Guitar Hero* imply that the games industry and the music industry are becoming ever more closely linked. We could also consider how record companies can promote their artists and ensure longevity for dead artists (see *Beatles Rockband* study in the section on Music Industry).

TASK

Look at the game's official website and at print based adverts for *DJ Hero*.

- What different strategies have been used to promote the game?
- Explore the benefits of convergence for the games industry.

Tomb Raider

Lara Croft and the *Tomb Raider* games are amongst the most successful and well-known games franchises to date. The original *Tomb Raider* was launched in 1996 by British company Eidos as an alternative to the traditional all male led games that previously dominated the games world. Steven Poole comments that prior to Lara it was widely believed in the industry that female characters never sold (2000). Lara proved that this was not the case. The game sold over 28 million units worldwide and to date has made more than £655 million in retail sales. She embarked on further adventures with *Tomb Raider Anniversary* and *Tomb Raider Underworld*. The launch of these games has once again seen Lara on the covers of magazines, in the press and keeping up to date with modern technology by launching her own My Space page. Lara has undergone many changes in the last ten years but her marketability and popularity have not diminished.

Looking at Lara – Representation of women in games

Helen W. Kennedy (2002) poses the question of whether a character like Lara Croft provides girls with an inspirational role model or whether she is nothing but a cyber bimbo in hotpants. The representation of women in games has often been a controversial issue. For many years female avatars have been shown as either props or bystanders; they are often heavily sexualised like *Ridge Racer*'s Reiko Nagase or Joanna Dark or offered as rewards and prizes to be won by the more dominant male characters. Lara Croft provided a different representation of women for the world of gaming.

Lara's creator Toby Gard admits that she 'showed some skin' (*The Guardian*, 15 June 2001) but he maintains that her wardrobe is practical and was a deliberate reaction to the spangly thongs, S&M corsets and spirally metal bras that many female games' characters wear. Lara's presence as a female lead in a very male dominated world, even today, is in itself challenging and her action packed exploits do indeed challenge typical and stereotypical gender roles. With the release of the *Tomb Raider Anniversary* the debate continued with computer magazine *The Edge* asking the question: 'Is Lara Croft sexist?' (http://www.edge-online.com/features/is-lara-croft-sexist?page=0%2C1).

However, despite being received positively by many women gamers, the shameless sexualised marketing of Lara and some of the close-up and personal camera shots in the game also turned off some women gamers. Feminist critic Elaine Showalter sees Lara as being an idealised character that 'no real woman can ever hope to equal' and worries that 'young girls will grow even more dissatisfied with their own bodies' because of her (Kennedy, 2002).

Female gamers on the forum of www.womengamers.com commented that the camera's focus on Lara's crotch when she swims, or the shower scene in *Tomb Raider 3* when she coyly asks 'Haven't you seen enough?' before disappearing from view, were more for the titillation of a male audience than about representing a female action hero.

ELSPA – the Entertainment & Leisure Software Publishers Association founded in 1989 to establish a specific and collective identity for the British computer and video game industry.

It has been suggested that the representation of women within the industry is one of the reasons there are fewer women gamers. This is perhaps demonstrated by the experience of female gamers who don't want to regard women characters just as prizes or victims and this emphasises the point that different users may respond differently to games and that gender is just one of the reasons why this is the case. But does this actually stop girls gaming? There is evidence to suggest that this is not the case and that women are a large part of the games market (40 per cent). The ELSPA points out that women age eighteen or older represent a significantly greater portion of the game playing population (34%) than boys seventeen or younger (18%).

So perhaps it is not so much that women are not gaming but rather that they are playing by their own rules and in their own ways – less of the 'hack and slash' and more 'pick up and play'. This may partly be dictated by the lack of leisure time available to them but women, it would appear, also want less complex controls and more depth to the story and the character. *The Legend of Zelda*, *The Sims* and *The Prince of Persia* all score strongly amongst women gamers, raising interesting questions about the nature of games targeted at women. In trying to develop and expand into the women's market for games, companies have apparently developed games that are feminine in appeal and appear to reinforce ideological gender stereotypes. Or do they?

Consider the range of *Barbie* games that deal with fashion shows, pet shows and horse riding competitions or the virtual pet keeping, *Nintendogs*. These titles reinforce nurturing roles for girls and do not, like many other games, prioritise competition or conflict. But, why are girls (and their mothers) so willing to accept a return to such traditional values? If Lara could be seen as a post-modern example of female representation in 1996 then what does the success of fairy princess *Barbie* in 2008 or the *Nintendo Imagine* series imply about how women perceive their place in the games world and beyond?

TASK

Does *Lara Croft Tomb Raider* reinforce or challenge typical representations of women?

Lara Croft and industry

Lara has been a marketing dream for many years. She was perhaps the first game character to move from being the object of a substantial advertising and marketing campaign to being a 'virtual' celebrity in her own right becoming the vehicle for the promotion of an entirely different product. The *Lucozade* campaign of 2000 saw Lara taking on the promotion of a drink that had hitherto been seen as a tonic for the ill or the elderly. As the (male) gamer takes a break so does Lara. After refreshing her energy levels with *Lucozade* she is able to fight on with renewed vigour. In another advert of the 'Gone a Bit Lara' campaign 'wannabe' Laras (this time real women dressed as the heroine) navigate the hazards of the more mundane real world thanks to the extra energy provided by their drink of choice.

Accompanying Lara's performance were celebrity appearances on the front covers of fashion and life style magazines. Lara appeared on the cover of *The Face* (June 1997), appeared in digital form on *U2*'s Pop Mart Tour and had a book dedicated to her in 1998 when cult author Douglas Copeland produced a series of essays about the fictional star.

Cut scene – a scene over which the player has no control. Often these scenes contain narrative information and form a cut or break in the narrative for players.

TASK

Draw up a list of the products and adverts that have featured Lara Croft.

Consider the ways in which other media forms are linked to the games industry:

- Advertising.

- Magazines.

- Film.

What is the impact of this convergence on gaming?

As we have discussed, games based on films and vice versa have become more and more common. The game versions of successful blockbusters or television programmes are to be found everywhere. Hollywood continues to license computer games in the hope of capturing a global audience of gamers. Attracting a pre-existing fan base is a way of ensuring success for your film. The original *Tomb Raider* film (2001) starring Angelina Jolie was one of the more successful game spin-offs. This was followed by a second film, *The Cradle of Life* (2003). Between them, these films grossed more than $450 million at the box office. However, the success of the *Tomb Raider* films is hard to pinpoint. Some believe the draw of Angelina Jolie was the main reason but it has also been suggested that the games have a cinematic quality which translates well onto the big screen. What is clear is that the films were able to attract a wider and more diverse audience than the original games and this, in turn, encouraged film-goers to become game players. Other games franchises have been equally successful and despite poor critical reception *Resident Evil* (2002) has been a big box office hit. However, a built-in fan base is not always sufficient to guarantee success; the $70 million box office flop *Doom* (2005) was a notable failure.

One thing is clear: the link between films and games is here to stay. Games adverts and cut scenes become ever more 'filmic', indeed some games' cut scenes are very complicated and they are continuing to become more elaborate. The games industry continues to provide ready-made narratives and heroes for film-makers. Perhaps one of the defining moments in the development of this game / film marriage is the involvement of producer Jerry Bruckheimer (of the *Pirates of the Caribbean* franchise) in the Disney film, *Prince of Persia* (2010). According to *Edge* magazine, such a big name with a celebrated track record:

'... gives the genre of videogame movies a kind of legitimacy'. (Mott, 2008:68)

TASK

- Watch the *Tomb Raider Anniversary* games trailer. How does this text use genre conventions?

- Watch the film trailer. What features of the game are evident in the film trailer?

EXTENSION TASK

Now you have studied three texts from the computer games industry, answer the following questions using ALL three texts:

Text

- Explore the ways that genre conventions are used or challenged in your chosen texts.

- How far do your chosen texts follow traditional narrative conventions? (Think here about conventional narrative theories and Ludologists' arguments against traditional narrative formats. Draw your own conclusions.)

Industry

- Briefly outline the ways in which the computer games industry is regulated. How has regulation impacted on the games you have studied?

Audience

- How do your chosen texts attract their users / audiences?

- How might different audiences / users respond to the games you have studied?

Bibliography

Atkins, B. (2003) *More Than a Game: The Computer Game as Fictional Form*, Manchester: Manchester University Press.

Carr, D. & Buckingham, D. & Burn, A. & Schott, G. (2006) *Computer Games Text: Narrative and Play*, Cambridge: Polity Press.

Howson, G. (2006) *Lara's Creator Speaks*, guardian.co.uk/technology (internet), 18 April. Available at: HYPERLINK. http://blogs.guardian.co.uk/games/archives/2006/04/18/laras_creator_speaks.html http://blogs.guardian.co.uk/games/archives/2006/04/18/laras_creator_speaks.html, accessed 20 January 2008)

Johnson, S. (2005) *Everything Bad Is Good For You: How Popular Culture Is Making Us Smarter*. Harmondsworth: Penguin Books Ltd.

Kennedy, H. (2002) 'Lara Croft Feminist Icon or Cyber Bimbo: On the Limits of Textual Analysis', *International Journal of Computer Game Research*, Vol. 2, Issue 2. (internet). Available at http://www.gamestudies.org/0202/kennedy/

McDougall, J. and O'Brien, W. (2008) *Studying Videogames*, Leighton Buzzard: Auteur Publishing.

Newman, J. & Oram, B. (2006) *Teaching Videogames*, London: BFI Publishing.

Meadows, M S. (2008) *I, Avatar: The Consequences of Having a Second Life*, Berkley New Riders (Pearson Education).

Mott, T. (ed.)(2008) *Reel Gaming. Edge* Magazine. Issue 186. p. 74–81.

Poole, S. (2000) *Trigger Happy: Videogames and the Entertainment Revolution*, Oxford. Arcade Publishing Inc.

Websites

www.elspa.com

www.theesa.com

www.blizzard.com

www.tombraider.com/anniversary

www.bit-tech.net

www.womengamers.com

www.imdb.com

www.dcsf.gov.uk/byronreview

www.theregister.co.uk

http://www.vgchartz.com/

http://thelinc.co.uk

The Music Industry

Cath Davies

This section will investigate media concepts and debates in relation to the music industry. The process of studying music involves analysing:

- Music as a 'text' that produces meanings to create appeal for a range of audiences.

- Music as a product that is produced and sold to consumers to generate money.

When investigating the music industry it is important to consider the strategies employed in order to make the artists and music sell successfully to a wide market to reap financial rewards. Therefore this chapter will highlight the ways in which artists and their music are promoted within the media. This process must also consider *who* the music is being aimed at, as the industry produces artists that will appeal to different tastes and age ranges.

Common strategies used by the industry to attract an audience are recognisable formulas generated by genre conventions and star personas. Like cinema, the music industry sells its products primarily by constructing stars. Singers and musicians are categorised within genres based on the style of music they produce and each mainstream performer contributes an image – a star persona – that contains a range of associations and connotations which are then used in all facets of marketing and promotion. Star personas and genre conventions create expectations of a particular 'type' of performer and 'type' of music produced. It is essential for the music industry to create and perpetuate these conventions in order to successfully sell their products to the relevant audience. Star personas are often constructed in relation to genre as new artists are categorised to fit in with the audience's familiarity of existing music genres.

Star personas are constructed in relation to identity and music artists assist in perpetuating hegemonic values – conforming to society's 'rules' and presenting lifestyles and identities that are considered to be admirable and desirable. Many music stars act as role models and are constructed to encourage teen listeners to, for example, conform to 'acceptable' traditional values and social identities. The music industry also offers star personas that highlight an alternative identity for listeners – ones that evoke rebellion and anti-social behaviour, offering challenges to hegemonic values in their music and identities. These artists are constructed by their differences to other, more mainstream singers and bands, and these are often artists whose music is categorised within less chart based genres. An alternative identity and ideology are promoted in more alternative music magazines for example. Woodward (2002) notes that all identities are based on their relation to 'the other', that is, those who are constructed as different. She suggests that identities are established through a process of binary oppositions that act as 'classificatory systems'. Identity is therefore 'marked' through *mise-en-scène* (visual style and appearance for example in music performances). It is important to analyse how song lyrics, music style and star persona can perpetuate or challenge traditional values and ideologies, and it is within music's visual images, working with song lyrics and music style, that ideologies are decoded.

The following three case studies offer opportunities to uncover meanings within music texts. **Beyoncé Knowles** is analysed in relation to representations of gender and race, with a consideration of how these meanings are encoded by the music industry in her songs and video performances. Similarly, **Marilyn Manson**'s star persona is investigated in the second case study, with attention to marketing and different responses to his alternative media image. Finally, the resurrection of 60s band **The Beatles** is analysed with reference to their re-released back catalogue CDs and the *Rock Band* interactive game. This section will address industry strategies used to appeal to a more mature fanbase in addition to generating new, younger audience interest.

Independent Women – Beyoncé and Gender debates

Beyoncé encapsulates a representation of the contemporary female who is sexually desirable but, at the same time speaks directly to a female audience. Her songs and music videos draw upon concepts of empowerment for women, often with narratives about walking away from unsatisfactory relationships.

A recurring theme in her work is that of independence for women highlighted by using motifs of strength, power and control. In this respect many of her songs are anthems for female audiences to sing offering an alternative gender ideology to the familiar traditional stereotype of feminine passivity. Her identity is not based on being 'a victim', singing about heartbreak and yearning for a man. When she sings about losing her partner, which is a conventional plot scenario in popular music, her mode of address outlines his loss rather than hers. Therefore she assumes a position of control and dignity in the break-up rather than one of 'pining' and suffering at the man's departure from her life. Beyoncé is no victim.

This is evident in the track 'Survivor', released in 2001 by her band, Destiny's Child. 'Survivor' is written in a first person mode of address with Beyoncé responding to her relationship break-up by speaking directly to the man involved. The lyrics highlight what she has gained from the break-up rather than what she has lost. Her success in her career, attitude to life and inner wisdom are all sources of liberation within the lyrics. The motif of surviving the break-up is transposed literally in the accompanying video illustrating the band 'shipwrecked' on a desert island surviving without a male presence. The video draws upon motifs of the jungle, female-as-hunter, combat clothing and choreography comprising powerful, aggressive stances. The final image of the three bandmates holding hands with their arms in the air triumphantly suggests female solidarity, visually reiterating the narrative of the song.

While Beyoncé's song lyrics advocate female empowerment and liberation, her music videos often position this power and control for women in relation to the female body. Beyoncé's physicality is a key factor in her star persona and her body is frequently on display through figure-hugging or skimpy clothing and is the focus of attention in the dance routines accompanying each song delivery (on video or live). Beyoncé's dance routines convey stances of power and control whilst reminding her ex-lover of what he is missing physically. An anthem of empowerment for women like 'Single Ladies (Put a ring on it)' (2009) outlines her discarding one man for another, suggesting 'now you gonna learn what it really feels like to miss me'. The video combines her piercing gaze at the camera, addressing the male viewer / voyeur, with close-ups of her body dancing suggestively – a reminder of the female body as a sexual spectacle. Beyoncé therefore displays her female physical assets (such as legs and backside) infused with connotations of liberation for women in this visual display. Her sexual movements and traditionally desirable female body become a 'weapon' to use against men, obliterating the feminist notion of the female body as a sexual object to be used by men.

'Single Ladies (Put a ring on it)' video

This is also apparent in her 'Suga Mama' (2007) video. The song offers a role reversal from the traditional stereotype of the female body as a commodity to be bought by a man. Beyoncé openly desires the masculine body and offers to pay for the pleasure of seeing him as a sexual object. However, this role reversal is then undermined in this video as the man is conspicuously absent. It is her body, rather than a male that is viewed writhing around in a sexual manner replicating a pole-dancing event.

Consequently, Beyoncé's star persona can be analysed as challenging hegemonic ideologies of the representation of women in the media but at the same time, it can also be viewed as reinforcing the stereotype of women identified primarily by their desirable, sexualised bodies.

TASKS

- Analyse the gender ideologies evident in the lyrics of 'Independent Woman'. What do you think is the message provided for the female listener?

- Discuss different interpretations of gender representations in the lyrics and accompanying video for 'Crazy in Love'.

- How does Beyoncé's persona differ (or is similar) to another female artist, within the r&b and rap genres? Provide evidence from song lyrics and video images

---

Bootylicous – Beyoncé and race debates

Beyoncé's desirable body is a key component of her star persona and this study can be developed further to consider her body in relation to her African-American identity.

The music industry often positions artists and their music within specific genres and many music genres are racially coded. Genres like rock, pop and country and western music are traditionally characterised as featuring white artists and marketed at primarily Caucasian audiences. Soul, blues, hip-hop, r&b and rap are stereotypically associated with African-American artists. Beyoncé's r&b music style incorporating hip-hop sequences, positions her within an African-American generic style. However, her mainstream popularity measured by worldwide sales, sell-out tours and accolades, suggests that she has transcended a specific racially-orientated genre and identity. She has become an important *crossover* star. Beyoncé's crossover status is empowering because it implies that her racial identity is not considered a barrier to mainstream success and as Cashmore (2002) notes:

> '...she, perhaps more than any other individual, convinced us that racism was outdated.'

This notion is reinforced in the symbolic gesture of her presence and performance at Barack Obama's presidential inauguration ceremony in January 2009.

The crossover appeal concept therefore is a useful motif in suggesting that the music and media industries celebrate all racial and ethnic identities without privileging a traditional hegemonic ideology of white supremacy. Beyoncé's 'otherness' as a black female performer is erased in a celebration of multicultural values where everyone is created equal and can succeed in the glamourous world of global stardom. When Beyoncé encourages women to identify with her through the anthems of female solidarity, she is speaking to all women regardless of ethnic identity. Her role as a woman takes precedence over her identity as a specifically

African-American woman. It would seem therefore that race is simply not an issue.

Nevertheless, it is possible to consider an alternative perspective on Beyoncé's racially-coded body. The erasing of her African-American identity can be viewed as problematic. Far from denying white superiority, Beyoncé can be seen as undergoing a *whitewashing* by the media that has consciously diminished her racial identity and difference to make her 'acceptable' to the white consumer. In order for her to appeal to the widest audience possible, it is suggested that her *difference* be less obvious than perhaps her real life partner, hip-hop musician Jay-Z (whose music articulates issues about racial identity directly).

Beyoncé's mixed-race is often highlighted as a key factor in her mainstream appeal and it is a theme evoked in the film *Dreamgirls* (2006). A study of the 1960s music scene for African-American performers, *Dreamgirls* highlights the need to create crossover appeal in both music genre and performers' appearances. Beyoncé's character Deena is singled-out as the figure who can achieve mainstream sales because her skin, hair and voice are less 'black' than the authentic soul-based performer in the band Effie (played by newcomer Jennifer Hudson). The issue of a thin, desirable female body is also addressed in Effie's replacement by Beyoncé's character. *Dreamgirls* articulates an important debate about ethnicity and 'difference' in the music industry, with specific reference to the industry's prioritising of image and a star's persona at the expense of their musical abilities.

Beltran describes crossover as 'non-white performers who succeed in becoming popular with white audiences'.

Dreamgirls

TASK

With reference to three scenes from *Dreamgirls*, analyse the representation of *either* gender *or* ethnicity.

Diva – Beyoncé as brand

The issue of Beyoncé's racial identity arises in the persona constructed beyond her music. Crossover appeal not only relates to music sales beyond the stereotypical market for a genre-based artist. In a celebrity obsessed culture, it is essential for a music star's image to be circulated far beyond the medium that made them famous and Beyoncé has achieved this by selling products other than music related ones. Her appearances in films like *Dreamgirls* and *Austin Powers: Goldmember* provide a direct link between her music stardom and the film narrative. She performs as a singer in both of these, thereby showcasing her music persona in another medium and attracting audiences to further sales (including the soundtrack of the films). The film also benefits by attracting Beyoncé's existing fanbase. This mutually beneficial arrangement between music and film companies is known as symbiosis.

TASK

Explore Beyoncé's crossover appeal. How has this helped to attract different audiences?

Beyoncé's endorsement of products – advertising Tommy Hilfiger, L'Oreal, Armani and Pepsi brands for example, is successful because of her crossover appeal; her attributes of glamourous stardom and charismatic 'extraordinariness' (Dyer, 1998) are evident in her Armani *Diamonds* perfume advert. Shot in black and white to evoke a bygone Hollywood glamour era, Beyoncé is placed on a platform singing 'Diamonds are a Girl's Best friend' in a sparkling dress. Her racial identity is diminished as she has stepped into the shoes of fifties Hollywood starlet Marilyn Monroe, albeit with slightly less blonde highlights and a stronger attitude! Her lighter toned hair is also certainly very visible in her L'Oreal advert causing controversy as a result of the airbrushing policy that appeared to have considerably 'lightened' Beyoncé's skin.

TASKS

- Outline the different ways Beyoncé's star persona can be interpreted. Use evidence from videos, album covers, star appearances and film roles to illustrate your answer.

- Research Beyoncé's music career development from Destiny's Child to solo performer, outlining strategies used by her record label to create mainstream appeal and global sales. How important are genre and star persona to these strategies?

Marilyn Manson and Ideologies of 'The Other' – The golden age of grotesque

Marilyn Manson is a music star whose persona is associated with a celebration of difference. He deliberately evokes an alternative identity by presenting himself as a binary opposite in his appearance to the conventional stereotypes of star beauty and glamour. Beyond the make-up and long hair that suggest an alternative masculine identity within contemporary popular music, Manson's persona actually defies gender categories. His androgynous appearance is less of a hybrid of masculine and feminine styles and more of a questioning of what constitutes the human form. He experiments with representations of the human body in his music videos and live performances, always evoking an otherness as a contrast to the 'perfect' body sold in advertising, cinema and fashion. It is Manson's appearance that is the vital ingredient in his persona – famous for his experiments in clothing, hair, make-up and his trademark contact lenses.

Manson's alternative identity is at the heart of his music and his songwriting examines themes of difference always positioning himself as an outsider to conventional society. His lyrics celebrate this role and act as social critiques of an American society that privileges physical ideals of beauty and in the process alienates those who cannot or choose not to conform to these hegemonic ideals. Manson's music speaks directly to those stigmatised as outside the rules of acceptability, evident in a song like 'The Beautiful People' (1996) which is an anthem for Manson's ideological stance.

The accompanying video constructs the song's message visually by depicting images of grotesque figures, fragmented body parts and drawing upon horror film iconography within the *mise-en-scène*. Menacing close-ups of Manson's metallic teeth and surreal contact lenses connote an inhuman quality assisted by angular camera work which creates a disorientating nightmarish scenario. These motifs reoccur throughout his videos and live shows perpetuating his persona as macabre, ghoulish and threatening. He revels in the guise of a horror film villain terrorising wholesome American suburban communities. After all, his stage name is a combination of two contrasting American figures – Marilyn Monroe as the epitome of sexual desirability and glamour and Charles Manson, the notorious satanic serial killer.

Whilst drawing on horror iconography to celebrate 'the other', Manson also performs alternative values in his anti-religious stance. Lyrics, videos and interviews frequently condemn and mock Christianity, accusing the faith of being perpetrators of fear and injustice within Western society. This ideology is an essential ingredient

'Poster boy for fear' – quote used by Manson during an interview in the film, *Bowling for Columbine* (2002). Manson is suggesting that he is an easy target to be blamed for the Columbine tragedy 'because I represent what everyone is afraid of'. It is also a comment on his star persona that he has constructed within his music – a musician who confronts and exposes people's anxieties and nightmares.

in the construction of Manson as controversial and shocking – an area that he has knowingly crafted in videos like 'Disposable Teens' (2000) that denounce Christ and parody Christian iconography.

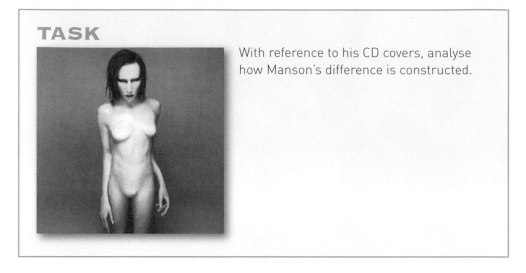

With reference to his CD covers, analyse how Manson's difference is constructed.

Manson as the '*Poster Boy for Fear*' – Responses to difference

The music industry uses star personas in the marketing of its products and in the case of Marilyn Manson it is important to package his alternative identity and ideology to make it desirable for a particular niche audience. Therefore his difference and anti-authoritarian ideology are packaged within a genre specific category that is familiar with these themes and visual styles. The rock / thrash metal genre and Goth visual identity are categories that are familiar within music from previous decades so Manson is able to fit within these familiar categories and be targeted at existing audiences. In doing so, his music speaks directly to those who are already embracing alternative music and identities. His guitar-based music and vocal style suit similar artists who are promoted and publicised within genre specific music magazines like *Kerrang!* and *Metal Hammer* and these often offer interviews with Manson where his ideologies are promoted uncritically – specifically due to an awareness of the target readership who embrace alternative ideologies within this genre themselves. The preferred reading is therefore one of acceptance of Manson's 'difference', he becomes a role-model for alternative identity in music for those who consume his persona in a range of media.

It is not surprising then that the mainstream, non music-based media, particularly in the US, have created a moral panic regarding Manson's persona. His anti-Christianity and anti-traditional values are the source of a potential 'threat' of Manson influencing American teenagers. This was especially evident in the aftermath of the Columbine school shooting in 1999, in which Manson become the scapegoat for the tragedy. As the two boys responsible assumed alternative black-clad gothic appearances, it was suggested by the media that they were fans of Manson who were re-enacting the singer's themes and ideology.

TASK

Using videos posted on *YouTube*, answer the following questions:

- What are the different perspectives presented on Marilyn Manson's influence on teenage audiences?

- What are Manson's responses to these?

The controversy surrounding Manson's alternative identity in the wake of Columbine has assisted in reinforcing his otherness within the media and his ideological stance (as displayed in his lyrics and videos) has surpassed his music-related persona. Mainstream publicity that presented Manson as a corrupting influence on youth culture has enabled his fanbase to thrive on their own anti-establishment identities. A binary opposition of 'them and us' is nurtured prominently during the moral panic when media coverage demonised Manson and those who resemble him. The construction of Manson as a threat to hegemonic values becomes a source of liberation for some teenagers seeking to rebel against society and their parents. In the wake of the Columbine moral panic (that filtered into mainstream condemnation of Manson), he became the figure that parents and teachers for example, did not wish their children and pupils to be listening to. Consequently, any anti-establishment persona becomes attractive to teenagers precisely for this reason.

Manson is a desirable role-model for some, not only because of the moral panic connotations that arose in the aftermath of the Columbine tragedy. His alternative ideology and celebration of difference can be empowering to those who themselves have felt that they do not 'fit in' with their peers. Manson's fanbase offer a space for acceptance in being different to others. Manson himself has spoken about music's ability to articulate these feelings of being different, and he references music stars like David Bowie who encouraged alternative identities when he was growing up. Manson's fanbase use his music and persona as an expression of their own identities, benefiting from a community of like-minded individuals who accept and enjoy their difference.

Manson's 'Fight Song' video

TASKS

- Analyse the *ideologies of difference* in the lyrics and accompanying video for 'The Fight Song' (2000). How does the video make it clear whose 'side' Manson is on during the game?

- What characteristics of Manson's star persona are evident in his official music online site: www.marilynmanson.com?

- Now look at unofficial fansites devoted to Manson. What similarities and differences relating to his representation can you discover?

The Beatles in the Twenty-first Century

The Beatles then...

This case study considers the role that the music industry and audiences play in maintaining the popularity of a band that disbanded over forty years ago. The Beatles, whose fame is synonymous with the 1960s, had their first chart success in 1963 and continued to make music together until 1970 (after which each member pursued solo careers). However, their success during the Sixties did not cease after the band's split and their recordings have continued to generate phenomenal global sales. In the twenty-first century, John, Paul, George and Ringo's recordings are included regularly on radio playlists, performance footage and interviews feature on TV and DVD, and their albums are frequently re-released with mainstream promotional and publicity campaigns.

In 2009, the entire album back catalogue was remastered, with a digital make-over that improved sound quality, and these releases coincided with the arrival of *The Beatles Rock Band* interactive game. This example highlights the strategies employed by the music (and other media) industries to perpetuate the global appeal of a band that no longer produces new music. It is possible therefore to use these products to investigate how the music industry makes artists visible to different target audiences, and also offers opportunities to study how audiences use these products.

TASK

- Using The Beatles official website (www.TheBeatles.com), outline developments within the band's career. What do you consider to be the key areas of their appeal?

Developments within digital technology have revolutionised the ways in which we consume music. It is commonplace to access music online and to carry whole collections on our MP3 players in the twenty-first century. The 'noughties' also witnessed a further development that has benefited the music industry and encouraged a new way of consuming music of the past – one that could not have been anticipated when a band like The Beatles originally performed. Game culture has provided a new platform for artists' music to be showcased, and 2009 saw the release of a game designed specifically to allow The Beatles to return for a virtual gig. Consequently studying games such as *Guitar Hero* and *Rock Band* can offer insights into the music industry's economic strategies, developments within media production and a profile of the active audience.

Along with *Guitar Hero*, *Rock Band* is an interactive game produced to be used with game consoles XBox, Playstation and Wii. *Guitar Hero* was first released in 2005 by Harmonix, who then collaborated with MTV and *Rock Band* was the result, released initially in 2007. The *Guitar Hero* franchise has since developed *DJ Hero* seeking to inspire would-be DJs (see section on Computer Games).

These game franchises all offer a similar concept. Players interact with music on screen by adopting the role of a musician within the band featured, and with the assistance of instruments (designed meticulously to resemble the original

... and The Beatles now (left)

guitars favoured by the stars), the user is encouraged to play along with the track to varying degrees of success. Points are achieved on the effectiveness of the mimicry – how well you are able to recreate the guitar solo, for example by emulating the chords flashing on the screen. *Rock Band* offers opportunities for four players at once who assume the different band members. *The Beatles Rock Band* therefore provides a choice of performing as John, Paul, George or Ringo, along with a choice of songs graded on different levels of musical complexity. Players develop their skills by progressing through different stages, acquiring points based on the accuracy of their performances. Success is rewarded with trivia information and access to rare and unseen photos of the band.

Unsuccessful renditions, however, can result in the rest of the band falling silent or a series of boos from the audience on screen watching you perform badly at, for example, the Cavern Club in Liverpool, Shea Stadium in New York or on the roof of the Apple Studios in London. The game's universe includes vivid recreations of many landmark occasions within the band's career, including surreal sequences to accompany the performances of their later musical output like 'Yellow Submarine' and 'Sgt Pepper' (often the tracks that the band never performed live). Snippets of the band chatting in the studio have also been included to create an authentic atmosphere, including comments on the performances of the three part harmonies that the game encourages from its players. Giles Martin, one of the game's producers, explained the attention to detail claiming:

> **'I wanted to put people in the position of being in the studio with the band.'**
> (Martin, 2009)

The Music Industry and Symbiosis

The rise of digital technologies has had an enormous impact on the music industry which has developed to accommodate the new ways of accessing music. Consumers are downloading singles and entire albums into their MP3 players far more than utilising traditional methods of purchasing CDs (and vinyl recordings) in high street stores. Music is increasingly consumed via game culture in addition to adverts, films and TV soundtracks and these provide substantial profits for the music labels that own the rights to the tracks being previewed in this way. There is a symbiotic relationship therefore between music companies and other entertainment industries – both benefit from this arrangement. The producers of *Guitar Hero* and *Rock Band*, for example, require access to artists' recordings and the use of their image to recreate within the game. The music industry makes money from providing this valuable resource to the game manufacturers, in addition to the game companies reaping profits from the sale of the product. It is estimated that *Guitar Hero* has sold in the region of twenty-five million copies which can result in additional sales to benefit the artists and tracks featured in the game.

The licensing departments of the major record labels have responded to digital technologies by putting the label's catalogues (the music produced by the artists under contract to them) on iTunes and other legal online sites, in addition to providing access for songs to be used on ringtones and games. *Guitar Hero* and *Rock Band* also provide downloadable 'track packs' to add to those featured on the initial game.

Materials such as these are a reminder that whilst music companies generate profits by offering their songs to be used in the game itself, they also benefit by generating interest in the artists featured. Re-releases of back catalogues and greatest hits compilations have been produced as a result of an artist's newly-found popularity via the game phenomenon. It is no surprise therefore that The Beatles entire album catalogue was released in a digitally remastered format to coincide with *The Beatles Rock Band*. The game becomes another 'shop window' to promote the band's musical career and secures new profits for the band and their record company EMI.

TASK

- Research the developments in the ownership of The Beatles' music with specific reference to Northern Songs, the Parlophone label, EMI and their own company Apple Records.

- What have been the advantages and disadvantages of The Beatles' involvement with a major recording label like EMI?

The Beatles for Sale – Marketing strategies

In order for the music companies and game producers to sell their products, whether a Beatles' remastered CD or a computer game, the products need to be promoted and publicised in order to generate interest from audiences. The marketing departments at the record labels are responsible for placing adverts for the products in a range of different media in the hope of appealing to the relevant target audience. They also create publicity within the media by encouraging editorial 'features' on their new products in magazines, radio and television programming. Promotion and publicity strategies tell the desired audience everything they need to know about the products available, generate an interest in buying these and then carefully placed adverts direct the audience to the purchasing of these items.

For example, there were editorial features on the origins and production of *The Beatles Rock Band* and remastered CDs in magazines ranging from *Mojo*, *The Word*, *Q*, *NME*, *The Observer* music monthly and *The Sunday Times* supplements. The *NME* featured articles on each Beatles album and offered different front covers as collector's items to mark the occasion. Most media coverage in editorial features was accompanied by actual adverts to buy the game and CDs, including invitations to buy these at specific locations like HMV and Play.com. BBC television celebrated the renewed interest in the band with a Beatles-themed evening broadcast on BBC2, and similar documentaries aired on BBC Radio 2. Beatles tracks were promoted on many commercial radio stations coinciding with the release of these new products. The HMV store in Cardiff dedicated a section of the shop to promoting the new products along with Beatles merchandise including books, T-shirts and mugs. Naturally, the store played Beatles music throughout this promotion period.

TASK

Compare the music industry's marketing strategies for The Beatles re-releases with the strategies used to sell Beyoncé and Marilyn Manson's music to audiences.

The Interactive Audience

The Beatles Rock Band encourages social interaction by offering group participation suitable for up to four players and this is an increasingly important factor in game culture promotion. Television adverts for consoles and specific games highlight group-based competitions amongst friends and suggest a multi-generational appeal for 'all of the family' playing at home.

In addition to the social factors present in playing a game like this, there are other possible gratifications to participating. The 'rewards' that materialise as the players develop their skills of performing , including the acquiring of trivia information, help to nurture a vital element of fan pleasure – the desire to accumulate knowledge of the band and gain access to previously unknown or unreleased materials. This helps fans become 'experts' in the playing of the game and at the same time learn more about the band's recordings and history. This is also encouraged in the digital remastering of the back catalogue as existing fans discuss and debate additions and changes to the previously released recordings. This was apparent in music magazine features about the new releases, with the journalists writing from their own fan-based perspectives on the materials.

TASK

Find examples of The Beatles on the official websites of two music magazines (e.g. *Mojo*, *NME*, *Q* or *The Word*). Analyse the writing style, mode of address and layout of your chosen examples. How far do the journalists convey their own music tastes in their writing?

In addition to the social interaction present when actually playing *The Beatles Rock Band* with friends and family, there is an additional social community for fans to interact with – online forums and sites that allow like-minded fans to interact and discuss their own opinions and experiences of playing the game and the remastered recordings. Fans regularly exchange information, experiences and knowledge in online forums and new products can rejuvenate interest in a band that split-up nearly half-a-century ago!

Like other versions of *Guitar Hero* and *Rock Band*, *The Beatles Rock Band* can also encourage players to develop their own musical skills by learning the instruments they have been mimicking. Many fans form their own bands from the enjoyment of listening to existing artists. John Lennon and Paul McCartney learnt music and formed The Beatles because of their teenage obsessions with Elvis Presley, Little Richard and Chuck Berry. Having a virtual 'taster' of the experience of performing in a band is another way of developing an interest and aptitude for such projects. Being a fan of a media text can therefore develop creative skills ranging from learning music to film-making. For example, online sites like *YouTube* have served as promotional vehicles for would-be performers who haven't as yet made it on to reality TV competitions, and fans are regularly showcasing their creative endeavours online. There are also many postings of players participating in the *Rockband / Guitar Hero* phenomenon with feedback on these performances. It is possible therefore to play to a much wider audience than immediate friends and family – the global gig is certainly possible online.

EXTENSION TASKS

- Analyse the official *Beatles Rock Band* site online. Start by summarising the content of the site and then outline the possible gratifications for both younger and more mature players.

- Who do you think are the key target audiences for The Beatles in the twenty-first century? Consider both *The Beatles* remastered CDs, and *The Beatles Rock Band* game. (You might like to bear in mind that editorial articles and advertising dominated publications such as *The Word*, *Mojo* and *The Sunday Times*.)

Bibliography

Beltran, M. (2007) 'The Hollywood Latina Body as Site of Social Struggle: Media Constructions of Stardom and Jennifer Lopez's "Cross-over butt"', in Redmond, H. (ed.) (2007) *Stardom and Celebrity: A Reader*, London: Sage.

Cashmore, E. (2006) *Celebrity Culture*, London: Routledge.

Davies, C. (2006) *Approaches to Pop Music*, Leighton Buzzard: Auteur

Dyer, R. (1998) *Stars*, London: BFI Publishing.

Woodward, K. (ed) (2002) *Identity and Difference*, London: Sage.

Male, A. (2009) 'You are the Walrus', *Mojo*, October.

Web

www.TheBeatles.com

www.youtube.com

www.thebeatlesrockband.com

www.marilynmanson.com

Further Reading

Bennett, A. (2001) *Cultures of Popular Music*, Milton Keynes: Open University Press.

Longhurst, B. (2007) *Popular Music and Society*, London: Polity Press.

Wall,T. (2003) *Studying Popular Music Culture*, London: Hodder Arnold.

NEWSPAPERS

Wendy Helsby

Newspapers, our oldest mass media form, began to flourish in the nineteenth century as a result of changing urban demographics, faster train transport, new printing technology and other commercial factors. However, after a long period of relative stability, they are now threatened by a combination of loss of advertising revenue and constantly developing communications technologies. Underpinning the study of newspapers therefore is this important question – will the press survive in today's multi-media world?

In the United Kingdom we pride ourselves that we have a *free press* which acts as a 'fourth estate' (McCauley, 1843) based on the ideology that newspapers give us the unmediated truth, a 'window on the world'. One of the main debates in the study of news is how far this is true and how far newspapers influence the hegemonic balance of power and set the political agenda. In other words how powerful are the press in today's world and are they still relevant to today's audiences?

This section focuses on a close study of three newspaper titles:

- *The Guardian*.
- *The Sun*.
- *The Basingstoke Gazette*.

And will cover the following:

- The power of the press – setting the agenda; representations; textual analysis.
- News gathering processes – producers and audiences.
- Regulation and ownership.
- Technology and the future of newspapers.

The coverage of these titles will be generic, but easily applicable to your own selected editions.

The Fourth Estate – in the nineteenth century there were three groups in government helping to create a balance of power. These were the spiritual Lords such as bishops, the temporal hereditary Lords and the Commoners. What Macaulay was suggesting therefore (in 1843) was that a Fourth Estate had appeared; namely newspapers and journalists, who could both influence, and be a check on, the balance of power.

News agenda
– which news stories are gathered, selected and treated sets the agenda for what is news and how it is received. The news agenda will reflect the decisions made by the professionals and the owners. For tabloids this is often ethno-centric and personalised. For the quality papers there may be a wider perspective and the setting of a different social and political agenda.

Approaches to Study

A **constructionist** approach to studying the newspaper industry was suggested by Noam Chomsky who referred to a process of 'manufacturing consent' in his famous critique of the American media. Chomsky considered that the media were being used to construct attitudes towards issues, such as the Vietnam War, in order to favour the views of the powerful elite. He stated that this was possible because the media were owned by a limited number of powerful groups with vested interests, such as selling arms, or with particular political agendas. The consumers of the news therefore were being led unknowingly by the way the news was constructed into a particular consensual position regarding political policies and actions.

Greg Philo (known for his work with the Glasgow Media Group) stated that news is not just *gathered* as if it occurred naturally, but that it is created by the process of journalism – choosing, selecting, constructing and therefore commodifying news.

This view suggests that newspapers have been fundamental in the construction of consensus (a hegemonic process) and therefore reflects the power of ownership.

A **functionalist** approach to studying the newspaper industry would see that the need to have revenue forces newspapers to be aware of, and reflect the interests of, audiences. A newspaper's main function is to provide topics of interest for a readership so that they will buy. These readers are then 'sold' to advertisers who are fundamental in financing papers.

Without advertising, newspapers would be too expensive to survive. Advertisers therefore can influence both the content and layout of the paper when they buy space; and they will react to public opinion. For example, an article on the death of Boyzone member Stephen Gately in the *Daily Mail* (16 October 2010) led to protests on Twitter and over 1,000 complaints to the Press Complaints Commission. As a result companies like Marks and Spencer removed their adverts away from the article online (Booth, 2009). Both producers and audiences are therefore seen to influence content and this suggests a more diffuse power to setting the news agenda and a more pluralistic or democratic view of the press.

Quality press
– these are the newspapers which cover stories in more depth, with the focus on serious issues. The level of language used assumes readers have a moderatelyhigh level of education.

The Guardian www.guardian.co.uk/

The Guardian, originally *The Manchester Guardian*, is owned by the Scott Trust which also owns *The Observer*, online *Guardian Unlimited*, *The Guardian Weekly* and (until February 2010) *The Manchester Evening News*. The Trust's aim is to be editorially independent and liberal without party affiliation; to display 'honesty, cleanness [integrity], courage, fairness, a sense of duty to the reader and the community' (www.guardian.co.uk/gnm-archive). Although the paper regards itself as editorially independent, because of its ownership structure, traditionally *The Guardian* has been seen as left-of-centre politically. However, in the 2010 General Election the paper surprised some of its long term readers by supporting the Liberal Democrat Party. Clearly, the political affiliations of the paper will influence its news agenda.

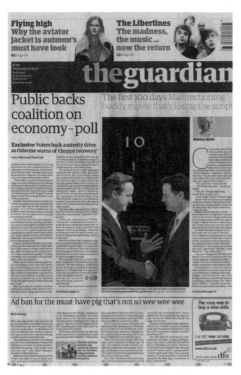

The number of column inches, the content of the news stories and the type of images tell you a lot about the readership of the paper, who tend to be in the A, B, C1 socio-economic groups and 'reformers' in terms of advertising. The weightier linguistic style combined with in depth articles means that newspapers like *The Guardian*, originally referred to as *broadsheets*, are sometimes referred to as the Heavies. The term *broadsheet* originally reflected the size of the *quality* newspapers.

In 2003 *The Independent* was the first UK broadsheet to move to the 'compact edition'. *The Guardian* has moved to the 'Berliner' format which is slightly bigger than the compact or tabloid size. To date the only national daily paper to retain the broadsheet format is *The Daily Telegraph*.

TASK

The Guardian has an interesting history. Look on its website and answer the following questions:

- When, why and where did the predecessor of *The Guardian* first emerge?

- What taxes were imposed upon the newspapers at the time? What effect did this have?

- How has the creation of the Scott Trust influenced *The Guardian* as a newspaper?

Today *The Guardian* appears Monday to Saturday with different specialist inserts, for example the Monday paper has the very influential Media section. Inevitably the style and layout have changed over time. The front page originally carried adverts with news only appearing on it from 1952. The weekend magazine began in 1988 as the Saturday edition followed the trend set by other quality dailies to expand into several pull outs and magazines. Research noted that people were spending more time reading the Saturday paper than the daily, consequently advertising volume increased on this day. But the Saturday boom has been countered by a slow down in sales on Sunday which has hit its sister paper, *The Observer*, bought by *The Guardian* in 1993.

News Production

The Guardian group employs over 600 journalists plus freelancers (stringers) and those who work online, all of whom could act as gatekeepers before a story gets to the editorial team who are the final gatekeepers deciding daily what goes to print. This process is informed by professional judgements, news values (see Television section), and is part of the working practices of journalists under deadline pressure. News production is never neutral; it is the result of news gathering and selection, at each point in this process a gatekeeper may allow the news item through or 'spike it'. As well as this process, the sources of the stories can also influence their content. These sources include:

1. News Agencies such as Reuters are an important source for all newspapers. These agencies provide information and news stories to subscribers of their services. National papers depend upon agency reports for their regional and international reporting as most national journalists are London-based. The agencies use their electronic services to provide financial, banking and business news; as a result this tends to be the priority for the news services and can result in bias in the news agenda.

2. Although *The Guardian* has its own excellent photojournalists, images from photo-agencies such as Magnum are also sourced. The use of photo-agencies often results in the same image, such as a foreign disaster picture, appearing in several papers. The dominance of first world agencies has meant that the selection of stories is often biased against the developing world. Stories from these countries often tend to be based on disasters and tragedies, like the January 2010 coverage of the Haiti Earthquake. This type of coverage has led to the accusation of cultural imperialism. However, today the use of digital photos and the internet means that the reliance on agencies for breaking news and pictures may not be as heavy as it traditionally was, although the question of reliability still remains.

3. Regular domestic sources such as the courts, police, hospitals and government agencies are the 'bread and butter' for a newspaper. These voices are privileged as, being important, they are frequently accessed (Hartley, 1982) regularly by journalists.

4. Regular events such as sporting or political meetings will be put in the news diary. However unexpected news may overcome these, for example a train disaster.

5. Newspapers are also the recipients of hundreds of press releases from commercial companies, trade unions, entertainment industries, charities, all hoping to get some 'free' coverage by a report or a review in the newspaper. Inevitably they will only provide positive views or angles of their organisations, and this will influence the 'spin' they put on the story.

6. Self-employed freelancers, or stringers, also cover particular interests or areas, whilst the paparazzi (freelance photographers) sell celebrity images.

7. Finally the internet and satellite / digital channels are always on in a newsroom to provide instant access to breaking stories.

Journalists do not have time within the pressure of meeting daily deadlines to check all the stories from these various sources so rely heavily on their integrity and accuracy. Although regular sources such as government spokespersons help to set the agenda for the daily news, news values are applied to decide what is newsworthy. In general journalists have a professional understanding of these values. This is combined with a view of their readers' expectations. This means that you may have the same story covered on the front page in national papers even if the treatment is different; or alternatively, completely different stories may appear when the news values suggest different stories, to different newspapers, for different audiences. There are occasions when a paper has a 'scoop' beating others to a story or where they have investigated a particular story, such as *The Daily Telegraph* breaking the news of MPs expenses (May 2009).

By-line – a line giving the name of the writer of the article. It is usually placed between the headline and the body of the text.

TASK

Here is a list of some of the news stories covered on 5 October 2009:

- The Conservative Party conference – national politics.
- The Irish vote on the Lisbon Treaty – international politics.
- Waitrose's reaction to Fox broadcaster racist comments – national news.
- Afghanistan General Election result – international politics.
- Social workers in child abuse cases – national social news.
- Cocaine use in under 25s – national social news.
- Asylum Seekers benefits cut – national social news.

From which source do you think they might have come?

TASK

Look through the stories in a copy of *The Guardian*.

What different news sources can you identify from the content and the by-lines?

Text

As with all newspapers, the front page layout of *The Guardian* includes the masthead with name, price, date, taglines for inside stories; the headlines for the lead story, sub-headings and by-lines and the picture which is usually linked to the lead story, but not always.

The front page below comes from a Berliner edition.

What makes a good news photograph?

Look at the image above; its meaning is immediate, but how is this conveyed? Dynamism is given by the diagonal line of the composition cutting across from bottom right to top left with police on one side and protestors on the other. This and the different dress codes and actions immediately connote confrontation. The white line along the road emphasises this opposition. The building at the back connotes location but also adds to the feeling of the protestors being hemmed in on all sides without escape routes. The attacking action of the policeman in the foreground leaning across the diagonal with arm and stick takes us on another diagonal from top to bottom adding to the trapped nature of the protestors and links with the defensive body language of the young man. A clear narrative is constructed and binary oppositions, (Lévi-Strauss) such as attacker/defender, order/disorder, police/rioter, emerge providing us with an image meaning which is anchored by the text. The 'anchor' of the photograph is seen in the sub-heading, 'Bottles were thrown...we had to move him'. Notice the use of quotation marks to suggest that this is a first person, primary source of evidence of the event and the ellipses which suggest that the comment has been shortened and there is more to say.

TASK

TASK

Using the front cover of your edition of *The Guardian*:

• Analyse the image and the text associated with it.

• What meanings are apparent?

Industry – New technology

Like other traditional media in the late 'noughties', *The Guardian* is struggling financially as advertising revenue declined and the web took more business and content. An advertising slump, combined with a falling readership as people move across to electronic sources, has created a 'double whammy' to which most newspapers, including *The Guardian*, have had to react to by developing online services.

The Guardian online site is now the biggest newspaper site in Britain. In 2006 they started publishing foreign and business news on the web before they appeared in the printed paper. This allowed them to supply a global audience with news in different time zones. *Guardian Unlimited* was the first British site to podcast and it uses the interactivity of the web for blogs and other services. All of these new innovations raise challenges for the printed paper. Will the traditional *Guardian* readers continue to buy the paper or will they move to the online site as it becomes more and more user friendly, interactive and audio-visual? You can now, for example, subscribe to read the paper in digital form.

TASK

Access the online version of *The Guardian* newspaper for the same day as the edition you are studying. What similarities and differences are there?

One response to the development of online news has been to create more interaction in the printed paper. As well as the traditional letters page, readers can now contribute obituaries, they can write reviews on restaurants and the site www.

guardian.co.uk/beenthere gives readers the chance to contribute travel stories. Alan Rusbridger (2009) editor of *The Guardian* said of their 'Comment is Free' (CiF) site launched in March 2006:

> '...there were thousands of people with voices and opinions worth hearing and something powerful, plural and diverse could be forged from combining a newspaper's columnists with those other voices.' (Rusbridger, 2009:9)

His view is that this interactivity moves power away from the press to the people.

This online activity has created the conundrum: how can the newspaper with a twenty-four hour deadline compete with a digital front page that can be altered at a moment's notice? What future is there for the traditional print version of *The Guardian*?

TASK

Using your edition of *The Guardian* newspaper, suggest its target audiences.

How might different audiences respond to the paper?

The Sun

The Sun is the best-selling daily newspaper in the UK so who sets its news agenda is an important question.

The Sun, *The News of the World*, *The Times* and *The Sunday Times* are owned by News International, part of the Rupert Murdoch empire. Rupert Murdoch, an Australian newspaper entrepreneur who took US citizenship, took over *The Sun* and *The News of the World* in 1969 and re-launched them in 1970. *The Sun* (which was originally the *Daily Herald* until 1964) was originally a left-wing trade union paper which Murdoch re-positioned to be a working man's newspaper with entertainment rather than politics at its core.

Murdoch has consolidated his control of other media by buying into telephone companies, television (FoxTV in the States), satellite transmission (Star satellite), electronic networks as well as films (Twentieth Century Fox) and sport (Sky).

Murdoch also owns MySpace. His company owns media companies in the US, Europe, Australia, South America, India and China. It is truly a global conglomerate.

Murdoch's ownership and wide portfolio of papers and other media forms give him unprecedented access to the opinion making mass media. He is one of few owners of the digital highway and in news terms is the ultimate gatekeeper. Today his son James Murdoch is in charge of the UK media business and as a free market supporter made his ideological position clear (August 2009) regarding the control and regulation of the media in a speech to the Royal Television Society in Edinburgh (www.guardian.co.uk/.../james-murdoch-bbc-mactaggart-edinburgh-tv-festival, accessed 21 March 2010).

TASK

- Read the speech given by James Murdoch.

- Summarise his key points.

How far do you agree with him?

Left - and Right-wing – refer to opposing political allegiances and ideologies. The right-wing ranges from conservative, generally middle class, to the extremes of people with views aligned to the British National Party; whereas the left-wing is the one aligned with socialism, the working class and, at the extreme, a Marxist / communist view of the world.

Both *The Sun* and its Sunday sister paper *The News of the World* are tabloids and are bought generally by the middle to working class readers, typically social groups C1, C2, D, E . Tabloids can be subdivided into family / female middle-market papers such as *The Daily Mail* and more working class / male or red-tops such as *The Sun*. A tabloid paper is populist in style with a high ratio of images to words and is sensationalist in tone using puns, alliteration, colloquialisms and neologisms. The syntax is simple with short sentences and paragraphs. Content is weighted towards popular culture and celebrity 'gossip' rather than politics and social issues.

Historical Backgound

Between 1960–4 five newspapers disappeared from the popular press as a result of loss of advertising revenue and those which survived responded by pushing down advertising rates so reducing further their profit margins. This meant they had to increase circulation and they did this through style and content. Murdoch's reaction for *The Sun* was to add sex and sensation to boost sales. His scantily dressed Page 3 Girl was introduced to *The Sun* in November 1970. It led to much criticism from feminists who attacked the images as demeaning, creating women as objects. Clare Short, an MP, was one critic of these images. Her attack on Page 3 type images led to the *News of the World* trawling through her private life to find any salacious gossip to damage her reputation (Short, 1996). The press can be a powerful enemy.

Other papers responded to the changes by adding more features and non-news articles such as fashion and celebrity gossip leading to the accusation of dumbing down news. This trend towards 'infotainment' in newspapers resulted not only from the loss of advertising revenue but also because newspapers like *The Sun* were having to compete for the visual immediacy of news stories with stories which had begun to appear on the internet. This move from political engagement to entertainment is also an effect of celebritisation of the news which is fuelled by paparazzi images.

The actions of owners like Murdoch plus the changes that were taking place in the media over the period from the 60s to the 90s led to market competition. For example, *The Daily Mirror*, under its then owner Robert Maxwell, which historically had been a highly regarded tabloid left-wing newspaper, tried to compete with *The Sun* and began to lose its traditional political edge.

In 1986, Murdoch challenged the traditional methods of producing newspapers by moving his enterprises from the then home of the British press, Fleet Street, to Wapping in East London where *The Sun* led the change from hand set printing to computer technology. This move triggered a union confrontation and weeks of strikes which Murdoch eventually won with the help of the Conservative Government at the time. A more recent move, virtually trouble free, was instigated in 2008 as Wapping in its turn had become out of date and new faster printing techniques have been employed.

As part of the convergent world of the media Murdoch bought into satellite transmission and his Sky services took over BSB to give him a satellite monopoly in the UK. By having such a broad range of media interests and the synergy it produces, Murdoch is able to bid for bigger slices of the media cake. It also means that Murdoch can subsidise the cost of producing his newspapers from other areas of his company and vice versa.

Text

Like other papers *The Sun*'s masthead contains its name in white on a red background (which is why it is also called a red-top), the date, price and issue. The headline is what people will read with a cursory glance at the news-stands and 'flags' or 'puffs' such as 'world exclusive' help to catch the eye. Images sell, which is why there has often been an attractive female figure featured somewhere on *The Sun*'s front page to target their younger male readership. It is a well-known aphorism that a picture can stand for a thousand words and how the image is framed, cropped, flipped or digitally manipulated are all significant contributors to meaning.

All newspapers tell stories and use narrative techniques. These stories belong to genres, such as crime and romance and so follow conventions. They are constructed through technical codes by the combination of images and words. Analysing these stories can help to unpick the discourses, the representations, the beliefs and values being conveyed.

TASK

1. Compare the images of the Conservative and Labour Party leaders at the time of the 2010 General Election on the front page of *The Sun*.

• Cover the words to reveal only the images. What does the image suggest about the leader?

Gordon Brown could be said to be quite powerful looking, with the patriotic flag behind, a low angle and a serious look providing a powerful image. Now look at the full front cover and see how the meaning changes. This is the front cover of *The Sun* when it told its readers that it was no longer supporting the Labour Party and Gordon Brown. On its masthead the language anchors the picture into a negative meaning with the phrase 'hard labour' – a pun on a prison sentence and the name of the political party. The 'flag' is of a poster inside listing a dossier of failures of the Labour government. The headline uses alliteration 'Labour's Lost it' referencing a well-known saying and the word 'lost' is repeated in the copy so emphasising the theme of the page. The image is of a faded Labour party, signified through the faded symbol of the red rose and the Union Jack behind Brown's face, with shadowed, downward eyes. The hand raised in a (perhaps) farewell sign rather than a powerful signal.

2. Now look at the front page on the general Election day 6 May 2010.

This front cover references the iconic 'Hope' poster of Barack Obama when he was running for US president in 2008.

The words 'Our Only Hope' are in white, a clean colour and increase in size so that 'hope' fits the same position as in the original Obama poster. The phrase 'In Cameron We Trust' references the phrase 'In God We Trust' which is the official motto of the United States. The message is pro-Tory and Anti–Labour. As in the original Obama poster, red is juxtaposed against blue and the serious eyes of Cameron are like Obama's looking upwards (or heavenwards).

Both images convey messages and *The Sun*'s front covers reflect the paper's clear ideological stance.

Like any genre we have expectations of the codes and conventions of the paper. Readers tend to be quite loyal and familiar with the layout and style of a particular paper, such as position of the sport, the weather, TV listings and so on, and take the preferred reading established by the editorial policy. However, what is left out because of space constraints or through choices is unknown and readers will be unaware if the selection of news is one that they would have made, or if the treatment is consistent with 'reality'.

TASK

With reference to the edition of *The Sun* you are studying:

- Explore how it uses genre conventions.
- Discuss how two main stories construct narratives.

Representation

Representation is an issue media watchers frequently criticise tabloid newspapers for. We have already touched upon the way *The Sun* has been criticised for its representations of women through Page 3, and it is obvious that the newspapers have a clear representation of its (predominantly male) readers.

TASK

With reference to the edition of *The Sun* you are studying:

- What is the predominant point of view? Male or Female?
- How does it represent women and women's issues?

TASK

With reference to the edition of *The Sun* you are studying, how do the language and images suggest its attitudes to current events and issues?

Industry – Regulation

Like other media, the press have to abide by the laws of the land in terms of libel, pornography, the Official Secrets Act and so on; these are statutory controls. Today newspapers in the UK also sign up to the Code of Practice of the Press Complaints Commission (www.pcc.org.uk). The PCC is self-regulatory, paid for by the press with seven press members and ten lay members. It has the power to fine and ask a paper to publish an apology and a rectification statement if it upholds a complaint such as inaccurate reporting. It tries to do a balancing act reflecting public attitudes without curtailing newspaper freedom.

The PCC can only be re-active not pre-emptive in its action. For the PCC one of the main criteria on which they are often asked to judge a story is 'in the public interest'. This is different from being 'interesting to the public'. In a high profile case the PCC demanded printed apologies to appear on the front pages of the *Daily Express* and the *Daily Star* because of the comments they had made about Kate and Gerry McCann. The stories fuelled suspicion that they were involved in their daughter Madeline's disappearance without any evidential foundation against them (see MediaWise Bulletin, 18 March 2008).

The Sun's often extreme attitude has led to it being criticised for its (mis)representations and it has frequently been reported to the PCC.

TASK

Look on the PCC website at www.ppc.org.uk:

- Can you find any recent complaints made against *The Sun*?
- What were they for?
- Were they upheld?
- How 'serious' do you consider them to be? Why?

There are two overriding principles which control the regulation of the press and which are paradoxically in tension – the right to free speech and the privacy of the individual. A newspaper might claim the right to freedom of speech in revealing the personal details of a celebrity to be in the public interest, whilst that celebrity might claim the right to privacy. Tabloids like *The Sun* often invade what some would regard as the private lives of public individuals. On 26 February 2003 for example *The Sun* 'outed' an MP with the headline 'Gay MP and the rent boy'. Should a celebrity or a politician who has used newspapers to publicise their careers then be able to insist that other parts of their life are not to be intruded into? Is it right that we should be able to gloat voyeuristically over the private lives of people, whether public figures or ordinary members of the public, when it has no relevance to their effectiveness as a member of society? This continues to be a hotly debated area.

Often articles can also be accused of mis-representation particularly of groups such as immigrants, asylum seekers and travellers who are often reported unfairly. For example, *The Sun*'s reporting of an incident in May 2009 was brought before the Press Complaints Commission. Ms Emma Nuttall of the 'Friends, Families and Travellers' Traveller Advice Project complained that an article about an attack on a police helicopter had attributed the blame for the damage to Gypsies, despite the fact that the official police position – quoted later in the coverage – made clear that the identity of those responsible was unknown. The complaint was resolved when the newspaper published a correction and an apology.

TASK

With a partner, select three different stories from the edition of *The Sun* you are studying. Discuss how they have been constructed in order to comply with the PCC code.

Industry – New technology

Like all daily newspapers *The Sun* has an online version of its newspaper which is constantly being up-dated. The website is quite interactive and has been opened up to readers:

'...we want videos as well as your great stories and pics.' (Gibson, *The Guardian*, 6 November 2006)

The Sun launched *MySun* to be part of the social networking explosion and to encourage reader contribution and therefore further develop its brand identity. The assistant editor of *The Sun* online stated that:

'It's not only a great new tool in terms of citizen journalism but also reminds us of why we are here – what *Sun* readers want to know and what they want to talk about.' (ibid.)

TASK

Compare your edition of *The Sun* with the paper's website for the same day (www.thesun.co.uk):

- What differences are there between the main stories?

- What does this tell you about their different news agendas and target audiences?

- What additional features does the website offer audiences?

- How important do you think the website is to the newspaper and to audiences?

The Sun continues to court controversy with its headlines and its use of celebrities to boost circulation. On the front page, reality TV stars, pop singers, politicians and notorious criminals jostle for space with other news. So will *The Sun* ever set? Looking at regional papers may help to begin to answer this.

Local Papers – *The Basingstoke Gazette*

[Note: Whilst the section looks specifically at *The Basingstoke Gazette*, the issues and concepts discussed can be transferred to the study of any local or regional newspaper.]

Although national newspapers are often more widely discussed in relation to the power of the press, it is in fact the local papers which are more avidly read by the majority of the population. It is estimated that three out of four adults read a local paper. However, like the dailies, regional and local papers are under financial threat through the loss of advertising revenue and the competition they face from electronic media sources which people are now increasingly using for accessing information such as house and car sales and local entertainment – traditionally the role of local newspapers.

A local paper has to be relevant to the community it serves but it still applies news values. It is essential that they reflect local concerns whether about rubbish collection or fund-raising for a good cause, because people buy the paper to find out what is going on in their community. People want to see or read about things which are directly connected with their lives reflecting an ethnocentric point of view.

Unlike the national papers, local papers are generally not politically biased. They see their role to support the local communities by mounting campaigns, providing information, covering stories which are linked to the local area. Because of this people pick up a local paper which they feel covers their area not because of its political editorial stance. But, what pleasure does it offer readers?

In my region there are four towns in a roughly twelve mile radius all of which have local papers covering their town and immediate villages. What is available in your local area?

The main local paper in my area is *The Basingstoke Gazette* which currently has three editions a week – on Monday a paid for edition is available, on Wednesday there is the free *Gazette Extra* and then the main paid for edition is published on a Friday.

The Basingstoke Gazette is produced in a dedicated building which houses the journalists, photographers and an advertising department. The material for each edition, once it has been approved by the editorial team, is sent via electronic form to a printing press thirty miles away. It is then distributed to local newsagents, shops and supermarkets. There is a website, www.basingstokegazette.co.uk/, should you want further information on this paper.

Ethnocentricity
– one of the news values identified by Galtung and Ruge. It means that we are more interested in stories which are closer (more central) to our culture and way of life (ethnicity), so these get priority in the news agenda.

How does the front page differ from that of The Sun and The Guardian?

TASK

Research your local newspaper to find out some factual information – for example:

- When was it founded?

- Who owns it today?

- How many editions are there per week?

- What are its circulation size and its distribution area?

- Where is it printed?

Analyse the front page of a recent edition:

- How has it been constructed?

- How typical is it of its genre?

- What does it offer for readers?

Access its website:

- Compare this with the printed version.

- Does it address or target the same audience?

News Sources

Local papers cover local news and where it has a local angle, national news. Like the nationals they rely upon news agencies and feeds from their group owners. Generally, local newspapers contain articles relating to:

- Campaigns about issues such as health and education linked to local schools and hospitals.

- Sport covering the amateur as well as professional games sometimes covered by a specialist journalist, whilst local minority sports will also send in reports.

- Business news linked to local commercial organisations.

- Entertainment, what's on and lifestyle articles are often sourced from a central 'library' of articles or press releases from the parent company.

- Charity events – using press releases from national as well as local organisations.

- Local schools, colleges and churches will also supply stories and pictures about their institutions.

- News will also be collected from regular or 'accessed' sources, like the magistrates' courts, council meetings, hospitals and police.

The bulk of the paper is taken up with advertising from small ads – offering services, items for sale, jobs; to display adverts – for promotions for, for example supermarkets and film releases.

Local papers cover little 'hard' news but tend to focus on 'soft' news subjects. Soft news, for example pictures of children on their first day at school, also often appear in the Monday edition. This creates a local targeted market.

Although local papers usually focus on parochial matters not of interest to people outside of their immediate location, occasionally an event will happen locally which is so newsworthy it becomes a national news item.

TASK

Select three stories from your local newspaper:

- How do they construct narrative?
- How do they represent the issues they are covering?

Soft news

– news generally about events which re-occur or are of minor importance, for example in the autumn pictures of children in their first year of school entry are often in local newspapers; whilst hard news would be a major accident or political row.

Industry – Ownership

Like many other local papers *The Basingstoke Gazette* is owned by a huge organisation. Newsquest is a regional paper group which is owned by Gannett, a US company. Gannett publishes papers read by over thirteen million people in the UK. It is the second largest regional media group in the UK publishing over 300 newspaper titles (see wwwmediauk.com/owners) as well as magazines and websites. There will be a Newsquest title near you (www.Newsquestmediapack.co.uk).

In 2006/7 advertising revenue fell 6.5% year on year at Newsquest. The continuing slide in advertising revenue, exacerbated by falling circulation income, is significant because it could lead to Newsquest pulling out of Britain altogether. Who could afford to take over these titles? Who would want to?

One issue for local papers is the steady drift of readers to the internet, particularly younger ones. Young people rarely pick up the local paper and *The Basingstoke Gazette* tries to attract the web generation and combat the same problems facing the national papers with various campaigns.

The Future of the Regional and Local Paper

In the past newspapers were delivered to most houses or picked up going to and from work. Today people may pick up a paper as they travel but are more likely to log in or dial up for their (free) local news putting the local (paid for) paper under threat. Greenslade quoted the Newspaper Society (the regional publishers trade body) as listing:

> '1,300 core regional and local newspaper titles plus 450 niche publications or magazines, and 250 ultra-local titles. Added to that are 1,200 websites and nearly 50 broadcast channels.' (2009)

In February 2009 Roy Greenslade conducted a survey of Britain's vanishing newspapers from January 2008. In thirteen months there was a net loss of forty-two titles.

TASK

Obviously, the primary target audience for a local paper is people living within a certain geographical area – but can you be more specific about some of the sections, articles, features within your own local newspaper?

Conclusion

In response to declining markets, the tabloids have re-vamped themselves to cover more gossip and the quality newspapers to include lifestyle sections. It could be argued that both have become less like newspapers and more like magazines. Other techniques to increase sales have been to have offers such as free DVDs; even so overall national readership has dropped by a fifth since 1990 and more worryingly young people, the readers of tomorrow, are not buying or reading papers. A number of newspapers have tried to launch editions targeting a younger readership but the number of readers under twenty-four has shrunk considerably since 1990. For example nearly a third of those buying the *Daily Telegraph* are the 'greying generation' of over sixty-five. It seems the younger generations are getting their news by 'news-grazing' electronic media, partly a result of convergence.

In the last decade newspapers have been competing with global companies like Google, Yahoo and BBConline to publish the news. The internet has also had another unforeseen consequence and that is the democratisation of access. Whereas celebrities have always featured in the papers, access to a national newspaper has not been easy for ordinary members of the public. But today blogging and tweeting allow people to participate in the construction of news, to become the news and to comment upon the news.

Another change is increased reader interactivity. The letters page of *The Guardian* has around half-dozen contributions because of space constraints, but numbers on the web can be almost unlimited – thus creating 'citizen journalists'. The flow of news is no longer one way and in the hands of the few. *Guardian Unlimited* users 'are now listening, watching, critiquing and participating' (2006: 6). Additionally the online audience can become their own online editors by picking out content in which they are interested or agree with. Are there dangers in this type of selection process? Are journalists under threat?

> **'Paid for national dailies were down another 1.6 per cent in sales in February and some nationals are reaching journey's end....The regional press ... is shrinking...evening papers produce only a single edition.'** (Preston, *The Observer*, 9 March 2008)

This trend, however, may be reversed in light of News International's decision to start charging for news access on the internet as of mid-2010. The rest of the newspaper industry looks on with interest.

Periodicals, magazines and newspapers have been circulated since it was possible to mass produce copies. Some have had serious political purpose, others have been mere 'rags' ready to sell the most salacious stories they could find like the 'Penny Dreadfuls' of the nineteenth century. Lord Macaulay's comment on the Fourth Estate gave the press status and showed their power. Napoleon was said to have stated that three hostile newspapers were more to be feared than a thousand bayonets. Is this still true today? Have the technical and economic pressures on newspapers undermined their position, power and purpose? Will newspapers and a 'free press' survive into the next century?

Resources

There are several films based on newspapers and journalism such as:

Citizen Kane (1941, Orson Welles)

The Paper (1994, Ron Howard)

The Front Page (1974, Billy Wilder)

All The President's Men (1976, Alan J. Pakula)

The Sweet Smell of Success (1957, Alexander Mackendrick)

Defence of the Realm (1985, David Drury)

Zodiac, (2007, David Fincher)

Websites:

www.indymedia.com

www.opendemocracy.net

www.holdthefronpage.co.uk

www.guardianunlimited.co.uk

www.thisislondon.co.uk – *The London Evening Standard* site

www.cultsock.ndirect.co.uk

www.bbc.co.uk

www.mediamagazine.org.uk (Issue 23 is on print, plus other archive articles)

www.cpbf.org.uk – The Campaign for Press and Broadcasting Freedom: an organisation which monitors the media, relying on subscriptions and donations.

www.mediawise.org.uk – MediaWise (formerly PressWise): an independent charity, set up in 1993 by 'victims of media abuse', supported by concerned journalists, media lawyers and politicians in the UK...on the principle that press freedom is a responsibility exercised by journalists on behalf of the public, and that the public have a right to know when the media publish inaccurate information.

www.bl.uk/collections/newspapers – British Library: history of the British newspaper.

www.reuteurs.com – Reuters news agency.

www.nrs.co.uk – National Readership Survey.

www.guardian.co.uk/commentisfree/ – *The Guardian* website for comments from readers.

References

Booth, R. 'Tabloid Columnist's Take on Death of Gay Icon Provokes Record Level of Complaints', *The Guardian*, 17 October 2009.

Boyce, G. and Wingate, P. (eds) (1978) *Newspaper History from C17 to the Present Day*, London: Constable.

Branston G. and Stafford, R. (2007) *The Media Student's Book*, London: Routledge, pp. 194–226.

Brownlee, T. (2005) 'Case Studies in Front Page News. Reactionary Royals and Fiddling Foreigners', *Media Magazine*, April.

Chomsky. N. and Herman, E. (1988) *The Political Economy of Mass Communication: Manufacturing Consent*, London: Pantheon.

Cohen, S. (1972) *Folk Devils and Moral Panics: The Creation of the Mods and Rockers*, London: Routledge.

Cohen, S. and Young, J. (eds) (1981) *The Manufacture of News: Deviance, Social Problems and The Mass Media*, London: Constable

Curran, J and Seaton, J. (1986) *Power without Responsibility*, London: Routledge.

Fiske, J. and Hartley, J. (1978) *Reading Television*, London: Methuen.

Galtung, J. and Ruge, M. (1981) in Cohen and Young (eds), *The Manufacture of News*, London: Constable.

Gibson, O. *The Guardian*, 6 November 2006.

Greenslade, R. (2009) www.guardian.co.uk/media/greenslade/2009/feb/19/local-newspapers-newspapers accessed 01/04.09).

Hall *et al.* (1978) *Policing the Crisis: Mugging, the State and Law and Order*, London: Macmillan.

Hall, S. (ed.) (1997) *Cultural Representations and Signifying Practices*, Milton Keynes: The Open University.

Hartley, J. (1982) *Understanding News*, London: Methuen.

Hollingsworth, A. (1986) *The Press and Political Dissent: A Question of Censorship*, London: Pluto Press.

Jempson, M. 'Behind Flat Earth News', reported in *Campaign for Press and Broadcasting Freedom*, May 2002, www.cpbf.org.uk.

Macaulay, T. (September 1828). "Hallam's constitutional history". The Edinburgh Review (London: Longmans) 48: 165.

Peters, C. 'Gag on UK's *Guardian* newspaper lifted'. International Press Institute, 13 October 2009, www.freemedia.at:gag.

Philo, G. (ed.) (1995) *Glasgow Media Group Reader; Vol. 2: Industry, Economy, War and Politics*, Lpondon: Routledge.

Richmond, S. www.blogs.telegraph.co.uk/technology/shanerichmond/9859537/ Interview_professor, accessed 12/10/2009).

Rusbridger, A. 'Power to the People', in *The Guardian Weekend*, 17 October 2009.

Short, C. (1996) 'Page Three, Indecent Display and the Roots of Concern,' in Collins, R. and Purnell, J. (eds) *Reservoir of Dogma*, London: London Institute for Public Policy Research, pp.33–41.

Wilcock, J. (2009) *The Popular Press: A Teacher's Guide*, Leighton Buzzard: Auteur Publishing.

Magazines

Naomi Hodkinson

This section explores three magazine titles which together investigate the areas of genre, narrative and representation. It will look at the relationships between them, and builds on those links in a text led way. The titles to be explored are *Total Film*, *Top of the Pops* magazine and *2000 AD*. However, before we focus on particular texts, you will need to be familiar with the media terminology associated with magazines, to investigate briefly the state of the magazine industry and each title's position within it, to understand the ways in which magazines target and appeal to their audiences and the ways in which different audiences respond to different magazines.

Magazines come in a wide range of sub-genres which include lifestyle magazines, comics and online editions. To highlight their conventions and appeal, consider how they differ from newspapers. Magazine coverage is often more detailed but with less timely information. You are more likely to find features than hard news. Whilst a newspaper covers the day to day story, a magazine will explore and profile the issues and people involved. Magazines are weekly, fortnightly or monthly while newspapers are daily and cover topics of general interest for a specific geographical area. Newspapers are ephemeral, but magazines are more permanent: we keep them for longer, re-read them and hand them on. Most importantly, magazines' content and audience are more specialised and focused. It's a bit like the difference between terrestrial and cable or satellite TV: mainstream channels have a broad audience but the cable channels are often more specialised or niche. Magazine consumers appreciate information which is specifically aimed at their needs and interests.

You will need to familiarise yourself with the conventions of the magazine genre and to use appropriate media terms. On the cover may appear: the title, the tagline, price, date of publication, main image with anchorage, possible straplines, sidebars or 'puff', trailing features or cover lines. Most magazines will have a contents page and editor's section, and most carry advertising. Magazines can also be divided into a number of different sub-genres.

'Magazines are printed and bound publications offering in-depth coverage of stories, often of a timeless nature. Their content may provide opinion and interpretation as well as advocacy. They are geared to a well-defined, specialised audience, and they are published regularly, with a consistent format.' (Johnson and Prijatel, 1999: 13)

Sub-genres
– smaller classes of a larger genre. For instance, hospital dramas and soaps are both sub-genres of TV drama.

TASK

In pairs, write down as many sub-genres of magazines as you can think of – for example, 'real life'. Find out how supermarkets or newsagents like WH Smiths break them down into categories.

Tagline
– a statement or catchy motto which captures the essence of a brand's identity. Magazines use taglines to offer clues about what they stand for, for example, 'for fun, fearless females!'.

Strapline
– a secondary sentence attached to the magazine's name which says something about its brand image.

House style
– relates to ideas about brand identity and mode of address. It provides continuity in language and is a term which describes a magazine's individual style and voice.

'Pap shots'
– photographs which have been opportunistically snatched by paparazzi.

Analysing a Magazine – The Cover

A magazine's cover is its 'face'. While books are sold with only the spine showing, the magazine's cover is on display. As with film posters or DVD covers, you can generally tell at a glance whether a magazine is for you. To understand how you make those judgements, consider a range of elements:

- The magazine's title. What connotations does it carry? *Nuts*, for instance, connotes craziness, but also crude masculinity. *Cosmopolitan* connotes someone who is at ease anywhere in the world, a city dweller.

- The strapline or tagline. These can be linked to brand identity / house style and to the title's values; and so to ideas about target audience. Is this magazine for 'men who should know better' or for 'women who juggle their lives'?

- The fonts and colours used. What do they suggest about the title's brand identity and target audience? Men's magazines like *Zoo*, for instance, frequently use a red, capitalised font, perhaps edged with black or gold to make it appear solid and bold; while teen girls' magazines like *Mizz* are more likely to employ pastel colours and round, 'friendly' fonts.

- The main image. Often a woman gazing into camera. How femininity is represented, however, varies widely between sub-genres. On some covers, she may be sultry and alluring, showing lots of skin for the male gaze, while on others, she will be friendly, unintimidating and fully clothed. Masculinity, similarly, is represented in a range of ways, from Hollywood stars in sharp suits on *Esquire*, to the black and white image of an idealised unknown on the cover of *Men's Health*. Some titles favour 'pap shots' over airbrushed, studio-shot perfection, which tells you something about their genre, content and audience.

- The anchorage and cover lines. These will reveal a great deal about the title's ideologies and target audience: what kinds of story does this magazine cover? How do the mode of address and the assumptions made position the audience? Are they boy-mad, insecure schoolgirls, fit and financially solvent gay men or politically aware ethical consumers of a certain age?

- Other tactics may range from the use of stars and celebrities, to sensationalism (count the exclamation marks!) and cover mounted 'freebies'. How else does this magazine cover seek to persuade the consumer to buy?

TASK

Identify the house style of *Total Film*, *Top of the Pops* magazine and *2000 AD*:

- How are their covers different in terms of design style and mode of address?
- In what ways are the covers similar?
- How are they different?
- What are the different discourses of each title?

Analysing a Magazine – Between the covers

Look at the following:

Note: See Rayner *et al.*, 2004: 27–39 for a useful chapter on image analysis.

- The contents pages – these offer not only an overview of the features but a sense of the title's brand identity through mode of address and design style. Are they formal and traditionally laid out or chatty, image-led and colourful?

- The editor's letter – this is part of the magazine's brand identity and connection with its audience; a personal touch. What assumptions does it make about the audience?

- Two-page spreads – these are still the primary unit of design, but how are they laid out? Traditional grids work in a two or three column format and are formal looking and book-like, but a more edgy or modern title might use horizontal, modular lines as well as the traditional, vertical grid, sidebars, text wrapped around photos and images which bleed across the grid lines. Compare the design styles of your chosen texts.

- The advertisements – given magazines' highly specialised audiences, the advertising they carry is also precisely targeted. Look at the proportion of advertisements to content and the kinds of brand which appear. What do they suggest about the target audience of the magazine you are analysing?

The magazine industry is generally dominated by major publishers, with a few notable exceptions like *The Big Issue* and *Private Eye*. Major magazine publishers include the following:

- IPC – IPC is American owned and part of the biggest media conglomerate in the world, AOL Time Warner. Titles in its stable include *Now*, *Nuts*, *Sugar*, *Marie Claire*, *Loaded*, *NME*, *TV Times*, *Woman's Weekly*, *Pick Me Up* and *InStyle*.

- EMAP – Emap was a major player in the industry but sold its magazine business to Bauer in December 2007.

- Bauer – Bauer is a German company and some of its titles are *FHM*, *New Woman*, *Empire*, *Closer*, *Heat*, *More*, *Bella*, *Real*, *Spirit and Destiny*, *In the Know*, *Take a Break*, *That's Life* and *Grazia*.

- Condé Nast – in the UK, Condé Nast's titles include *Vogue*, *Easy Living*, *Glamour*, *Tatler*, *GQ* and *House and Garden*.

- The National Magazine Company (NatMags) – owned by Hearst, some of their titles are *Good Housekeeping*, *Cosmopolitan*, *She*, *Prima*, *Zest*, *Country Living*, *Esquire*, *Best*, *Reveal* and *Men's Health*.

- BBC magazines – a good example of commercial intertextuality or synergy, many BBC magazine titles are spin-offs from successful shows, so they already have an established audience. They include the *Radio Times*, *Teletubbies* magazine, *Dr Who Adventures*, *Gardener's World*, *Top of the Pops* and *Top Gear*.

Many popular commercial magazine titles are global and are published in different countries. *FHM*, for instance, publishes twenty-eight international editions and *Cosmopolitan* has fifty-nine editions worldwide (hearst.com). This globalisation of the magazine industry suggests that magazine producers make stereotypical assumptions about their audiences. Mainstream, global titles like *Cosmopolitan* appear to target a homogenised audience and appear to assume that those audiences all think the same way and want the same things. However, most titles thrive by offering specialist subject matter to niche audiences.

The magazine audience is an increasingly fractionalised one, with niche titles as obscure as *Trout and Salmon* or *Your Caravan and You*. Even within sub-genres the audiences are divided, for instance, *Kerrang!* targets a very different music fan than *Mixmag*. However, magazine titles have a clearly defined and focused target audience. They target these audiences with a mode of address which 'speaks their language' and they generally contain preferred readings which their target audience is likely to agree with. This precisely defined readership enables publishers to 'sell' their audiences to advertisers, and this is how they make most of their money.

Until recently the magazine industry was generally characterised by increasing growth. In recent years, however, the industry appears to be doing less well and circulation figures for many titles, especially monthlies and teen girls' magazines, tell a more worrying story for the industry. Felix Dennis, the previous publisher of *Maxim*, is quoted in the *Economist* magazine as saying that 'it's a long, slow sunset for ink-on-paper magazines' (29 September 2007).

Nonetheless, competition remains fierce among the main publishers. New titles keep launching and most of the growth is in the newer titles (with notable exceptions like *Cosmopolitan*). Magazines need to keep up to date with new technologies: most have websites and at least some of their content is available on mobile phone downloads.

Magazines are associated with 'me-time' and have a tactile quality and a portability which TV and computers struggle to match: they can be enjoyed in bed, in the bathroom or on the bus.

Total Film, Future Publishing, £3.99 monthly, ABCs: 81,029

The issue referred to is March 2010.

Future Publishing was started on a kitchen table in Bath in 1985 and now publishes over 150 magazines worldwide. Their biggest are *XBox 360*, *Total Film*, *T3*, *Official Playstation2*, *Digital Camera*, *Classic Rock*, *Total Guitar* and *Fast Car* (*The Guardian*, 30 November 2007). Future also holds the official licence for magazines from Microsoft, Sony, Disney and Nintendo to publish titles like *Official Nintendo Magazine*. These associations with new technology companies can be linked to ideas about target audience and synergy. Over one hundred international editions of Future's magazines are published in thirty other countries around the world and they have offices in the US and Australia.

Future have extended the *Total Film* brand. In 2009 they launched The Total Film Red Carpet Preview event across eleven cinemas in the UK:

> 'It was the first event of its kind, allowing film fans to get early and exclusive insight into films in production and meet some of their on screen heroes. Total Film has gone on to launch the Total Film Red Carpet Screening Club, which enables thousands of readers to preview films exclusively before their release date.' (http://www.futureus.com/)

The Totalfilm.com website was redesigned in 2009 and has seen an uplift in traffic to 450,000 unique visitors a month globally.

Total Film features reviews of new films but also celebrates old ones and countdowns, for instance, of 'the top one hundred Hollywood players' or 'cinema's saints and sinners'. The magazine has an extremely consistent format and narrative structure:

- Buzz – film news and gossip, for instance an Oscars preview in this edition.

- Screen – reviews and ratings for new releases.

- Features and interviews of mainstream heavyweight film stars and directors, for instance in this edition Robert Duvall, Mel Gibson and Daniel Day-Lewis.

- Lounge – home entertainment news and features.

- Every edition starts with a contents, the editor-in-chief's letter, readers' mail, and rounds off with quizzes and a film-related competition.

Readers' Mail is all from men and the advertisements *Total Film* carries appear to support the idea that the magazine is targeting a predominantly young, educated, male audience. Most advertisements support the film industry. DVD retailers HMV and Play feature frequently, along with adverts for computer games, gadgets, technology, occasional cars and beer, and pornographic phone lines at the back.

The mode of address in *Total Film* is humourous, masculine and youthful. The March 2010 edition includes a feature called *Buzz Baldie Bingo* which tries to work out which films are likely to win which upcoming Oscars by highlighting what they have to offer which might impress the Academy, for instance 'triumph over adversity' or 'will make you cry'. However, the magazine manages to avoid being either too specialised or too laddish in its mode of address by using a knowing yet informal tone. For example, the anchorage on film stills is frequently irreverent, funny and occasionally rude. In March 2010, caption anchorage on an *Invictus*

ABCs – the Audit Bureau of Circulations audit the average circulation figures per issue of each magazine title over a six month period. They also track whether sales are up or down, and so offer useful information to the industry about trends. This figure means that *Total Film* has sold, on average, 81,029 copies per issue over the last six months.

Demographics
– this approach
to understanding
the character
of an audience
makes
generalisations
about social
groups.
Demographic
characteristics
can be easily
inferred, such
as age, gender,
ethnicity and
educational level.

**Psychometric
profile** – these
profiles 'measure
thought'
and classify
audiences by
their values,
attitudes and
beliefs. This can
also be linked
to audience
classification
systems like
Young and
Rubicam's
'4C's', originally
from the field of
advertising, which
characterises
consumers by
their needs and
values.

Stars
– are culturally
significant
because they
represent shared
cultural values
and attitudes.

(2009) film still of Matt Damon surrounded by black South African children reads: *No, I said 'who likes the Springboks?' Not 'Who wants an XBox?'* and the review's sub-title is *Freeman finds inspiration in funny shaped balls.* A still of Jeff Bridges and Maggie Gyllenhaal's *Crazy Heart* (2009) characters gazing soulfully into one another's eyes is anchored *Him: 'Any requests?' Her: 'Have a shave'*, in reference to his impressive facial hair. *Total Film* clearly positions its audience as young, predominantly male, knowledgeable film lovers with a sense of humour.

The stereotypical representations of gender in *Total Film* reflect the gender bias in the mainstream Hollywood film industry. The magazine favours male actors and directors with talent and gravitas but does also feature occasional interviews with particularly attractive and sexy actresses. For example, March 2010 features an interview with Mila Kunis from *The Book of Eli* (2009) accompanied by an image of her in underwear and a skimpy leather jacket – as well as stills from the film. However, audience profiles for the magazine suggest that these stereotypical representations don't completely alienate female readers (it claims that 25 per cent of its readers are women) perhaps because the magazine is about films rather than being a celebration of laddishness like a more traditional men's magazine like *Zoo*.

Future Publishing sells this audience to advertisers in a range of ways. They claim that the average demographic is 75% male and is twenty-six years of age. The psychometric profile describes the *Total Film* readers as 'dedicated film-goers' who are 'first in the queue on the opening night' and 'love showing off their film knowledge to their mates' (http://www.future-advertising.co.uk/ads/portfolio/print.jsp?brand=18&print=30).

In your analysis of *Total Film*, you could also consider their use of stars and celebrities. Stars are manufactured by the industry: they are commodities. You might explore how and why stars and celebrities are used and this could be linked to ideas about star image. In his book *Heavenly Bodies* (1986) Richard Dyer suggests that star images are constructed and mediated identities, defined by their historical context and their culture. His approach considers how star images are formed by, and reflect, the ideology and belief systems of the society in which they are created. They are not only attractive and talented; they have to be culturally significant in some way.

TASK

What does *Total Film*'s use of stars suggest about the symbiotic relationship between the magazine, the film industry, the stars themselves, and the audience?

Top of the Pops Magazine, BBC Worldwide, £2.30 monthly, ABCs: 107,576

The issue referred to is 10 January 2010.

Top of the Pops magazine was first published in 1995. Originally a music magazine for young pop fans, its early popularity contributed to the demise of *Smash Hits*. Teen music magazines suffered from the increasing availability of the internet and the fact that young people could find their favourite music videos, pop celebrity gossip and song lyrics online without parting with their pocket money. Originally a spin-off of the BBC1 television show which it has outlasted, it is now classified as a teen girls' magazine.

On the cover, the title's name is at the top of the page in a large, consistent retro font. Along with the use of vibrant pink and yellow, this creates a familiar visual identity for the magazine so that it will be easily recognised at the point of sale.

This use of colour may indicate *Top of the Pops* magazine's status as a possible precursor to titles like *Closer* or *Pick Me Up*, which also frequently use magenta and yellow and belong to the same sub-genre of gossip style magazines, although they target older audiences. The main image is usually either of a teen heart throb like Robert Pattinson from *Twilight* or boy band JLS or it may be of an aspirational female role model like Cheryl Cole. This edition is graced by Joe McElderry, who had just won *X-Factor*. Previously, the cast of *High School Musical* have featured prominently.

Its design style is bright and colourful, almost scrap book-like in its informality, and image led. It is constructed more like a website than a book, perhaps reflecting the way its readers read it, not from front to back like a book, but with a 'pick and mix' approach, dipping in to find the bits they want. *Top of the Pops* magazine doesn't have a contents page. It just offers page numbers on the cover for each feature. It does follow a repeated formula, however; each edition includes characteristic features like:

- Gossip.

- Your oops! (cringes).

- Shameful celeb slip ups – like *Heat*'s 'circle of shame', this feature comprises un-Photoshopped images of celebrities looking tired or scruffy, with spots or eating junk food, anchored with 'witty' captions.

- Interviews with celebrities.

- Pin-ups of boy bands or up and coming film actors.

- Beauty 'news'.

Symbiotic relationship – synergy in industry is a symbiotic relationship, different arms of the industry engender, rely on, support and benefit one another.

- High street fashion.

- 'The surgery' problem pages.

- True life stories, for instance, 'Frazzled by a sunbed!'

- Horoscopes, puzzles and letters.

- Quizzes with titles like 'Will your summer love survive?', 'Could you handle life in the limelight?' and 'What's your shopping style?'

The magazine's tagline is 'More gossip! More scandal! More you!' The discourse offered by Top of the Pops magazine makes topics like celebrity gossip, fashion and boys appear normal, and it makes assumptions about the target readers' lifestyles and interests. It constructs and positions its audience as young heterosexual girls.

Mode of Address

Linked to the idea of audience positioning is the concept of mode of address. This is defined as 'the way a text "speaks" to its audience' (Branston and Stafford, 2006: 543). By addressing its audience in a certain way, media producers make assumptions about them, for instance, as Branston and Stafford explain, you might position a teacher, friend or bank manager by the way you address them in different ways. The mode of address of a magazine can be identified by looking at its design style, its images and the language it uses. For instance if the subject is looking directly into camera, this is an example of a direct mode of address which assumes a relationship with the reader, as does the use of the personal pronoun, 'you'. Mode of address also refers to a text's overall house style.

On the cover, Joe, winner of the 2009 X-Factor smiles into camera. This direct mode of address suggests a personal relationship with the audience. Some of the anchorage of cover images is written in a handwriting-style font, adding another personal touch. The cover lines address the reader directly as 'you' – 'Joe needs you! But are you his perfect match?' The language is appropriately informal for the target audience, for example, 'wanna be famous?' and 'we're lustin' for Justin' (Bieber, a sixteen-year-old 'hot new Canadian cutie'). Celebrities are referred to as 'celebs', boyfriends are 'boyfs' and best friends are 'bezzies' or 'bffs'.

> ## TASK
>
> Look at a recent edition of *Top of the Pops* magazine. How does the front cover position its readers?

Representations of Gender

The representations of young men and women in the magazine are encoded with assumptions about how males and females 'should' look and behave. The aspirational cover images and female celebrities featured are often older than the target audience because, stereotypically, young girls aspire to look and to be a little older than they are. Girls in *Top of the Pops* magazine are represented as being interested in appearance, fashion, celebrity gossip and the opposite sex. This is a stereotypical, conformist and simplified representation of girls – it assumes that the reader is attractive, chatty and frivolous. The 'cringes' featured also represent young girls as being self- or image-conscious.

These representations position the reader and invite her to judge, admire or condemn the young women depicted. It is assumed that she will relate to them and aspire to be like them and she is invited to see them as role models with features like 'Get Cheryl's Life!' These representations appear to reinforce traditional patriarchal notions about women's role in society. However, it could be argued that the audience of media literate readers are well aware of the assumptions being made about their age and gender and may reject the magazine's preferred reading.

Angela McRobbie describes how post-feminism is an:

> '...active process by which feminist gains of the 1970s and 80s come to be undermined.' (McRobbie, 2004: 225)

Post-feminism, she suggests, asserts that feminism's work is done, that it is 'no longer needed'. She explores how:

> '...elements of contemporary popular culture are perniciously effective in regard to this undoing of feminism, while simultaneously appearing to be engaging in a well-informed and even well-intended response to feminism.' (ibid.)

So the representations offered by *Top of the Pops* magazine and the ideologies behind them encourage a mainstream, hegemonic view of young women and may undermine feminist values of female achievement in, for example, the fields of education or work. These ideologies about issues like gender, sexuality and friendships can perhaps be linked to the magazine's mainstream producer, the BBC.

Males in the magazine are represented as heart throbs, pin-ups, 'hotties' and 'crushes'. The 'stars' featured tend to be safe, 'boy next door' types. The mothers of the target readers (who probably pay for the magazine) will not feel threatened by Joe from *X-Factor* or Aston from JLS. Boys are represented as enigmas, but also as something to be desired. Boyfriends and 'crushes' are status symbols. This issue includes a poster of a shirtless Taylor Lautner from *Twilight New Moon* (2009) for teenage girls to look at, suggesting perhaps that voyeurism isn't just for men looking at women and subverting Laura Mulvey's notion of the male gaze.

Hegemonic – hegemony has its roots in Marxist theory. It refers to 'the social and cultural control which the elite and privileged members of society have over the rest' (Burton, 1990:162). A hegemonic view is that there are fundamental inequalities in power between social groups.

TASK

Look at an issue of *Top of the Pops* magazine and read the quizzes section. What ideologies, values and attitudes are encoded about how young women 'should' look and behave?

Industry

Top of the Pops magazine is owned by BBC Worldwide, a commercial arm of the BBC, and any profits from it go towards the funding of the BBC:

'BBC Magazines publishes over 50 popular consumer titles including Top Gear, Radio Times, BBC Good Food and Gardeners' World. As the UK's fourth largest consumer magazine publisher, it sold around 85 million copies in the past year. BBC Magazines also has growing audiences round the world.' (bbcworldwide.com)

Top of the Pops magazine sells an average of 2,238 copies overseas each edition, reflecting its small but growing global status.

Teen girls' magazines are regulated by TMAP (the Teenage Magazine Arbitration Panel), a self-regulatory body set up after magazines like *Sugar* were accused of glamorising promiscuity with lurid sexual content. TMAP guidelines were designed:

'to ensure the sexual content of teenage magazines is presented in a responsible and appropriate manner.' (tmap.org.uk)

TASK

Read the guidelines on the TMAP website. Summarise the main points

---

Unusually for a magazine of this genre, *Top of the Pops* has no digital edition, but users can sign up for a fortnightly gossip e-mail at www.totpmag.com – a marketing tool to persuade them to purchase the next edition. It offers a 'swapitshop' feature, which enables users to link to exchange posters, games, films and other related swag. The brand is extended on Facebook, Twitter and Flickr.

Many of the features in the magazine link into BBC Radio 1 web pages or bands' websites, so *Top of the Pops* magazine is a good example of media convergence and synergy. This edition advertises links to the JLS website, the *Twilight New Moon* website, CBBC and Radio 1. Fans can send their 'Oops' cringes into Radio 1's Greg James and the problem pages 'surgery' with Aled and Dr Mel is also a spin off from the Radio 1 show, which links into advice pages. Other advice pages have to use a tiny url, for example, an article on peer pressure links into www.tinyurl.com/193surgery-peerpressure, which further links into the BBC *Slink* website, an online magazine for teenage girls which shares many of the magazine's characteristics. (http://www.bbc.co.uk/switch/slink/).

Top of the Pops magazine also offers its readers further incentives in the form of freebies and giveaways like stickers, posters, sparkly stationery or make-up and is often sold packaged in a polythene bag, possibly to make it look as if it is bulging with goodies (or maybe so the freebies don't 'fall off').

The magazine benefits from commercial intertextuality with its close relationship to the pop and television industries. The 'stars' it features on its cover are often from *The X-Factor* or younger American stars from Nickelodeon, Disney or from the pop world: members of the *High School Musical* cast, Miley Cyrus, Rihanna, the Jonas brothers or Taylor Swift. These stars are represented as idealised objects of pleasure and identification for the target audience.

Audience

The target audience for *Top of the Pops* magazine is 13–17-year-old female mainstreamers and aspirers. Young and Rubicam's 4Cs (cross-cultural consumer characterisation) suggests that aspirers are driven by the need for status, so the supposedly glamorous lifestyles of young stars are one of the appeals offered by the magazine.

Negotiated and Oppositional Readings

The preferred reading of the magazine supports the dominant mainstream ideology that young girls should be heterosexual consumers who love popular culture, shopping, their mates and boys. The target reader is positioned to accept this preferred reading, but not everyone will. There are three possible responses to a media text suggested by Stuart Hall's encoding/decoding model. Our gender, experience, social and cultural backgrounds and the representations within *Top of the Pops* magazine are likely to impact upon our reading of it.

For instance, the target reader's feminist mother may generally consider her daughter's magazine harmless fun and buy it for her, but may worry about the stereotypical representations of gender and boy-mad tone. She may feel that the focus on celebrity is shallow and encourage her daughter to read more challenging books as well. The same reader's father may not understand the mode of address or recognise the celebrities and may consider the magazine boring and silly. Her grandmother, if perhaps she is religious, with strict ideas about sex before marriage, may take an oppositional reading to the magazine on those grounds.

Tiny url – a tool which makes an impossibly long URL much shorter, thus minimising the chances of making mistakes when it is typed into a browser or of it breaking.

Young and Rubicam worked in marketing and classified audiences by the needs that motivate and drive them. Look at http://www.4cs.yr.com/global/ to find out how Young and Rubicam stereotype audiences.

TASK

Analyse the front cover of a *Top of the Pops* magazine. How does it attract its target audience?

2000 AD, £1.90 weekly, ABCs: 20,000 approx.

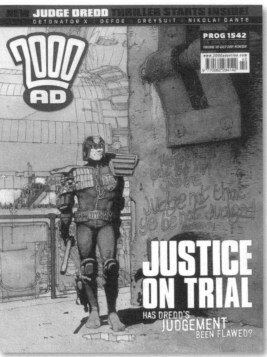

2000 AD emerged in the era of punk sensibilities, when traditional children's comics like *Wizard* and *Hotspur* were losing readers. It was originally published by IPC / Fleetway, then Egmont, but is now owned and published by Rebellion, who own intellectual property rights and are also well known for developing computer games like *Alien vs. Predator*. *2000 AD* is stable and growing, although only marginally profitable as a small part of a bigger industry which includes graphic novels and games. It carries very few advertisements: perhaps one for *2000 AD* merchandise and one for similar comics or video games on the back page.

The genre of *2000 AD* is difficult to define because it has elements of a range of genres, including war, science fiction and action/adventure – but ultimately, it is a comic book.

TASK

In what ways is a comic different from a magazine? Consider the following:

- The codes and conventions of comics such as framing, onomatopoeic sound effects and different shapes of speech bubble.

2000 AD feature five different comic strips a week, with Judge Dredd the only constant fixture, while others like Strontium Dog or Nikolai Dante come and go. While each story is self contained to an extent, the strips are serialised within each 'prog' and often end with cliff-hangers.

Characters depicted are generally aggressive, macho, tongue-in-cheek, male and white. Settings are generally dark, post-apocalyptic, dystopian and futuristic, which links to the science fiction genre. We could arguably criticise *2000 AD* for violent content and the way it represents women. The absence of female characters in some editions could be considered a negative representation. The comic's ideology is hegemonic, although it positions the audience in contradictory ways. Characters aren't black and white and it can be difficult to know who to cheer for. The most violent character is a policeman, so *2000 AD* encourages readers to: '...decode the various texts in complex ways and so form their own opinions on a variety of social and political issues.' (http://medal.unn.ac.uk/casestudies/dredd.htm)

It could be argued that *2000 AD* foreshadows trends with parody and political satire. Previous stories have included one about a show called *Sob Story in Mega City One* (Judge Dredd's post-apocalyptic home town) in which people moan and bewail their lives in the hope that viewers will give them money: foreshadowing, perhaps, the recent popularity of 'reality' shows featuring very ordinary people who will do pretty much anything for a bit of money or fame. Another strip in a previous edition, the *Militant League of Fatties*, parodied the idea of fat rights, although of course ultimately the militant fatties were too overweight to achieve much. This knowing, satirical tone may appeal to fans because it assumes that they have their own political opinions. Given the fluid and shifting nature of the preferred readings, *2000 AD* challenges its reader and is not just for children.

The fictional editor of *2000 AD* is Tharg the Mighty, with his customary greeting: 'The Mighty One speaks! Borag Thungg, Earthlets!' This idiosyncratic mode of address is part of the comic's appeal: understanding the language is one of the pleasures offered by the text and may encourage audience identification. 'Zarjaz', for instance, means good or cool. The comic contains many self-conscious 'in-jokes' and intertextual references: in one strip, *Kingdom*, the heroic dog-soldier is called Gene the Hackman, after the American actor. His foes are giant ants which he refers to as 'Them', in an intertextual link to the 1954 'creature feature' of the same name. The cover of prog 1674 makes an intertextual reference to the multiple Oscar-winning 1976 film about the US Watergate scandal with its cover line *All the President's Men – the Battle for the Red House Begins*.

 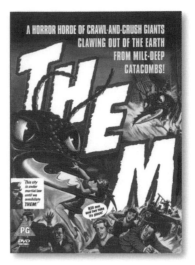

2000 AD fans are particularly loyal. The comic has its own fanzine, Zarjaz, and the average demographic of the 2000 AD reader has aged alongside the comic itself.

TASK

Look at a copy of *2000 AD*.

- Who is its primary target audience?

- How might this target audience be compared to that of *The Beano*? Compare an issue of each.

TASK

Investigating representations in *2000 AD*.

- With a focus on three specific strips or stories, compare the representations of heroism.

- Explain the representations of crime, law and the police in Judge Dredd.

EXTENDED TASK

Explore the ways in which *2000 AD* reinforces or challenges typical representations of masculinity.

DC Comics – one of the largest and oldest comic books companies in the world. It brought us *Batman*, *Superman*, *Wonder Woman* and thousands more characters.

Moral panics – in the media they stem from the idea that elements of popular culture can be blamed for wider problems in society, for example, we see computer games like *Grand Theft Auto IV* being blamed for violence and youth crime. They are cyclical in nature: concerns about the issue are raised in the media and reinforced by further coverage until action is taken to curb the 'problem'.

While *2000 AD*'s peculiarly British style and humour may exclude some international audiences, it is popular in the States, Australia and New Zealand: generally anywhere that English speakers can be found. It has a thriving online edition at 2000adonline.com. DC Comics owns the North American publishing rights to *2000 AD*. It has spawned various films and computer games: not just Judge Dredd, but *Shaun of the Dead* was originally a comic prequel in prog 1384 (April 2004) written by Simon Pegg and Edgar Wright. Rebellion have developed games like *Rogue Trooper* (Eidos), which won two BAFTAs and is based on a character from *2000 AD*. So *2000 AD* is a global brand.

Today, *2000 AD* is less widely distributed than many other comics although it can be found in larger branches of supermarkets and WH Smiths. Back issues can be ordered online and they remain on sale at collectors' and fans' specialist shops like Forbidden Planet, instead of being taken off sale and returned to the distributor like most periodical magazines. When a new edition of *Total Film* or *Top of the Pops* magazine comes on sale, the old ones are destroyed or returned and the retailer only has to pay for the copies sold. *2000 AD* will stay on sale even if it is an older issue because it is a collector's item. *2000 AD*'s cult status and relatively small circulation mean that traditional marketing methods are not the most efficient. It is mostly marketed on the internet and by word of mouth, due to its peculiarly loyal and long-lived readership, although Rebellion also attend conventions.

Conclusion

Since magazines became popular more than a hundred years ago thanks to increasing leisure time among a growing literate middle class, cheaper printing, electric light and better distribution, they have often been scapegoated as inferior elements of popular culture. The moral panics about the 'penny dreadfuls' in the Victorian era and the violent horror comics in the 40s and 50s can be linked to these debates about popular culture, 'dumbing down' and the intrinsic worth or value of comics and magazines. The implication is that the content of comics like *2000 AD* may have a detrimental effect on audiences. While it is difficult to either validate or refute these suggestions, you may have learned from your studies that audiences are able to negotiate their own understandings and meaning from media texts. You might like to research these debates further in Martin Barker's *Comics: Ideology, Power and the Critics*.

SUMMARY TASKS

Consider all three magazines you have studied:

1. How do they market and promote themselves in different ways? You might like to consider the following:

- Launches.
- Marketing and advertising.
- Press and media packs.
- Giveaways, incentives and competitions.
- Mobile services.
- Subscription offers.
- Websites and fan sites.
- Conventions.

2. How do your chosen texts attract their audiences?

3. To what extent are the magazines you have studied global?

Bibliography and Further Reading

Books

Alden, C. (ed.) (2007) *Media Directory*, London: Guardian Newspapers, Ltd.

Barker, M. (1989) *Comics: Ideology, Power and the Critics*, Manchester: Manchester University Press.

Branston, G. and Stafford, R. (2006) *The Media Student's Book*, 4th edition, London: Routledge.

Dyer, R. (1986) *Heavenly Bodies*: Film Stars and Society, Basingstoke: Macmillan.

Helsby, W. (2004) *Children's Comics: A Teacher's Guide*, Leighton Buzzard: Auteur.

Johnson, S and Prijatel, P. (1999) *The Magazine from Cover to Cover*, NTC Publishing Group. [AQ: city?]

Rayner, P., Wall, P. and Kruger, S. (2004) *AS Media Studies: The Essential Introduction*, 2nd edition, London: Routledge.

O'Sullivan, D. and Rayner, P. (2003) *Studying the Media*, 3rd edition, London: Arnold.

On the Web

http://www.2000adonline.com

Audit Bureaux of Circulations: http://www.abc.org.uk/

www.magforum.com, useful profiles of UK publishers and their titles.

National Readership Survey: http://www.nrs.co.uk/

www.natmags.co.uk, useful core reader and brand profiles.

Press Complaints Commission Code of Practice: http://www.pcc.org.uk/

Total Film website: http://www.totalfilm.com/

Web References

Daniel Chandler, *Notes on 'The Gaze'*: http://www.aber.ac.uk/media/Documents/gaze/gaze09.html

Charlton, M. *Let the Punishment Fit the Crime: Evaluating Judge Dredd*: http://medal.unn.ac.uk/casestudies/dredd.htm, accessed 4 June 2008.

Economist magazine 29 September 2007: http://www.hearst.com/magazines/

http://www.futureus-inc.com/archives/2005/09/official_xbox_m.php

McRobbie, [A 2004] *Post-feminism and Popular Culture*, from *Feminist Media Studies*, Vol. 4, No.3, London: Routledge. http://weblearn.ox.ac.uk/site/human/women/students/biblio/historiog/McRobbie per cent20- per cent20postfeminism.pdf, accessed 19 March 2010.

Young and Rubicam's 4Cs: http://www.4cs.yr.com/global/default.asp?tid=b0c57e2f-6b8f-4e32-8b20 5bcf74124349

Advertising

Wendy Helsby

In this section you will:

- Closely study advertisements for perfume including *Chanel No. 5*, concentrating on the areas of text (genre, narrative and representation), industry and audience.

- Study how the advertising industry works to target audiences at both a local and global level through the textual study of Nike adverts.

- Consider the use of celebrity by the advertising industry and their appeal to audiences.

- Look at regulation of the industry and its impact on advertising alcohol with reference to Guinness adverts.

Advertising is the financial engine house of commercial media. Its purpose is to target and deliver markets to producers which it does by converting the messages in an advertising campaign into action on the part of the audience – be it a change of attitude, a change of behaviour or a purchase. Producers see adverts as giving audiences information about products and services, so providing them with choice, but a choice which they hope to control. Adverts use a variety of methods such as promises of improvement, magical solutions and fear. However audiences are influenced by many factors and they can be fickle in their reading of texts. Advertisers therefore research their needs as well as the zeitgeist of the times to appeal to them in various ways.

TASK

Collect a range of adverts for different products; for example, perfume, cars and mobile phones. Try to get adverts from different media such as print, film, television and the internet.

Look at them carefully and then put them into categories according to their lines of appeal, for example, sexual attraction or sophistication, and their specific audiences, such as the independent woman, the successful business man, the cool teenager.

- How do the adverts group themselves?

- Are there similarities in the design of the adverts or their use of genre?

- Are there similarities in their use of conventions / style or narrative techniques?

- What can you say generally about the ways in which these products target their different audiences?

'This is *No 5: The Film*, a three-minute movie or the world's most expensive advertisement, depending on your stance....
The film to revolutionise advertising...at £18 million, it is certainly a first in terms of budget. Miss Kidman's £2 million fee alone is equal to the entire cost of the Oscar-nominated 1995 film *Trainspotting*. Although shot in five days in Sydney, Australia, *No 5: The Film* took "many more months to complete".' (Charlotte Edwardes, *Daily Telegraph*, 22 November 2004, www.smh.com.au/news/Film/Every-second-counts-in-42m-threeminute-film/)

EXTENSION TASK

Choose one of the products and investigate their advertising campaigns in more depth.

Consider the following points:

- Genre and appeal.

- Narrative themes.

- Gender or other representations.

- Audience targeting.

- Producers and market positioning.

- Regulations that might influence content or placement.

After you have completed your research prepare a short presentation on your selected campaign discussing the key findings.

Chanel No. 5

The referenced advertisement can be viewed on www.YouTube.com alongside 'the making of' with commentary, released 2004.

Background

Many actors and directors have been lured into advertising campaigns and Chanel has been a regular user of 'star status' to sell its products. After the success of *Moulin Rouge* (2001) Chanel brought the winning combination of Nicole Kidman (star) and Baz Luhrmann (director) to the campaign for their upmarket perfume Chanel No. 5. They were knowingly using the link between the genre, star and director (and the audiences' knowledge of this intertextuality) in the hope of transferring the film's success and the glamour of the star onto Chanel No.5.

Chanel claimed that the result was a 'creative first: the film to revolutionise advertising' (Chanel website). Globally its 'premiere' was preceded by its own advertising campaign and in the UK it was even included in Channel 4 listings so that people would not miss it.

An advert – whether costing millions like this and with a global name or for a local market – is made up of technical codes such as composition, lighting, colour, camera, *mise-en-scène*, sound and graphics. These combine with genre and narrative conventions, symbolic and cultural codes to construct a line of appeal and to deliver messages about the brand image.

Text – Genre

The Chanel No. 5 advert is in the genre of the unrequited love story, a 'brief encounter'. It mixes the loss of love theme which has appeared throughout time in stories such as in *The Lady of the Camellias* (Alexandre Dumas, 1852) and *Moulin Rouge* with the more optimistic romantic theme of films like *Notting Hill* (1999). The message is that inside every celebrity there is a 'real' individual who may fall in love with an 'ordinary' person (the purchaser) in a chance meeting. An important convention of the genre is 'the kiss'; although as a romance and with an eye on scheduling, sex is not seen. Other conventions of romantic genres, such as love at first sight, barriers to love, memories of love, doing one's duty (as with classic films like *Casablanca* [1942] and *Brief Encounter* [1945]) are all encapsulated in this advert. There is also the trans-historical (Propp) fairy story theme of finding the 'prince/ss' even if a pauper!

In a reverse of the Cinderella story the ball gown becomes ordinary clothes in an edit flourish, a 'magical' solution that adverts frequently use (Williamson, 1978), but here there is a twist – it does not hinder romance but allows it to flourish. Chanel had based a previous advert on Red Riding Hood, so the references to a fairy story subtly linked these two campaigns together.

Narrative

As with most stories, a series of enigmas and their answers help to move the narrative forward. The key enigmas to be resolved are:

- Where can you find real love?

- Should you abandon a career for love?

As the narrative unfolds these questions are answered through micro questions, such as: Who is she? (we find out – 'the most famous...'); Who is she running from? (we see – the paparazzi); and so on. The non-diegetic male voice over helps to tell the narrative from the point of view of the young male hero and so positions our identification with both the protagonists. Time and space are rapidly changed (ellipses) as we move from the streets of New York to a garret rooftop (a similar location and *mise-en-scène* to *Moulin Rouge*) and back to the red carpet.

Brand – a unique and identifiable symbol, association, name or trade mark which serves to differentiate competing products or services. Both a physical and emotional trigger to create a relationship between consumers and the product / service. (allaboutbrands.com)

Brand identity – a unique set of associations that the brand strategist aspires to create or maintain. These associations represent what the brand should stand for and imply a potential to customers. (allaboutbrands.com)

Brand image – a unique set of associations within the minds of the target customers which represent what the brand currently stands for and implies the current promise to customers. (NB: Brand image is what is currently in the minds of consumers, whereas brand identity is aspirational.) (allaboutbrands.com))

Trans-historical – means that beliefs or myths are carried across periods of time to provide continuity of ideas. For Propp the ideas inside fairy and folk stories were deeply rooted in society through many ages. They are merely updated in texts to fit a contemporary context.

Mythic level – this lies beneath, therefore hidden within, the story but provides the ideological base in which the ideas (beliefs / ideologies) of the narrative are rooted.

The advert opens with the initial equilibrium of the hounded celebrity. The montage editing, slightly monochrome colour and camera angles connote her flight. The disruption is that in running away from the paparazzi she enters a taxi, where she finds a young intellectual who does not recognise her because he is so engrossed in his books. She says 'drive' and escapes with him and they have a brief affair in which she leaves the trappings of celebrity, signified visually by clothes and location, to be an ordinary person, a dancer. Then she is told by her controlling impresario / secretary (father role) and by her lover that her responsibility is to her public. She accepts her fate and returns to the red carpet. The new equilibrium suggests that she is now in control of her fame, signified by the groomed hair and smooth black dress; but she has always got that moment of escape, that 'brief encounter' to remember. She looks back to see the Chanel sign on the roof top with the young man hanging off the crescent (C) moon shape. The camera zooms in to a close up of the jewel hanging down her bare back, a (diamond) ring with the logo No. 5 inside. Her backward glance over her shoulder conveys the memory of love as well as the belief that even a star is accessible.

The ideological message conveyed within the advert is that if only briefly love is possible however seemingly impossible the circumstances. This fleeting moment, will be remembered by the man through 'her kiss; her smile; her perfume'. The message is also that everyone has responsibilities and that sometimes sacrifice is necessary in order to meet them. Some of the binary oppositions which help to convey these meanings and resolve the fictional narrative are based on:

- Being out of – or in – control.

- The conflict between personal and public life.

- The differences between rich and poor.

- Being a celebrity or being ordinary.

- The tension between duty and emotion.

The dominant beliefs (ideologies) that are (re)established are those of duty and responsibilities but also the idea that a career, glamour and romance are all possible. However, these resolutions are at the mythic level of meaning.

Representation

The Kidman character moves though three representations. In real life Nicole Kidman is a beautiful, blonde, female, white, successful star which adds meaning to the role she plays here. In the advert she becomes the hounded female celebrity on the run, conveyed through an extravagant stereotypically pink, disorganised, flouncy dress and her dishevelled blonde hair, signifying how far she is out of control of her status as 'the most famous'. The stereotype created by the blonde hair as well as the pink dress again references *Moulin Rouge*, but also references a stereotypical Disney Cinderella look. It is a classic stereotype and would be easily recognised by the audience. However, even though a stereotype it is still a powerful image seen countless times in media texts. This creates a certain ambiguity for the reader who may identify with the character. Then the 'star' is transformed. Wearing a black and white suit, she becomes a 'dancer' her movements are alluring not panicking, as she falls for the young man in a love scene on the rooftop. Finally she is seen in a black fitted gown sleek and strong with hair pulled back and controlled as she moves calmly up the red (connoting fame) carpeted stair case in front of the paparazzi as she accepts her (celebrity) destiny. Lighting helps to establish these changes in the role and narrative. Starting from high key lighting with the paparazzi, we move to low key romantic lighting on the roof top with the darkly lit space when she is told by her (male) lover and by her (male) secretary to return to the 'real' world; and finally to be spot lit as the star on the staircase.

The young impoverished (Latin) lover, Rodrigo Santono, stereotypically wearing glasses signifying intelligence, is unworldly and unaware of her fame. He is attractive, muscular, but ordinary, as suggested by his clothes, such as the white vest. The impresario / secretary in control of the star persona, an older male shadowy figure stands formally dressed in the background. So each character also represents a (stereo)'type'.

Representation of Place

The New York cityscape is seen as a romantic, glittering city. The yellow cabs and the architecture convey this sense of place. The swirling cameras, fast editing and bustle signify the energy at the centre of the celebrity world. Fireworks signify emotion and celebration. Romantic Paris is signified by references to the *mise-en-scène* seen in *Moulin Rouge* particularly with the roof top scenes; and the French connection is underlined by the romantic sounds of the non-diegetic music, Debussy's *Claire de Lune*.

Audiences

This advert is primarily targeting a young reasonably up-market audience. The line of appeal is that romance will overcome differences. The brand image is of exclusivity but its repositioning for the young is that this does not deny romance to lesser mortals. The company's logo of two intertwined Cs is identified with the message throughout the advert. In the UK the advert was shown in cinemas and on Channel 4 targeting the young and alternative viewers of the channel as well as cinema audiences for films like *Moulin Rouge*. Audiences would have experienced the pleasure of recognising the intertextual references to *Moulin Rouge* referenced in the design through the *mise-en-scène* and in the cinematography. This pleasure is consciously exploited by the advert in a knowing way.

Identification for females would be with the glamour and status of the celebrity, both in the advert and with Kidman herself; and for young men (possible purchasers) with the lover, handsome, strong, a South American romantic who captures the heart of this star. He is the narrator and we follow his desire. The genre and narrative of lost love may also have appealed to an older, secondary, audience with the possible connections to texts such as David Lean's *Brief Encounter*. The element of the man making the decision for the woman may also have links with the dominant

Advertising Agencies – they are independent from the company they represent. They provide a service which researches the audience and the brand profile for a company's products. From this evidence they advise their clients on how to promote their products and produce new adverts and promotional ideas.

ideologies of gender roles and may have appeal for older, more traditional, male purchasers.

For both primary and secondary audiences buying Chanel No. 5 might link into the dream or myth of romance. In a simple way therefore this advert demonstrates how different ages and genders may read and respond to the same narrative.

Audiences may also be enticed through the adverts intertextual references – the overt link to *Moulin Rouge*, and the more subtle link to other stars such as Marilyn Monroe (the icon of the paparazzi hunted and haunted star) might add to their engagement with the advert. The link with Monroe is also a clear link with the product. Marilyn Monroe had famously claimed in 1954 that all she had on when she went to bed was 'a couple of drops of Chanel No. 5'.

Industry

This is part of Chanel's ongoing high profile campaigns linking celebrities to their brand image (which they continued with Audrey Tautou in 2009). It appeared in television schedules and was even shown on news broadcasts when first released. Campaigns like this have to build upon previous messages. Whilst Chanel has done its own creative work in-house it has also used a digital advertising agency to provide online expertise.

This campaign aimed to reposition itself in the market place and to bring down the age of the purchaser of Chanel No. 5 which was seen to have gained an old-fashioned image. People who bought it were characterised as middle-aged men buying it for their mistresses at airport shops or as a birthday present for their grandmothers. Chanel needed to revitalise the brand by getting young men to purchase it for their partners and for young women to wear it.

TASK

Discuss how linking *Chanel No. 5* with the film *Moulin Rouge* might have helped to lower its audience age profile.

The advert itself was a 'media event'. It was accompanied by a twenty-five minute film of 'the making of...' when screened in cinemas and it had rolling credits at the end in order to help signify its filmic credibility. Although the logo appears a number of times, the perfume bottle never appears – which again helped to position it as a film rather than an advert. Why would this be seen to be important? Is it that showing the bottle would have broken the fairy story spell?

Below you can see one of the display adverts that appeared with the movie campaign. There are obvious visual references to the film but the significant difference is the position of the bottle and the brand name. This identifies it as an advert. Magazines have quite strict rules about what appears as an advert and what appears as editorial material. Without the bottle the advert might appear to be an image based upon a story around Kidman.

Chanel No.5 display ad

TASK

Consider how Nicole Kidman – actress, wife, mother, 'celebrity' – reflects the image of Chanel.

Although we do not generally think of adverts belonging to their own genres, perfume adverts such as Chanel No. 5 can be divided into sub-genres and this shows how far discourses create meanings and beliefs; in this case the discourses of romance, beauty and celebrity. Many contemporary perfume adverts use celebrities, promise fame, allure and romance – the use of celebrity endorsement is not new. Stars of the silver screen, such as Barbara Stanwyck, Debbie Reynolds as well as Marilyn Monroe all appeared in adverts for products such as Lustre-Crème shampoo in the 1950s.

In 2009 Chanel produced a new advert, this time with Audrey Tautou the star of *Amélie* (2001) and the biographical film of *Coco Before Chanel* (2009). It was directed by Jean-Pierre Jeunet, director of *Amélie*. The advert is two and a half minutes long and represents a woman travelling on the Orient Express train from Paris to Istanbul. Her perfume attracts a young man and we follow them as their paths cross and eventually meet. The non-diegetic song is Billie Holliday's 'I'm a Fool to Want You' which anchors the meaning of the 'film'. The advert was released on networking sites such as Bebo before its official launch on 5 May 2009, the same day that Coco Chanel had originally launched Chanel No. 5.

TASK

Using the discussion on the Chanel advert starring Nicole Kidman as a basis, analyse the Tautou advert (found on the web in various sites including the Chanel site).

- List the textual differences and similarities between the two adverts: use style, form, content and message as areas to study. For example, do you think the lines of appeal are similar or not?

- Explain why you think the differences / similarities exist.

- Is the audience appeal the same or not?

- Why do you think Chanel decided to commit to another expensive advert in 2009?

TASK

Look at the advert below. Although this is a print advert, can you see similarities with the Chanel adverts in terms of the conventions it uses?

The advert is targeted at both women and men and is typical of perfume adverts where the people in the advert personify the bottle of perfume. What you are buying here are bottles that are selling dreams, desires and aspirations.

How is this achieved? Textual analysis can be used to deconstruct the advert and reveal the meanings:

The advert is divided into two with the dark borders framing a lighter central section where our focus goes first; the background re-emphasises the pale / dark binary opposition of the people. The bottles are laid out on the left border in a V shape reflecting the graphics above them. The graphics contain the initials of David and Victoria Beckham with the V given a feminine drape and below the words 'intimately Beckham'. Their lay out is reflected in the 'intimate' position of the people, so emphasising the link and the transfer of connotative meaning between bottles and people. The pale bottle is personified by the pale blonde female image with her dress a similar colour to the bottle and her hair to the bottle top, and the drape of her dress reflecting the graphic V. The darker one is reflected by the darker male image. The man looks at us – a direct and active mode of address whereas the female passively clings to the man although (intimately) she is pulling his shirt open.

The female wears a revealing evening dress, with bare back and leg, suggesting sexual availability. The man however is fully clothed; he is in control, his watch band stands out as an icon of masculinity. He is wearing a ring on his wedding finger connoting a relationship and is suggestively – 'intimately' – holding the woman's leg. We buy into this intimacy. The iconic levels of denotation and connotation refer to the images of two famous celebrities and there is intertextuality in the form of the personas developed by the Beckhams. Cultural knowledge allows us to read the text and to take the underlying message about relationships and success in the shape of celebrity being available in the bottle. There are many similarities to the Chanel advert.

Like the Chanel advert this provides a 'mythic' message which we are being sold. But what is actually being sold here? Do you find out what the contents of the bottles smell like? What quantity you are buying? How much it costs? Where to buy it? If not, what are you buying? The 'myth' is that the perfume can give you the glamour of a beautiful woman and a strong masculine, but tender sexuality; in other words: a relationship like the Beckhams. It is carefully constructed not to send the wrong messages, particularly to men. This is not about androgyny CK style, nor about gayness. This is about getting female attention and a relationship if you smell good.

TASK

Look back at how the advert is constructed and answer the following questions:

- How does the advert reflect contemporary gender relationships?

- Do you have a different reading to the one above?

- Do you think this advert provides positive roles?

Try to explain your points of view clearly.

The 'Swoosh' and Global Branding – 'To the Next Level'

Although David Beckham wears Nike as a professional footballer, he does not (currently) endorse it as a brand. Given Beckham's global celebrity status it is an interesting point to consider – why doesn't he? The answer may lie in the brand image and brand identity of Nike.

Nike's 'swoosh' is probably one of the most recognisable global sports logos. Nike's image is based on urban 'edginess' and they often use renowned sports personalities who have had a 'bad boy' image, such as Eric Cantona and, lately Wayne Rooney, or popular marginal activities such as break dancing hoping to appeal to alternative audiences.

In America, Nike's message often appeals to particular minority ethnic groups and their advertising campaigns have focused on black athletes and the sports to which the black audience have an affinity, such as basketball.

A study of Nike raises questions about globalisation and about cultural and global imperialism. When you go to buy locally (in the UK, for example) are you really buying globally? What else have you bought apart from a pair of trainers or a cap? Have you, perhaps bought in to a global fashion trend and contributed to global homogenisation? Nike, it appears, understands this global / local contradiction

and with their global campaigns such as the 2008 football campaign 'To the Next Level' (a two minute film, directed by Guy Ritchie of *Lock, Stock and Two Smoking Barrels* and *Snatch* fame, played during the European Football Championships), they referenced the local. Ritchie's global video was given a regional feel by focusing on particular footballers depending on which continent it was being viewed. The advert combines scenes on the football pitch with off pitch glamorous nightlife and typical (male) humour such as 'mooning'. The narrative subject, from whose point of view (camera) the game is played is the viewer who 'plays' for a premiership club against the world's greatest footballers, such as Ronaldo. The edgy style links with the edgy urban nature of previous campaigns and also offers intertextual reference to Ritchie's black comedy gangster movies.

The campaign, like other Nike ads, was globally released on television and online on the Nike website. It also provided interactivity as you could sign up for a training programme, allowing the viewer to become more deeply engaged in the Nike message. In 2008 Nike also released adverts for the Olympics in China made specifically for Chinese audiences. These showed apparently ordinary Chinese suddenly performing extraordinary athletic feats (www.altogetherdigital. com/20071002/chinese-olympics-adverts-from-nike/).

In February 2009 Nike released 'Show Your 5', a three month ad campaign in the UK. This was backed by a band called The View with their track 'Wasteland'. The ninety second television advert had Wayne Rooney, Joe Cole and Rio Ferdinand playing five aside football with local players from inner city clubs. The gritty, urban feel is conveyed through the use of simulated CCTV footage as well as the style of music. Like Chanel the campaign had a pre-launch on the web with teaser clips on blogs and social networking websites. Its aim was to link with the popularity of five aside with young players and with Nike's sportswear line of five aside clothing. The shots and the young players were all based around the city of Manchester in the north of England.

Commodification
– this is the way that things not normally bought and sold as in a shop, are created as commodities to be sold to consumers. This can be seen in areas such as ideas or the use of celebrities who become 'commodities' within the media.

EXTENDED TASK

Text

View 'Show Your 5' on www.youtube.com.

The overall theme is of a group of friends coming together in the evening to have a football kick around:

- How do the images and editing work together to create and represent an urban environment?

- Look at the quality of images, the use of black and white, the way some images are seen through wire mesh; the surveillance style of filming and so on.

- Listen to the sound track, including all elements of music, voices and sound effects, such as police sirens. How do these add to the overall message?

- How would you characterise the ordinary people seen in the advert?

- Consider the famous players / celebrities seen in the advert. What does their image add to the overall message? What do they represent?

Audience

Having completed the textual analysis, look at what you have written and now link those elements, such as the style and the players, to a target audience:

- How does Nike brand its image to appeal to the target audience? What is the message of the advert? How does it fit the Nike brand?

- Consider age, gender, class, ethnicity, etc. How do the elements, such as technical codes and subject, help to target audiences?

- What are the lines of appeal? What are purchasers of Nike buying into in this advert?

Industry

This advert suggests that Nike as a brand is aiming to provide a local UK message. It was shot in the urban environments of the city of Manchester but it does have a global link. How does this advert link to Nike's other local/global campaigns?

Sport, and particularly football, is a commercial and cultural global industry and advertising is there to promote it and to commodify the aspirations and inspiration it provides. Nike hopes the world will buy into this commodification by purchasing the global Nike logo and the local Nike message of grass roots sport.

In sport advertising it is possible to see how power and representations are reflected through the adverts, and how this in turn is influenced by globalisation of sport. One debate raised is how far global imperialism, the trans-national control by a few conglomerates, imposes identities onto local cultures. But the other side of the argument suggests that, perhaps, there is an exchange of ideas through the ability of the global economy to reach local consumers and react to their needs – so that global imperialism is not a total one way process.

Nike's base is in the US but they have relatively few employees there; the production is done by workers in factories in countries like Indonesia. Interestingly the co-founder of the company (Phil Knight) stated that the 'three-legged stool' of Nike's success consists of celebrity endorsement, product design and advertising (Hatfield, *The Guardian*, 17 June 2003). Efficient economic production is omitted from this metaphorical stool and Nike has been criticised for the exploitation of developing world workers particularly those in the Far East. Whatever the outcome of these debates one fact is undeniable: the majority of the profit is bound for American shores and this economic control could be regarded as the clearest form of global as well as cultural imperialism.

Further discussion on globalisation can be read in various sources, such as at: www.mediaknowall.com/advertising/globalad and in Hesmondhalgh, 2006.

For further information look at the ASA website at: www.asa.org.uk and OFCOM's site at: www.ofcom.org.uk.

TASK

Investigate how Nike uses global events, such as the Football World Cup, World Athletics Championship or the Olympics to promote itself.

The advertising of sports shoes and trainers are often targeted at young people. How does Nike brand its image to appeal to this audience?

Regulation and Advertising – Alcohol and Guinness advertising

The regulation of print advertising began in the 1960s with the establishment of the Advertising Standards Authority. Since 2003 this organisation regulates most mass media adverts under the auspices of Ofcom. The ASA uses the CAP code (Code of Advertising, Sales Promotion and Direct Marketing) produced by the Committee of Advertising Practice, against which it adjudicates complaints received about advertisements.

An advert has to deliver its message quickly as a reader flicks through a magazine or watches a screen. This encourages the use of shorthand cultural references and can often lead to stereotypes and other potentially biased messages. However media texts can be polysemic (several possible meanings) and audiences are not homogenous (all the same), so that even if some of the target audience take the message as intended (preferred reading), others may not (negotiated or oppositional readings). For producers this means that they cannot guarantee that audiences will take the intended message, and at the extreme they may even be offended by it. It is rarely the intention of the advertiser to cause offence or to misguide audiences (although some advertisers actively attempt to do this, an infamous example being some of Bennetons). If they do then the ASA may become involved to adjudicate.

Another factor influencing regulation is the belief that advertising is a very powerful conveyer of messages and that advertisers should: act responsibly, especially with regard to vulnerable groups; be honest in their claims and not mislead, or encourage certain anti-social behaviours.

TASK

Study the advert below. It was banned in 2009. Before looking at the ASA ruling suggest why this advert might have contravened the CAP code. Look carefully at all the elements.

The ASA decided that the advert linked seduction with the consumption of alcohol. It also suggested that alcohol changed the woman's mood and enhanced her confidence and contravened rules 56.8 and 56.9 of the code.

The advertising of alcohol is one of the key concerns of the ASA particularly where vulnerable and young people are concerned. The CAP code for Television Advertisements (rule 11.8, pp. 72–4 of the code) concerns this area. The basic message is that the advertising of alcohol should not suggest that drinking can contribute to popularity, success, be therapeutic or increase sexual activity. It should not link with aggression or activities such as driving or working machinery and there should be no encouragement to excessive drinking. Because there is a particular concern about the appeal of alcohol to young people, alcohol adverts have to use actors who appear to look over twenty-five years old in an attempt to make sure that the advert (and therefore the product) does not appeal to a younger demographic.

How far do you think this rule might help to protect young people?

Recently social concerns about binge drinking and the sale of 'alcopops' and other alcoholic drinks to young people (an example of a moral panic) have been discussed and have forced regulators to introduce stricter rules (in 2005 and 2007).

In September 2009 the ASA reported that their latest survey revealed a compliance of 99 per cent to the code on advertising alcohol (www.asa.org.uk/asa/news/news/2009/ASA+Alcohol+Compliance+Survey, accessed 7/12/09). You can see how seriously the advertising industry takes the code.

Guinness

A long standing alcohol advertising campaign is Guinness. It began advertising in 1929.

TASK

Look at or watch some of the old Guinness adverts – they are freely available on sites like www.youtube.com and the Guinness website, as well as in books (see references):

- How have they changed over time with regard to suggesting success, popularity, sexual appeal, aggression, etc.?

- Can you spot any ways in which they might contravene today's much stricter code?

TASK

Consider two contemporary Guinness adverts:

1. Look at the 'planetary engineering' advert from 2009 which can be found at: www.visit4info.com/brand/Guinness-Draught/2375. Click on 'planetary engineering'.

Consider the technical codes employed to create the message. Answer the following:

- How has a narrative been established?

- Who is the hero of this story?

- What is the genre?

2. Look at the Guinness 'dot' advert from 2008 which can be found at: www.visit4info.com/advert/Guinness-The-Dot-Guinness-Draught/55183, accessed 15 February 2010.

- This narrative is the story of a dot, a point that could evolve into anything.

- How does this advert target the Guinness drinker but also try to appeal to younger drinkers?

EXTENSION TASK

Who owns the Guinness brand? Where are they based? What other popular brands do they own?

Guinness has traditionally been associated with Ireland. How have Guinness built a global brand image? Consider the implications of the local / global link for Guinness.

If you click onto the Guinness website (www.guinness.com) you will be asked for some personal details. Having considered the regulations in the UK why do you think Guinness has put in this page?

In the 1980s Guinness began to use more sophisticated styles of advertising than the often comedic approach they had adopted earlier. With the help of techniques such as psychographics – drawings done by consumers of the inner qualities of Guinness – they produced a campaign which emphasised the Celtic spirit and the warmth audiences associated with the brand. The slogan used was 'pure genius'. It reflected the, 'mysterious, elemental, nourishing, rewarding and relaxing' nature of Guinness (York, www.independent.co.uk/news/media,, accessed 21 February 2005). This became its brand identity.

In the late 1980s a trend towards individualism in popular culture was identified resulting in adverts which used the actor Rutger Hauer (Replicant Roy Batty in

Blade Runner, (1982), a cult film) to personify the glass of Guinness – with his black clothes representing the body of the drink and his pale face and hair representing the foamy head of the drink. The early 1990s adverts reflected changing social status and used irony with slogans such as 'a woman needs a man like a fish needs a bicycle'. In the mid 1990s Guinness began the campaign 'good things come to those who wait' based upon the time it takes to pour a Guinness and for the head to settle out. This famously produced the Guinness surfers advert which was based upon a man waiting on a beach for the wave of his life: 'He sits and waits ...that's what he does...tick...tock.' The advert won many awards and was voted by the public as number 1 in Channel 4's '100 Greatest TV Ads'.

None of these adverts would seem to contravene the regulations. However the market for Guinness, which has typically been seen as a niche male drinker, was, like Chanel, seeing its audience profile ageing. So, in order to appeal to a younger audience Guinness had to reinvent itself, without contravening the CAP code. As a drink it is visually very distinctive and the company wanted to convey the message of hidden depths, of being an individual and being 'macho'. For a recent campaign (2007), BBDO, the advertising agency used by Guinness, adopted the tactic that challenged the Guinness drinker to 'find the advert'. In order to create interactivity with the 'tipping point' advert, the consumer could follow a series of clues left on the website where they could enter a competition of interlinked tasks. This is a type of viral marketing obviously more appealing to a younger web wise generation.

The Guinness Surfers ad (left)

The 'tipping point' advert showed 1000 villagers in South America building a domino chain with objects such as old tyres and fridges – a sort of dominoes for giants. The final image was of a glass of Guinness made out of stacked books with the slogan – 'Good things come to those who wait'. Like the previous surfers advert this one takes 1 min 29 seconds to run.

Guinness believed that this advert showed community working together but how far does that fit in with Guinness's brand identity?

In November 2009 a new Guinness advert, 'Brings a world to life', was produced showing a group of young men braving the elements, moving around dressed in dark colours to contrast with the spray, bubbles, snow and so on swirling around them. They were said by the company to reflect how the pint of Guinness is poured, stirred around and settled; the advert ends with the figures successfully posed together on top of a waterfall.

TASK

Study three Guinness adverts. How do they conform to the Cap code?

EXTENSION TASKS

Consider the three campaigns: *Chanel No. 5*, Nike and Guinness.

Text

- How do these texts use narrative and genre to maintain audience's interest?

- How do they convey ideas, or beliefs, of, for example, romance; sophistication; individualism; urban life styles; male bonding, through the technical codes of camera, sound, editing and through the mise-en-scene?

Audience

- How do these adverts target their different audiences? Consider, for example, the textual elements, the lines of appeal, the use of celebrity (or not), the cultural references and intertextual references.

- Look at the ways they address their audiences. Do you think audiences are persuaded to buy products by such advertising?

Industry

- How have ASA regulations affected these campaigns?

- How global are the campaigns?

Conclusion

Advertising has always worked on audiences in many ways through lines of appeal, such as fear and one-up-man-ship, using psychology and social trends. Producers have always delivered messages with meanings, ideas, values and beliefs, 'selling us ourselves' (Williamson, 1978:13) Today advertisers use a wide range of platforms, global as well as local, which increasingly have meant their target audiences are more diffuse than mass through the additional use of technologies such as new forms of the web and the 'blogosphere'. These can provide a 'free' media buzz for consumers and producers.

Consider the story of the *Dove* Campaign for Beauty, where *Dove* introduced a dialogue between its consumers on the definition of beauty. 'The Real Truth About Beauty' is shown in the advert '*Dove* Evolution' where an ordinary female face is manicured and then digitally enhanced to create a 'perfect' image finishing with the tagline 'No wonder our perception of beauty is distorted'. *Dove* is owned by

Unilever and at an economic level this advert was a risk, but one which appears to have worked in its favour. It has been viewed on YouTube millions of times. The *Dove* advert illustrates that even if the power behind media messages is in the hands of a relatively small group of producers such as Unilever, another model of 'bottom up' messaging facilitated by new technology may be an increasingly powerful alternative. The '*Dove* Evolution' campaign for example was parodied by a 'slob evolution' response where a good looking man was converted into a slob.

Like other industries in this brave new media world much is uncertain for advertising. But unless a different system of paying for our media is devised, advertising and its various forms, such as sponsorship and product placement, will remain fundamental to the media's survival. A major question for the advertising industry is how far the new technologies and changing economic structures will change the world of advertising.

Bibliography

On the web

www.screenonline.org.uk – a fantastic site for background into advertising on British television and film. Also contains clips to view such as the tombstone AIDS campaign advertisement.

www.paintedcows.com/international -- this is a website that will lead you to many other national sites and discusses both national and international issues in advertising and marketing.

www.ipcmedia.com – magazine media packs includes *Nuts, Loaded, Uncut, NME.*

www.warc.com – World Advertising Research Center. This is a subscription website for professionals in the media, marketing and advertising but it does have a free trial. It has, for example, case studies, research, brand, consumer target groups, marketing intelligence.

www.asa.org.uk – Advertising Standards Authority. Find out about the CAP code and adjudications; it has an excellent college / schools site with downloadable material.

www.mediamagazine.org – excellent resource with case studies on campaigns written with A level students in mind. Can access archives if a subscriber to the magazine:

Dugdale. H. 'Product Placement and the Fast Forward Generation' at: www.mediamagazine.org, September 2006.

Dugdale, H. 'Goodbye Mr Linekar' at: www.mediamagazine,org, Number 18, September 2007.

www.mediaknowall.com – good resource for clear explanations of key concepts such as media effects and good links.

www.YouTube.com – where you can find video clips of television and film adverts.

In addition the websites of specific companies provide ample material for researching campaigns.

www.metro.co.uk/home/20267-too-wkd-for-television -[En rule] alcopops and the ASA.

Books and Articles

Armstrong, K. (1999) 'Nike's Communication with Black Audiences: A Sociological Analysis of Advertising Effectiveness via Symbolic Interactionism', in *Journal of Sport and Social Capital*, Vol. 23, No. 3: 266–86.

Cook, G. (1992) *The Discourse of Advertising*, London and New York: Routledge.

Curran, J., Collins, R., Garnham, N., Scannell, P. and Wingate, P. (eds) (1986) *Media, Culture and Society: A Critical Reader*. London: Sage.

Davies, J. (1998) *The Book of Guinness Advertising*. London: Guinness.

Dyer, G.(1982) *Advertising as Communication*, London: Routledge.

Dyer, R. (1985) 'Taking Popular Television Seriously' in D. Lusted and P. Drummond (eds), *TV and Schooling*, London: BFI.

Fiske, J. (1982) *Introduction to Communication Studies*, London and New York: Routledge.

Goffman, E. (1978) *Gender Advertisements*. Cambridge, MA: Harvard University Press.

Gumbel, A. 'Boom in "Brand Integration" Gives Advertising the Break it Needs', *The Independent*, 5 November 2005.

Habermas, J. (1989 / 1962) *The Structural Transformation of the Public Sphere* (trans. T. Burger and F. Lawrence), Cambridge: Polity.

Hall, S. (ed.) (1997) *Representation: Cultural Representations and Signifying Practices*. London: Sage.

Hatfield, S. 'What Makes Nike's Advertising Tick?', *The Guardian*, 17 June 2003.

Hesmondhalgh, D. (ed.) (2006) 'Media Production DA204' in *Understanding Media*, Milton Keynes: Open University Press.

Helsby, W. (2004) *Teaching Television Advertising*, Leighton Buzzard: Auteur.

Leiss, William, Kline, S. and Jhally, S. (1990) *Social Communication in Advertising*, London: Routledge.

Mahmud, S., 'Nike Takes Soccer to "the Next Level"', *Adweek Online*, 1 May 2008.

Monahan, J., 'TV Sponsorship', 3 February 2003 at: www.mediamagazine.org.

Morley, D. (1980) *The 'Nationwide' Audience: Structure and Decoding*, London: BFI.

Williamson, J. (1978) *Decoding Advertisements: Ideology and Meaning in Advertising*, London: Marion Boyars.

RESEARCHING, CREATING AND EVALUATING YOUR OWN MEDIA PRODUCTIONS

I am grateful to Johnnie Blows (magazine cover, pg. 263), Maria Khafizova (public health campaign, pg. 267) and Leanne Crook (CD artwork and video production, pg. 251) of Royal Russell School for allowing us to reproduce examples of their media pre-production and production work in this chapter.

Researching, Creating and Evaluating Your Own Media Productions

Colin Dear

Media Studies at AS and A Level not only allows you to explore all aspects of the media, it also offers you the opportunity to be creative by carrying out your own production work. Creativity and originality are vital to all productions but it is also important, particularly at AS and A Level, that you demonstrate an understanding of genre conventions and construct appropriate narratives and representations in the productions you create. In order to do this successfully, you need to think carefully about your aims before carrying out research and, possibly, pre-production work. At the end of the process, it is also likely that you will need to evaluate the success of your work and demonstrate what you have learnt.

This section aims to give you advice on how to make good decisions throughout the completion of your production work, which may well involve the following:

- Writing or choosing a brief so you are clear about the aims of your work.

- Conducting research and reaching conclusions.

- Completing planning and pre-production work (e.g. storyboarding, or creating samples of potential production ideas).

- Producing a media text.

- Evaluating your production.

It is worth noticing that the production of the media text occurs fairly late in the process. You should complete research and pre-production planning before you begin producing your text because what you produce will be improved by the knowledge, understanding and skills you gain from these tasks.

Completing a major project like this involves making a series of good decisions. Remember, the decisions you make today will affect what you can do throughout the time you are working on your production. Many factors will affect your decisions: resources, deadlines, other people. This chapter is intended to help you think them through fully before you begin any production work.

Your Aims – Writing or choosing a brief

Before you start to do any research or production work, you need to have a clear idea of what you're aiming to produce and the main stages of your work. This is generally established through a brief. You may be given a brief by your teacher, you may have to choose one from a range of options or you may be asked to write one for yourself. A typical brief might give you a choice of tasks for the pre-production and production elements of the project.

Sample brief:

1. AN INDIVIDUAL PRE-PRODUCTION

Your task is to produce either:

1. A storyboard for a music video featuring a new artist.

OR

2. A cover and the insert pages for a new musical artist's CD.

2. A PRODUCTION ASSIGNMENT

Your task is to produce either:

1. The music video for ONE OF YOUR GROUP'S storyboards. You may work on this together but please plan and discuss your individual roles carefully before you begin.

OR

2. A magazine front cover and double page spread featuring a new musical artist. THIS TASK MUST BE DONE INDIVIDUALLY.

3. A REPORT

THIS TASK MUST BE DONE INDIVIDUALLY. It should be between 1,200–1,600 words and should focus on:

- The research you completed to inform your pre-production.

- A justification of the target audience for your production.

- An evaluation of the production, highlighting strengths and weaknesses through a comparison with existing music videos or magazine pages.

This kind of brief, the kind your teacher might give you, offers very clear instructions about what you need to do. As such, you can use it as checklist and should work to a series of deadlines – a deadline to complete the research, one for the storyboard, and so on. This will help you manage what may seem like an overwhelming project. If you are given the freedom to set your own task, then you should aim to produce a similar brief to the one above. Make sure, however, that you agree it with your teacher and check that it meets your Awarding Body's requirements, which will be on their website.

Factors to consider when writing or choosing a brief:

- What resources do you have available to you? It is important to be realistic at this point. You will need access to, and knowledge of, the appropriate technology. For print productions, you will need a digital camera and desktop publishing software. If you are planning to produce a video, you will need a video camera, a tripod and some editing software.

If you're producing a video, think about your cast, costumes, props and locations. Genres which use everyday settings, such as horror movies or soap operas, may be more achievable than science fiction or television news. That said, you can still be creative. It may be possible to create a post-apocalyptic world using the empty corridors of your school, some derelict land nearby and some expressive camera positions! In order to create a new celebrity magazine, you don't need access to real stars. You can construct your own, using a friend or a parent as your model. How you use costumes, props, body language, locations, camera positions and language codes to construct their star persona is what will be assessed.

- When are the deadlines? How much time have you got? Be warned, production often takes far longer than people expect. If possible, talk to students in the year above about their experiences. Effective video productions are often based on simple narratives with limited people involved. For print productions, you could organise a joint photoshoot with a member of your class and appear in each other's photos. All of these ideas can make it easier to meet your deadline.

- Should I work in a group? Working in a group may sound like an easier option than working individually, but this is not necessarily the case. You must first check with your teacher if your Awarding Body allows group work and how many are allowed in a group. Then make sure your group size is appropriate and the roles of each group member are agreed at the start. This should help your group work effectively together, ensuring that everybody contributes equally. Each group member will need to take on a technical role because your teacher will be assessing you individually. Members of the same group can get dramatically different results!

If you are worried about working in a team, it might be better to choose a project that you are confident you can complete individually. Whilst video production is often a group activity (though not necessarily), other print or new media forms are best completed individually.

- Does what you are planning meet the requirements of your Awarding Body? If you are not given these by your teacher, check on the Awarding Body's website. Check the requirements before you start. There are often rules about how long video and radio projects can be, how many pages of a print production you need to create and whether all your photographs have to be original or whether you are allowed to use found images.

Once you are clear in your mind what your aims are, you should be ready to start your research.

Researching

There are two main types of research you might undertake in your Media Studies course: one type is called primary research and is mainly used in the media industry when new media products are being developed – it leads onto pre-productions and finally productions. The other type, called secondary research, is often linked with academic and formal study as it focuses on books, journals and websites about the media. However, investigative research of this kind can also be used to create more sophisticated media productions as it helps you to focus on why the media is constructed in the way it is. So whatever kind of research you undertake, it should help you create better productions because you will know more about how to use genre conventions, structure narratives, construct representations and appeal to audiences.

In this section we will consider:

- Different types of research and what they can help you to discover.

- Writing up your research, and in particular the difference between blogs, reports and investigations.

- How to use research to help you create your pre-productions and / or productions.

Different Types of Research and What They Help you Discover

Before you start your research, you need to know what you are trying to find out. For example, if you are going to produce a teenage magazine, an important task would be to identify the generic conventions of magazines targeting teenage girls. Once completed, this research may raise other questions leading to new forms of research. You might want to ask, 'which conventions do teenage girls find most appealing in magazines that target them?' This type of research gives you a much better understanding of how you should construct your text.

You will also need to consider the audience your text is going to target. It might be useful to write a profile of the type of person you are intending to aim your text at, to ensure your research is focused. The type of text you are producing may be popular with a range of audiences and this is something that might be useful to look at as part of the research. Are there differences between the responses depending on, for example, gender, age, or personality type?

Research Methods

Primary research refers to information that you collect first hand using methods such as:

- Content analysis.

- Textual analysis.

- Questionnaires.

- Focus groups and interviews.

Secondary research refers to information that someone else has already collected and can be found in books, journals, DVDs and websites for example. Both forms of research can be useful tools for a media student. In order to help you choose the most appropriate combination of research methods for your project, each technique is explained and evaluated below.

Primary Research Methods

Content Analysis

Content analysis refers to the process of counting how many times pre-selected features occur in a text. For example, in the past researchers into media violence would count how many acts of aggression occurred in certain genres of TV programmes. They would then produce alarming statistics about the number of violent scenes children would have seen by the time they reach a particular age. The main problem with content analysis is that it depends on how you define what you are counting. Acts of aggression might include tackles in a football match, fights between cartoon characters and good guys defeating bad in order to save the day.

If you were researching the representation of women in TV drama it might be a useful starting point to count the number of female characters occupying positions of authority in the workplace. However, counting these characters does not tell you how they are represented. You would also need to know whether they are represented as being good at their jobs. Do they have good working relationships with their colleagues? Is the impact of their job on their relationships and / or families a key theme in the narrative? Clearly, *Ugly Betty*'s Wilhelmina Slater is a very different character to Dr Nikki Alexander in *Silent Witness*. Content analysis might not necessarily tell you this, so you will also need to complete some detailed textual analysis.

Ugly Betty's
Wilhelmina Slate and
Silent Witness' Dr
Nikki Alexander

Textual Analysis

Textual analysis is a key research method. You should use the skills described in the earlier sections to analyse your chosen texts in detail. Use annotation for print texts, labelling key features or a viewing grid to analyse moving images.

If the main aim of your research is to find out how you should construct your own production then it may help if you focus on identifying conventions. All media forms have conventions. Music videos use a mixture of illustration and performance, newspapers have mastheads which help define their brand identity and adverts end with pack shots. As such, textual analysis can help you identify the features that are essential if your text is going to be effective.

Textual analysis can help you identify how similar texts to your own construct representations and narratives. Conventions are not rules so you don't have to stick to every single one. However, they do offer useful guidelines for you, and will help guide your audience's expectations. Deliberately breaking one convention, or mixing the conventions of two genres to create a hybrid, can help you to produce a text which is more interesting and exciting and is a common practice in the media. Think of television programmes like the various versions of *Big Brother* which combine (at least) game show, documentary and soap opera conventions or films like *Slumdog Millionaire* which combine comedy, romance and social drama conventions in order to attract a wide audience.

It is also worth bearing in mind that you will need to analyse your texts several times to get a really detailed understanding of how they are constructed. As a starting point you should aim to analyse accurately the visual, symbolic, technical and audio and/or language codes used in the text. Always make sure that you use subject-specific terms and concepts. The initial analysis you completed will help you pick key scenes, pages or characters for closer scrutiny. Once you complete your first attempt at analysis you may need to undertake secondary research, which is explained below, before returning to look at your texts in more depth. Further detailed analysis may be required to look at how representations and narratives are constructed.

Asking the Audience

As discussed in earlier sections, a text doesn't simply convey the meaning the producer intends. Audiences can respond in different ways to texts, interpreting them in ways other than the producer intended. This means that it is often valuable to ask audiences what they think, rather than simply assuming that analysis has all the answers. When completing audience research you will need to choose between questionnaires, interviews and focus groups.

Questionnaires

Questionnaires can be an effective method of finding out what relatively large numbers of people think or feel about a particular issue. However, questionnaires are difficult to design well. Poorly designed questionnaires often produce results which tell you more about the way in which the questions were written than about what the audience think. To avoid this pitfall, think carefully about what you need to find out before you devise your questions. Think about 'who' you are asking and what they are actually able to tell you. If you are researching film trailers, is it enough to know what your respondents do or don't like, or do you need to know their reasons? Most people can tell you what they think but may find it harder to explain why they have those opinions.

Open questions are often more useful than closed ones. An open question is one where the respondent is left space to compose their answer rather than choosing from options such as Yes/No. If you are asking respondents to do more than circle choices, you will need to be able to give them the time and an appropriate space to answer them properly. A questionnaire with open questions may be harder for respondents to complete but a few good responses may tell you more than large amounts of repetitive information.

Quantitative and Qualitative Data

You may want to use both, or either, of these data collection methods but think carefully how useful the results you get will be to you. Quantitative research aims to put a numerical value on the topic being researched, in other words, to measure it. The results may be reported in the form of statistics. An example of quantitative research might be to record the amount of time people spend on social networking websites. Qualitative research aims to uncover the reasons behind something happening, for example, why young people spend more time using social networking sites than watching television. For many media projects, qualitative research is more useful as it is more likely to answer questions such as why people like or dislike certain media texts.

Although you may need the respondents to think carefully about their answers, a questionnaire should be as user friendly as possible. Try to do the following:

- Keep it short – no more than six questions.

- Make it clear and easy to read with no spelling mistakes.

- Avoid jargon.

- Avoid media terminology in the questions.

- Test the questionnaire so that you know your questions deliver the information you need.

- Thank your respondents at the end of your questionnaire!

When you write up your results and interpret the answers, you are likely to want to relate the respondents' comments to media concepts and theories. For example, if a respondent talks about money, mansions and expensive cars in r&b videos, then you may later link this to Young and Rubicam's concept of 'aspirers' and discuss the significance of this. You should distribute questionnaires to members of your target audience as it is their views you are trying to establish.

Interviews and Focus Groups

One limitation of questionnaires, even those that are well designed and qualitative with open questions, is that they tend to provide brief answers. Questionnaires are frequently used to gather a limited amount of information from a large amount of people. However, you will probably want to get more in depth views from fewer respondents.

Interviews and focus groups allow researchers to find out more about what people think and crucially can help reveal why they think the way they do. The ability to listen to the respondents' answers, pay attention to their non-verbal communication and ask supplementary questions can allow you to research your audience's feelings in much greater depth than using questionnaires. You can also adapt the interview according to the answers you receive.

It is important that your respondent feels at ease. Take notes, rather than recording what they say. Conduct the interview somewhere they feel comfortable and where you will be free of interruptions. Ensure confidentiality and get parental consent if you are interviewing children, even if they go to your school. Another issue to consider is the impact that your behaviour has on the results. Just as you don't want the way you write questions to influence the answers you receive when conducting a questionnaire, you must minimise your effect on what is said in the interview. You should encourage your respondent to express themselves but remain neutral yourself. Your job is to ask open questions, it is not to offer your opinion or criticise the responses you receive.

Focus Groups

Focus groups typically involve seven to ten participants, although you may find smaller numbers easier to manage. You will need prompting questions especially at the start of the focus group in order to stimulate discussion. However, the aim of a focus group is for the participants to talk to each other, asking questions and stating opinions. The main advantage of this method is that discussions often involve participants justifying their opinions. This can give an insight into why people think the way they do, rather than simply revealing what they think.

You will need to select your participants carefully; focus groups usually include people with something in common. For your project, they should all be members of your target audience. The management of the group dynamic is important too. You don't want one person to dominate as this defeats the object of the method which is provoking discussion. This means you will have to manage the debate whilst trying not to influence what is said.

Stimulus Material

One good technique for stimulating discussion in focus groups and getting useful answers from interviews is to show your participants existing media texts. Simply asking people to rank texts in order of which is the scariest, the most attractive, stylish, attention grabbing, or whatever is relevant to your research can be a revealing process. Choose your texts carefully as this will help provoke debate and justification of the order.

For example, showing a focus group pictures of women and men with a range of body types might help generate discussion regarding representations of gender. It is much easier for your participants to discuss how women are represented in the media if they are looking at well-chosen pages from, for example, lifestyle or fashion magazines.

Secondary Research

The aim of secondary research is to use books, websites and journals to improve your knowledge and understanding of a topic, often by referring to expert opinion. This does not mean you are only looking for books about the media texts you are studying. Researching a key concept, such as narrative, genre or representation, and applying the points you discover to the texts you are studying can help you gain much better understanding. You might use a book that discusses the genre which your text conforms to, but does not specifically discuss your examples, such as *The Cinema Book* edited by Pam Cook (2008).

Photocopying or printing off pages and highlighting relevant sections can feel like a quick and convenient method of conducting this kind of investigative research but there are advantages to making notes as well. Note-making encourages you to put what you read into your own words, forcing you to interpret and think more carefully about how the ideas you've read about apply to the texts you are analysing. When making notes write the information you need for referencing and the bibliography (see bibliography later) at the top of the page. Write the relevant page number in the margin next to each point. This will save you time and stress at the end of the process.

Get to know your library. If in doubt ask the librarian. Firstly, identify sections with relevant books. Look for books about media concepts; for example, genre, narrative or representation as well as books about your particular media form such as film, television or advertising (which may all be in different sections). You will need to browse through the books to find relevant chapters. Use the index to quickly check for relevant information in the book. Academic books often have introductions which summarise the key content of each chapter. Reading the introduction can help you evaluate whether the book will be helpful to your research, and if it is, which chapters you need to use.

The internet can be an extremely useful source of information as it will allow you access to documents that you would not be able to find locally. However, as there is so much information on the internet it can take a lot of time and effort to find what you want. Don't assume using the internet will be more efficient than finding books in the library. Avoid sites which offer trivia about your text or genre. The aim of your research is to find out more about theoretical perspectives not to discover information about the people and processes involved in production.

If you are using any internet site for research you need to be able to identify who has written the information so you can evaluate their expertise and motivation for writing. There are some very useful sites for media students including those produced by academics and universities such as David Gauntlett's www.theory.org.uk and the University of Abersystwyth's www.aber.ac.uk/media.

Most students use search engines. You should try different ones as they will give you different results. Remember you are trying to narrow the search as much as possible so you can screen out irrelevant information. You can narrow a search by using more terms. Simply adding the term 'genre' to horror narrows your search considerably. If you put the word AND between each of your terms, the search will only find documents which include all, not just some of the words:

Genre AND horror AND women

Speech marks allow you to search for exact phrases:

'horror genre' AND 'representation of women'

It can really help your search if you can identify the name of a relevant theorist who has written about your topic, and add them to the search:

'horror genre' AND 'representation of women' AND Carol Clover

Investigations

You may be required to write an account of key conclusions you've reached following your research. Titles are an important part of this process. Focused titles, which give a clear indication of the area you are concentrating on, allow you to construct a clear central argument. You may be basing an investigation on a key media concept such as narrative, genre or representation. This concept should be incorporated in the investigation title, so that you can refer to it throughout your investigation.

Avoid studying too many texts in your research as this is likely to result in a superficial investigation. Choose one or two specific media texts. Avoid studying the whole of *Dr Who*: base your study on a specific episode, even though you may refer to other episodes to provide context and comparison. If you are researching newspapers, check what is reported on the front pages for a few weeks and choose the editions with the most interesting stories. Possible titles for investigations might therefore include:

- To what extent do the representations of youth in *skins* and *Gossip Girl* conform to, or challenge, stereotypes?

- Analysing horror films and genre conventions – with reference to *Scream* and *Saw VI*.

- How do newspapers construct narratives? A detailed study of the same story as reported in *The Daily Mail* and *The Guardian*.

The investigation question or title can also help you structure your investigation effectively and help you construct an argument out of your research. Choosing two texts allows you to compare and contrast them, which can give your work a sense of purpose. The examples above give straightforward grounds for comparison: British versus American, older with newer texts, and texts with radically different ideologies. You might also want to compare mainstream with niche, high budget with low budget or even across media forms, for example film versus television. Comparison is not a requirement of research essays but for many students it is a helpful approach.

Once you have worked out what you need to know, or decided upon your question, you will be able to choose the type of research you need to undertake in order to get the answers you need.

Research investigations in Media Studies should aim to link together primary and secondary research. You should research what other people have said about texts that are similar to, but not the same as your own. You should also have a set of notes generated by your detailed textual analysis. In writing your essay you are aiming to compare your analysis with the findings of your secondary research, and in doing so evaluate whether what people have said about other texts can be applied to the focus of your study. For example, David Gauntlett has written about the representation of masculinity in monthly magazines aimed at men including *FHM* (http://theoryhead.com/gender/MGI2008-extra1.pdf). Your essay could focus on evaluating whether his ideas about these magazines, written in 2001, can be similarly applied to weekly lad mags such as *Nuts* and *Zoo*.

This does not mean that you should include large sections lifted from your research, even if they are clearly referenced. Where possible you should interpret secondary research in your own words and apply it to your texts for yourself.

The investigations you can expect to write are often towards 1400–1800 words in length. It is essential to have a clear structure and plan before you write. Such an essay is too long to launch into without a plan, but you may also find that it is quite short and you will need to state your points and evidence as concisely as possible. This means you will need a detailed plan. This plan should identify the content of every paragraph you are planning on writing. This will also help you divide your investigation up into a number of sections. Writing six sections, each approximately 300 words long, is a much more achievable task than trying to complete the investigation as a whole. It will also allow you to schedule your time and set yourself interim deadlines. These paragraph headings will also provide you with guidelines for your production, which will need to reflect your research findings.

Referencing an investigation

Referencing is the process of indicating the ideas that you have discovered through your research. Borrowing other people's ideas without acknowledging their source is plagiarism, or cheating! You need to indicate in the main body of your investigation which ideas are not your own. If you reference them you have conducted legitimate research. Most mark schemes reward students for completing substantial research and so, to an extent, the more references you have the better. That said, research is supposed to support your ideas and arguments. You need to apply the ideas you gained through research to your texts, rather than simply filling up your investigation with quotes. Even if you summarise or re-interpret your research findings in your own words, you will need to provide a reference.

There are several referencing systems but the basic principle of all of them is that references should be clear and accurate. The reader should be able to find the original source of the information using your references.

A straightforward option is to use the Harvard Referencing System. According to the Harvard System, you include the name of the author and the year their work was published alongside the idea you have borrowed. The full details of the publication are then listed at the end of the essay in a bibliography.

For example:

> According to Gauntlett (2002), 'representations of masculinity on the internet are likely to be very similar to those found in film and television...'

If you need to reference a newspaper or a journal, the full date when the article was published should be provided. For example, 'plans for the new Bond film have been shelved due to MGM's financial problems' (*The Guardian*, 20 April 2010).

Bibliography

Your bibliography should include all the sources referenced in your investigation and the other resources you have used. The sources should be organised in alphabetical order according to the writer's or producer's surname. The reader ought to be able to follow your references and access the original information, thus allowing them to check ideas or explore a topic further you must include the following:

Surname, first name (year of publication), *the title*, and the publisher and place of origin.

For example:

Gauntlett, David (2002) *Media, Gender and Identity*, Routledge: London.

The layout is important, the author's surname must be placed first and the title of the book or journal should be in italics. This all helps clearly identify the sources of your information.

If you need to reference an article you found on the internet, you do the same for the author's name and give the title of the article. You also include the web address, again so that the reader can find the article easily for themselves. The date you first accessed the information should also be included as information changes rapidly on the internet.

For example:

Chandler, Daniel, *Semiotics for Beginners*, http://www.aber.ac.uk/media/Documents/S4B/, 11 June 2009.

Producing – Pre-production work

Once you have completed your research, of whatever kind, you will be ready to undertake your pre-production work. It is essential that your pre-production work incorporates what your research has suggested. It may be helpful to summarise your research findings and use these as objectives for your practical work. For example, women's lifestyle magazines:

- Inclusive and personal mode of address.
- Women represented as balancing careers and relationships.
- Female cover stars represented as role models.

These research findings could be used as a basis for your pre-production and production work as well as when writing an evaluation.

Pre-production refers to the tasks needed to be completed before production can begin, such as scripting or storyboarding video projects or producing final stage mock-ups of print material.

Below are some suggested combinations of print-based pre-productions and productions:

	Film	Music	Magazines
Pre-production	A teaser and a trailer poster for a new film.	Covers for a new r&b artist's CD.	Two magazine front covers (April and July) for a new magazine.
Production	DVD cover and insert for the special edition of the film (four pages).	Front cover and double page spread of a new music magazine featuring this artist.	A double-page spread and front cover of the Christmas edition

Pre-production
– (process of constructing) a planning arefact for example a script, storyboard or 'mock-up'

However, you might like to mix audio / visual with print, for example creating the storyboard for a new film, as pre-production work and making the DVD cover and poster for production.

Scripts and Storyboards

When you are writing a script or making a storyboard you should aim to demonstrate your understanding of genre, narrative and representation. For example, if you are scripting the opening scene of a new crime drama you may want to start with a crime being committed. Alternatively you might begin with the discovery of a body. What your detective does and says in the opening scene will form an important part of their representation. Are we introduced to them at the

Shot Length	Visuals	Camera Instructions	Sound Track	Comment

crime scene or does your script cut to their personal lives? How does your character relate to stereotypes of gender, age and ethnicity? All of these elements need to be considered because these factors will be the focus of how your work is assessed.

Storyboarding

Storyboarding is an essential element of video production, regardless of whether the storyboard itself is being assessed. Hollywood films are fully storyboarded before production begins. Spielberg storyboards his movies although he hires artists to do the pictures, as apparently, he can't draw. If your drawing is not up to much either, you need not worry. Artistic talent is not what is being assessed. You need only draw well enough so that each shot matches its description. You can use photographs instead, but whichever method you prefer, it is essential that the camera is correctly positioned and labelled. Every shot will need a frame on the storyboard and you must label the camera position, audio, the duration (length it lasts) and the transition (cut, fade, dissolve) for each one. Unless your drawings are excellent you might find it helpful to include a brief description of the mise-en-scène.

Some tips for storyboarding:

- You should aim to use a variety of camera positions and movements, remembering to include close-ups to show the characters' emotions.

- Avoid positioning the camera to the side of the action too frequently.

- Make sure you demonstrate an understanding of the continuity system.

- Label transitions using correct terminology such as cut, fade, dissolve or wipe.

- Indicate the audio codes that will be used including both diegetic and non-diegetic sound.

- The more complex the action, the more shots you will need to use.

- Presentation is important – you will need to be able to understand what you planned to do when it may be cold and wet, and you are tired, hungry and stressed.

- Watch similar texts to the one you are planning. How long are the shot durations? How many shots will you need to plan?

Understandably, many students are keen to get on with filming, but a good storyboard can make filming and editing straightforward. If all you have to do is shoot what you drew, and then put the shots in sequence on a timeline, it will save you lots of time and effort, reduce the likelihood of mistakes and mean that your finished product is of a much higher standard.

Scripts

You will need to present your script in an appropriate format. The BBC Writers' Room website at: www.bbc.co.uk/writersroom/scriptsmart/ provides guidelines on

Mock-up – a final version of a planning artefact for a print production which lays out the images and text for a designer to review the page/s.

how to structure a television script: finding out what is the appropriate format for your script should form part of your research. So whatever format you choose you should be able to justify it in the report on your research.

Some scripts include important camera directions. Adding these may allow you to demonstrate more of the knowledge and understanding you have gained from your studies.

Print Pre-productions

Pre-production activities for print work usually mean making mock-ups of the finished pages. A mock-up is a term used for a draft of a project that might be presented to clients (in advertising) or publishers (in the magazine industry). Mock-ups need to be as close to the finished product as possible, so *must* be made using original photos and desktop publishing software.

As you are aiming to produce as a good a mock-up as possible, you will hopefully find that the mock-up is actually as good as a finished production. In this case it becomes essential to develop your ideas across some new pages of print material for your production, rather than making minor adjustments to your pre-production.

Producing

Production work is an opportunity for you to demonstrate your technical skills. Your aim should be to achieve as professional a finish as possible. This means you need to be organised (for example, tick shots off your storyboard as you shoot them), pay attention to details (fully justify the columns in your print work) and follow the production methods you have been taught (such as using a tripod).

Below are some guidelines to help you with the production of your audio / visual and print work:

1. Producing print based texts:

- Make sure your page is set up with appropriate dimensions. Simply measure existing media texts for yourself and use these as a template.

- Most media texts are dominated by images. Make your photographs central to the layout and make the text fit with the images, not the other way around.

- Try to make your work cohesive. This means that the pages need to work together as a whole. Limit the number of different colours you use. Don't use too many fonts. Some texts, such as gossip magazines, break many conventions of the magazine form by using colours that clash and layouts that are really busy. This is quite a hard style to imitate and you need to pay even more attention to the design so that it looks visually exciting, rather than just messy.

- Think through the connotations of everything you choose. Not just the words you use for your title, but the font and colour of the masthead as well. If you aren't sure about a decision, get audience feedback using the research methods described previously.

- Take a step back and look at your work as if you were not the producer of the text. Is the page clearly laid out? Can you read all the words? Are they spelt correctly? Is the genre recognisable? Do the images and masthead grab your attention? It may help to put your cover next to a real one to compare them.

- Include barcodes, issue numbers, dates, price, copyright information, etc. These details are essential features of media texts.

2. Filming and editing:

- Use a storyboard. Make sure you shoot all the shots you have planned. You can shoot extra shots or try more creative camera positions if you have good ideas on the day, but these should be filmed as well as, not instead of what you planned. When editing, have the storyboard in front of you. You may adapt what you have planned but the storyboard will help you organise your shots on the timeline.

- Conduct a location 'recce'. This means go and look at where you are filming. Try to anticipate any problems you might encounter. Are there any strong sources of light which might make your shot look very dark and shadowy? Is it noisy? Will we be able to hear the characters speak? This is particularly important if you haven't got an external microphone. Will you be able to control your locations or will passers by interfere with what you have planned? Most importantly a good point is to consider the Health and Safety implications of what you have planned.

- Press record then say 'action' clearly so all involved know that you are filming. Once the action has been completed, wait a few seconds before you stop recording. This will make editing easier.

- Always check that the camera is focused, or that you have set it to autofocus. If the camera needs white balancing check that you know how and when to do this.

- Avoid too many camera movements. Panning, tilting and tracking are hard to do smoothly. In many cases you might be better to shoot two or three shots with the camera in a static position. If you have to move the camera, shoot several attempts so that you can choose the smoothest in the edit. Too much zooming tends to look unprofessional in students' work.

- When editing you should aim to produce a 'rough cut' as early as possible. This is where you place all the shots on the timeline which will allow you to check that your narrative makes sense and that your continuity is good. Once you have completed a rough cut you can tweak what you have done as much as you like to reach your desired effect.

- Use any effects available to you sparingly and only when they have a purpose. Most film and television programmes are edited simply, without complicated transitions. You want your work to demonstrate that you understand narrative, genre and representation, not show off everything that the computer can do.

Evaluating – Reports and evaluations

Once you have completed your production you will be expected to submit some written work to support what you made. This will often include:

- Aims.

- Summary of research.

- Target audience profile.

- Evaluation.

Check the requirements of your Awarding Body – you may have a choice of format, for example a report, a discursive essay (possibly illustrated) or a suitably edited blog. Often the word count is quite short so it can be useful to use a report style format to make the most of the available words.

Reports

A report can include bullet points, annotated images, quotes and tables. Use these to summarise your points but remember everything you write will count towards the word limit. If you have produced a video you can often export individual frames as still images, by saving them as jpeg files, which can then be opened in other programmes.

Some students might like to produce a suitably edited blog. It is important to remember that the content will need to be similar to that of the report described below, only the format is different. Choosing this option does encourage you to write up each element as you complete it. However, you must be careful to avoid simply describing the process of completing the project. Blogs often take the form of an online diary and you must ensure that yours does not.

Aims

Set out what you intended to do in a couple of sentences. Write as if you are completing the project professionally: 'My aim was to launch a new British, female R'n'B star...' is more focused than 'I had to make a music video...'.

Research

This should be a summary of your results, rather than a description the research itself. You should focus on key themes of representation, genre conventions and typical narrative structures identified through textual analysis. The word count will not be high enough to include every text you analysed, however you may want to include key examples as images in the report. Annotating key features is a good idea, although these words will still need to be included in the word count.

If you undertook quantitative research then obviously tables and statistics are an appropriate form to report these results. When reporting qualitative questionnaires, interviews and focus groups, select your best quotes, include them but add your interpretation. Try to link what your respondents said to the media concepts that underpin your work.

Audience Profile

Target audience profiles should include more than one group of people, often we talk about texts having primary, secondary and tertiary audiences. You may want to summarise key information about their demographic profiles (age, gender, etc.) in bullet point form. To discuss their psychometric profiles (personality types) you might use groups suggested by advertising agencies such as Young and Rubicam (explorer, mainstreamer, etc.) but these categories are not the only way to discuss audiences. You could describe your audiences' attitudes, lifestyles, relationships and whatever else is relevant to the text you have constructed.

Evaluating your Work

The first step in evaluating your work is completing detailed textual analysis as if it were any other media text you might be studying. If you produced a print text, annotate it and use a viewing grid for audio/visual material. A traditional evaluation, where you are simply required to comment on the strengths and weaknesses of your finished product should focus on two elements. Firstly, how well the text works creatively, and secondly, how well produced is it from a technical point of view. In the first instance you might talk about how successfully you have represented your characters and the second might talk about the choice of fonts. Obviously there is some crossover between the two. For example, how you positioned the camera may have an impact on your representations.

All evaluations must relate to the initial aims of the project. You need to evaluate if your text appeals to its target audience. Conducting some audience research can give you valuable feedback. Conduct a focus group but make sure the participants belong to your target group.

Does your text conform to genre conventions? Comparing your text with professionally produced texts can help you be critical of your work. You should be able to identify some weaknesses and highlight limitations. The lack of budget, technical constraints and limited resources will have had a negative impact on your text and you should explain this. This is not the same as making excuses or complaining about people who let you down. Your comments should all be focused on the finished text. If you have worked in a group you should evaluate the success of the production as a whole but should also aim to draw attention to the strengths and weaknesses of the parts of the project for which you were responsible.

Some evaluations are less focused on the general construction of the text and require that you focus on the ways in which the production reflects the research you undertook. In this case you should approach the evaluation in one of two ways:

1. Use your key research findings as headings. Then evaluate how your text reflects these findings. Reflecting research does not necessarily mean simply imitating your results. You may have deliberately challenged conventions, and you will need to explain this in your evaluation.

2. Use key features of your text as headings. Then explain how your research justifies the creative decisions that you made.

In this kind of evaluation your strengths and weaknesses relate to how well you used the knowledge you gained from researching a specific topic, such as the representation of gender. As such, only specific elements of your production, in this case how you represented gender, need evaluating. Basic technical skills need not be discussed at all. As you are not focused on how the text relates to its target audience, you will not need to complete audience research for this type of evaluation.

Conclusion

In completing this project you will have demonstrated your research, planning, technical and creative skills. You will have managed a complex project with numerous deadlines and a range of resources and will want to achieve the best possible mark, especially as this project will be a substantial part of the assessment of the course. It is worth remembering that the best projects are always the ones in which each individual element clearly relates to the rest of the project. For example your pre-production mock-up should reflect the discussions that took place in your focus group, which in turn was designed to answer some questions raised by your textual analysis. This is not to say you will have copied the texts you looked at, but your work should have been improved by what you studied. The marker should be able to tell that you did relevant research and completed effective planning by looking at your production.

Finally, remember that at every stage of the project you are being assessed on your understanding of key media concepts: genre, narrative and representation. These concepts must underpin every decision you make. A successful project is one that uses genre conventions, structures narratives and constructs representations that appeal to its target audience.

INDEX

Picture Credits

The publisher believes the following copyright information to be correct at the time of going to press, but will be delighted to correct any errors brought to our attention in future editions.

Page 17 – *Skins*: L-R Merv, JJ, Naomi, Freddie, Effy, Cook, Pandora, Emily, Katie and Karen © John Wright/amarang.com; *Spooks*: Series 7, Hermione, Peter and Richard © Kudos Productions/BBC; page 19 – *Dracula* (Terence Fisher, 1958), Christopher Lee as Count Dracula © Hammer Film Productions/Warner Home Video; *Twilight* (Catherine Hardwicke, 2008) Robert Pattinson as Edward Cullen © Goldcrest Pictures/Twilight Productions/Summit; page 21 – *CSI Miami* © CBS Television Studios/Jerry Bruckheimer Television; *Waking the Dead* © BBC; page 23 – *Tombraider: Underworld* © Eidos Interactive/Crystal Dynamics]; *Return to Castle Wolfenstein* © Activision/Raven Software; page 25 – *Life on Mars* © Kudos Productions/BBC; pages 26–8 *Strictly Come Dancing* © BBC/Format Entertainment; page 32 – *Bullet Boy* (Saul Dibb, 2004) © BBC Films/UKFC/Shine; *Call of Duty: World at War* © 2008 Activision/Treyarch Invention; page 37 – *Psycho* (Alfred Hitchcock, 1960) Janet Leigh as Marion Crane © Paramount Pictures/Shamley Productions; *The Fast and the Furious* (Rob Cohen, 2001) © Universal Pictures/Original Film/Mediastream Film GmbH; page 49 – *The X Factor* © Fremantle Media/Syco Television/Talkback Thames; page 51 – *Hungry* by Crystal Renn, published by Simon and Schuster, 2010/© Crystal Renn; page 55 – *Professor Layton and the Curious Village* © 2007 Nintendo/Bee Train; page 56 – images © 2008 Ubisoft/Nintendo; page 57 – *Tombraider: Underworld* © Eidos Interactive/Crystal Dynamics; page 62 – © L'Oréal; page 64 www.dolcegabbana.com; page 65 – www.lorealparis.co.uk; page 66-7 © Dove; page 68 – Kelly Holmes at Athens, 2004 © 2008 Russell Garner; page 69 – *Whole Foods* © 2007 André 3000/Altered Ego; *Catch 22* © 2009 Tinchy Stryder/Island Records; page 75 – *Closer* © 2008 Bauer London Lifestyle; *Men's Health* © National Magazine Company www.natmags.co.uk; *GQ Magazine* © Condé Nast Publications www.gqmagazine.co.uk; *Heat Magazine/Heat World* © Emap London Lifestyle <www.heatworld.com>; page 78 – *Men's Health* © National Magazine Company <www.natmags.co.uk>; page 82–4 – *Slumdog Millionaire* © 2009 Celador Films/Film4/Pathé Pictures International; pages 90, 93 & 94 – © BBC; page 99, 100 & 102 – © Company Pictures/E4/Stormdog Film]; pages 103 & 106 – *The Wire* (David Simon, 2002–8) © Blown Deadline/Home Box Office; pages 111–2, 117–18 – © BBC; page 119 © Planet Rock/Blacksheep; page 126, 129, 130, 13–3, 137 & 148 – *The Dark Knight* (Christopher Nolan, 2008) © Warner Bros./Legendary Pictures/DC Comics/Syncopy; page 128 – © DC Comics; pages 138–9, 140 & 148 – *Shifty* © 2008 BBC Films/Between the Eyes/Film London; page 141, 144 & 148 – *This is England* (Shane Meadows, 2006) © Big Arty Productions/Film4/Screen Yorkshire/UKFC/Warp Films; pages 153–4, 156 – *World of Warcraft* © Blizzard Entertainment; page 155 – *Second Life* © Linden Research, Inc.; page 160 – *South Park* © Comedy Central/Comedy Partners; page 162 – *PaRappa the Rapper* © 1996 Nana On Sha/Sony Computer Entertainment; page 162 & 165 – *DJ Hero* © 2009 Activision; page 169 – GlaxoSmithKline/Eidos Interactive; *The Face* (Emap) <www.emap.com>; pages 174 & 175 – © Columbia Records; page 177 – *Dreamgirls* (Bill Condon, 2006) © DreamWorks/Paramount Pictures/Laurence Mark Productions;

ALSO AVAILABLE FROM AUTEUR

The Film Genre Book

John Sanders

Studying TV Drama

Michael Massey

The first stop for Film and Media Studies

Notes

Notes

Notes

Notes

Notes

Notes

Notes

Notes

Notes